PHILADELPHIA UNITARIANISM

1796-1861

OCTAGON CHURCH, Tenth and Locust Streets, Philadelphia, 1813
First church edifice built by the Unitarian Society, designed by Robert Mills.
Courtesy of the First Unitarian Church of Philadelphia.

PHILADELPHIA UNITARIANISM
1796—1861

by
Elizabeth M. Geffen

Assistant Professor of History
Lebanon Valley College

Philadelphia
University of Pennsylvania Press

Printed in Great Britain
by W. & J. Mackay & Co Ltd, Chatham

TO MY PARENTS

PREFACE

THIS STUDY IS CONCERNED WITH UNITARIANISM IN THE LIFE OF Philadelphia—from its first appearance until the outbreak of the Civil War. The history of New England Unitarianism has been amply set forth but the Philadelphia story has not been told until now. Here, in part, is that story.

Based on the author's doctoral dissertation, "Philadelphia Unitarianism (1796–1861)," at the University of Pennsylvania, 1958, this account has been slightly amplified, but the main outlines and conclusions remain the same.

It is the particular distinction of Philadelphia Unitarianism that it was not, in its origin, an outgrowth of the American experience, but an import from England. Unlike New England Unitarianism, which, with the single exception of King's Chapel, Boston, evolved from native American Congregationalism, this society was transplanted full-blown to American soil by a small group of British immigrants. The Vaughan family, distinguished English Unitarians, came to Philadelphia in the 1780's. How many others of the sect there were in the city at that time, or previously, is not known, nor how many of Unitarian persuasion who did not declare themselves. Some historians go back to the seventeenth century and claim William Penn as a Unitarian on the basis of his disquisition on the subject of Divine Unity in *The Sandy Foundation Shaken*. The first religious society to be named Unitarian in Philadelphia, however, was organized in 1796. This group, known then as the Society of Unitarian Christians of Philadelphia and surviving today as The First Unitarian Church of Philadelphia, is, in fact, the oldest permanent Unitarian church to bear that name in America.

The records of the First Unitarian Church for the period before the Civil War contain no complete list of members. Accordingly, the congregation had to be recreated from references to individuals in the extant church journals and manuscripts, including minute books, financial records, the pastor's registers, and the like. These names were then traced through the Philadelphia *City Directories*, histories, biographies, memoirs, family papers, and similar materials. Specific data thus gathered concerning members of the society have been listed in three appendices: A. Officers of the Society; B. Occupations of Members; C. Organizational Activities of Members.

Inevitably, since church records are not complete, many volumes being missing and those available not kept as fully as an historian would desire, some members of the society may have been omitted from the present study; others may not have had justice done them in this narration. For all such omissions, failures, or faulty inferences drawn from extant data, the writer asks the indulgence of members and friends.

No attempt has been made to describe or to discuss the theological aspects of Unitarianism in Philadelphia or elsewhere, for such consideration is beyond the intention of the author. For the purpose of this work it suffices to state the definition given by Dr. James Mease in his *The Picture of Philadelphia*, published in 1811. Describing the Unitarians of his day, with whom he was intimately connected, Dr. Mease said: "Their leading tenets are a denial of the catholic doctrine of the Trinity, and an adherence to the literal sense of those passages of Scripture which assert the unity of God and the humanity of Christ." Unitarianism, of course, rejects any universal, exclusive, or binding definition in terms of creed. However, the writer believes that Dr. Mease's definition fairly states the case for the group under consideration.

Part of this material, dealing with the antislavery activities of the pastor of the Unitarian Society, was published by *The Pennsylvania Magazine of History and Biography* in July, 1958, in an article entitled, "William Henry Furness, Philadelphia Antislavery Preacher."

Annville, Pennsylvania
June, 1959

ELIZABETH M. GEFFEN

ACKNOWLEDGMENTS

SPACE LIMITATIONS MAKE IT IMPOSSIBLE TO RECORD HERE THE names of all who have assisted me in this study, but my gratitude to them is none the less real.

Special thanks are due to professors at the University of Pennsylvania: Wallace E. Davies, who supervised the dissertation on which this work is based; Robert E. Spiller, Anthony N. B. Garvan, Thomas P. Haviland, and Don Yoder, who read the manuscript and offered helpful criticism. Mrs. Dorothea H. Williams, Custodian of the Edgar Fahs Smith Memorial Collection; Mrs. Delphine Oakie Richardson, Interlibrary Loan Librarian; and Mr. Reuben Goldberg, Photographer of the University Museum, all gave generously of their talents. I am also indebted to Mrs. Gertrude D. Hess and Mrs. Ruth Duncan of the Library of the American Philosophical Society, to the staff of the Historical Society of Pennsylvania, and to the custodians of the Archives of Harvard University. Mr. Francis James Dallett, Secretary and Librarian of The Athenaeum of Philadelphia, has put at my disposal in unstinted measure his rich knowledge of Philadelphia history.

The members of the First Unitarian Church of Philadelphia have given me heartening support, among them most especially the Rev. Harry B. Scholefield, former minister; the Rev. Dr. Anders S. Lunde, present minister; Dr. Oscar S. Nelson, former President of the Board of Trustees; and Hayward H. Coburn, Esq., present President of the Board; Miss Lucretia T. Gartrell, Parish Assistant; and Miss Alice L. Farr, former Church Secretary. My gratitude to the first Unitarian who extended to me the right hand of fellowship, the Rev. Dr. Frederick R. Griffin, Minister Emeritus, is immeasurable.

The Rev. Max F. Daskam, minister of the Unitarian Church of Germantown, made the records of that society available. The Rev. Mason McGinnis, Assistant to the President, and Mrs. Martha

Acknowledgments

S. C. Wilson, Librarian, of the American Unitarian Association in Boston graciously assisted my research in the association's Historical Library.

Mr. Horace Howard Furness Jayne most generously gave me from his family's records the collected manuscript correspondence and printed sermons of his great-grandfather, William H. Furness, which constitute a major part of my primary source materials. Dr. Charles L. Chandler, Professor Emeritus at Ursinus College, shared with me his accumulated store of Unitariana. Professor Frederick B. Tolles, Director of the Friends Historical Library of Swarthmore College, responded generously to a call for assistance with Quaker history. To my former colleague, Professor Samuel M. Bradley, I am grateful for assistance in the final preparation of the manuscript.

Two faculty awards granted me by Lebanon Valley College made possible much valued technical assistance in the processing of the manuscript.

To the late William H. DuBarry I am deeply indebted—for unfailing kindness, and encouragement, and tireless guidance through the maze of Philadelphia's present and past.

Greatest of debts is that which I owe to Professor Roy F. Nichols, who wanted this history written and who made it possible. His wisdom, his patience, but, above all, his enjoyment of both life and history have been a constant source of inspiration.

CONTENTS

CONTENTS

ILLUSTRATIONS

PHILADELPHIA UNITARIANISM
1796-1861

I

English Genesis

Sunday bells tolling in Philadelphia at the end of the eighteenth century summoned the city's seventy thousand inhabitants to worship at twenty-seven churches.[1] Unhappily, the Reverend Dr. Helmuth, pastor of the German Lutheran Zion Church, estimated that "at times hardly one-fourth of all the numerous inhabitants . . . would vouchsafe to hear the call of the Lord, much less suffer themselves to be gathered under his wings."[2] Vice-President John Adams, fresh from devout New England, admitted that Philadelphia offered the Godly a limited choice, between "the solemn gloom of the religion of that City, on the one hand . . . and the licentious Spirit of Pyrrhonish and Credulous Philosophy on the other."[3]

On June 12, 1796, however, a new alternative was offered by a small group of British merchants, recent immigrants to the United States, who on that date organized in Philadelphia the first permanently established Unitarian congregation in the New World.[4] They had brought their religion with them from England, where Joseph Priestley had given them a theology a full generation in advance of the liberal Christianity slowly evolving out of New England Congregationalism and, in the single instance of King's Chapel, Boston, out of the Episcopal Church. Denying the dogma of the Trinity, asserting the unity of God, the humanity of Jesus, and the perfectibility of man, they had still been "wandering sheep without fold or shepherd," according to one of their number,[5] when Priestley arrived in Philadelphia in June, 1794.

17

Only by the grace of linguistic derivation was Philadelphia in that year the City of Brotherly Love. It was the capital and the seat of the federal government of "one nation indivisible," but no amount of political eloquence could blind even the least observant to the obvious cleavage within the ranks. The Revolution was over; the enemy without had been vanquished; and the citizens of the new republic now concentrated upon fighting each other. The conflict was basic, deeply rooted in the eternal dichotomy of human nature—liberal versus conservative. Politics provided the framework for the struggle.

Though political parties in the modern sense had not yet formed, well defined political differences separated the liberal Democratic Republicans headed by Thomas Jefferson from the conservative Federalists led by Alexander Hamilton. George Washington, serving his second term, presided over the nation's affairs with an icy dignity and superhuman calm which the Federalists not only considered appropriate but found congenial, while the Democratic Republicans saw in the President's bearing a presumption to aristocracy which galled them personally and seemed to them to threaten the very existence of democratic government. Given as their leader a famous soldier, who had just won a war and saved the country from unmentionable calamity, the Federalists had unfortunately made too much of their opportunity. If Washington had ever had the common touch which makes all men kin, he lost it in Philadelphia while he was President. Built up into superhuman proportions by those who made a business of hero-making, he became remote and withdrawn from the average American whose future welfare he had done so much to secure. William Maclay, junior senator from Pennsylvania, ran the gamut of public reaction. At the beginning of his term in April, 1789, Washington was for him "the greatest man in the world."[6] By 1792 he was convinced that "the President has become, in the hands of Hamilton, the dishclout of every dirty speculation, as his name goes to wipe away all blame and silence all murmuring."[7]

The political division was not a friendly one nor did it stop at the top level. Quite to the contrary, it split all of Philadelphia into two opposing camps, which warred upon each other with every available weapon, neither giving nor asking quarter. Reputations were torn to shreds in the public press on both sides; physical violence degraded the proceedings in the halls of Congress. Diametrically opposed in their approach to domestic problems of life and government, the two parties also took divergent views of the great drama being played overseas in France, the Democratic Republicans favoring the cause of the French Revolution, the Federalists believing it a threat to all vested interests everywhere. In the ensuing war between France and England the two American factions maintained the same lines of allegiance, the Republicans wildly pro-French, the Federalists grimly pro-English. The excesses of the pro-French mobs in Philadelphia, aggravated by the notable eccentricities in the behavior of the French minister, Genêt, did nothing to allay the bitterness of the domestic conflict. There seemed to be no middle ground. Even the foreign traveller, spending only a short time in the city, had to make his choice between the two parties. Benjamin Henry Latrobe, visiting Philadelphia briefly in 1798, testified:

Political fanaticism was, during my residence in Philadelphia, at its acme. To be civilly received by the fashionable people, and to be invited to the President's, it is necessary to visit the British Ambassador. To be on terms with Chevalier DYrujo [*sic*], or General Kosciusko even, is to be a marked democrat, unfit for the company of lovers of good order and good Government. [8]

Onto this stage, strewn with the wreckage of verbal and physical battle and torn with the continuing conflict engendered by political extremists, stepped Priestley in June, 1794, seeking a refuge where he might live in peace. A scientist, scholar, and ordained minister of the Unitarian faith, he innocently demonstrated the unworldliness of his three callings when he declared that he had no intention of becoming involved in politics in America but was interested only in "philosophical pursuits . . . and my still more favourite pursuit, the propagation of Unitarianism." [9]

Priestley had had a distinguished career as a scientist in England, his discovery of oxygen in 1774 having given him international fame as a chemist, but he had also supported the French
Revolution and he had preached Dissenting sermons. His twofold
unorthodoxy, in both politics and religion, had eventually proved
to be too much for some of his Birmingham neighbors to endure.
What Pitt whimsically referred to as "the effervescence of the
public mind" had bubbled over and on Bastille Day, July 14, 1791,
a mob had burned the meeting-house in which Priestley preached
and had destroyed his home, reducing to rubble his library, his
laboratory, and such of his personal belongings as he had not had
time to salvage in making his escape. He had found immediate
shelter with a former pupil and old family friend, William Vaughan,
in London and shortly thereafter had obtained a post with a congregation at Hackney. Here he had been reasonably happy for a
time with his writing, teaching, and lecturing, but public hostility
could not be evaded. Harried by the increasing pressure of political
and religious intolerance, Priestley had finally decided that his only
hope for peace lay in exile. France, his first thought, he had discarded in favor of America, and in October, 1791, he had begun to
send funds to John Vaughan, younger brother of William and also
a former pupil, now in Philadelphia, whom Priestley asked to look
about for a future home for the Priestleys in the New World.

This was not to be an isolated dwelling in the wilderness, however. It was to be the center of a grandiose scheme for an ideal
society, dedicated to political, civil, and religious liberty, and by
February, 1793, at least one hundred English families were interested in the project.[10] Priestley's son Joseph, Thomas Cooper, and
two other young men had been sent to the United States to choose
a site for the proposed utopia and, after considering the land
from New England to the Carolinas, in February, 1794, they had
chosen a tract of land on the Susquehanna River, forty miles north
of the small settlement of Northumberland in Pennsylvania. Cooper
gave six reasons for this choice. As defenders of human dignity and
freedom they had been pleased by the fact that in this area there

was no slavery and white men lived at peace with the Indians. Economically, the tract was presently cheap but offered the prospect of increasing in value upon cultivation, while large adjoining areas were available for expansion. As Englishmen they were attracted by the climate, which was much like that of their native land. Finally, they found in Northumberland a larger proportion of English settlers than they had found elsewhere, a most important factor, since above all else they intended to make of their settlement a community of English gentlemen. By the middle of 1794 the Priestley group had purchased 300,000 acres, which they proposed to offer to settlers in lots of approximately 400 acres each.

Priestley arrived in New York on June 4 and received an enthusiastic welcome from such groups as the Democratic Society of New York, the Tammany Society, the Associated Teachers in the City of New York, the Medical Society of the State of New York, and the Republican Natives of Great Britain and Ireland, resident in the City of New York. He was greatly pleased. "I never saw any place that I liked so well as New York. It far exceeds my expectations, and my reception is too flattering, no form of respect being omitted. . . . This must be a glorious country, and I doubt not of finding a peaceable and useful establishment in it."[11]

Two weeks later he was welcomed to Philadelphia by the *Philadelphia Advertiser* of June 21 as "the justly celebrated philosopher." The American Philosophical Society, of which he had been elected a member in 1785 through the offices of William Vaughan, sent greetings by its president, David Rittenhouse, to a colleague whom they regarded as "an enlightened republican."[12] He was also warmly received by the scholarly circle of the University of Pennsylvania, where he met fellow scientists like Benjamin Rush and James Woodhouse. For Rush, Priestley's arrival in America was important enough to cause him to reopen his Commonplace Book, which had been neglected since August, 1793, because of the yellow fever epidemic, to note: "June 4, 1794—Dr. Priestley landed at New York."[13]

But Priestley was welcomed perhaps most heartily of all by John Vaughan, his former pupil, now a prosperous Philadelphia merchant.[14] Vaughan had come to Philadelphia in 1782, bearing recommendations from Benjamin Franklin, who had for many years been a close friend of the Vaughan family in England.[15] That an Englishman could travel thus freely between the two belligerent nations then involved in the American War for Independence might seem strange, but the Vaughans had actually been intimately connected with the American cause for many years. John Vaughan's mother had been the daughter of Benjamin Hallowell of Boston, Massachusetts, whom his father, Samuel, had met in the course of travelling the triangular route of his mercantile interests between England, the West Indies, and the American colonies. Benjamin, John's eldest brother, actively worked for the Americans during the Revolution as a confidential agent for the Earl of Shelbourne, and in 1782 went to France as an associate of Lord Shelbourne and of Franklin to participate in the Anglo-American peace negotiations. When John Vaughan in 1778, at the age of twenty-two, had begun his mercantile career, his father had sent him to Franklin, then in France, for guidance.[16] Though John had diligently applied himself to the study of French and the learning of the wine business, he had also watched "with great anxiety, the Event of so interesting an affair" as the struggle for American independence.[17] In May of 1778 he had illegally registered himself in Bordeaux as an American in order to avoid possible deportation but had asked Franklin's advice about really making himself an American citizen.[18] By November, 1779, he had made up his mind to settle in America before the war was over and in 1781 he was seeking through Franklin a short-cut to American citizenship.[19] When he finally left Europe in 1782 he took with him Franklin's letter commending him to Robert Morris, which, together with his father's business connections with Morris, secured for him a place in Morris' counting-house.[20] Here he applied himself diligently and prospered, so that by 1791 he was able to establish himself as a merchant in his own right.[21]

Vaughan's family had for many years been closely associated with Priestley[22] and zealously followed his religious teaching, but the young Vaughan had found no congenial church home in Philadelphia when he arrived there. In 1783 the Rev. William Hazlitt, an English Unitarian, father of the essayist and a friend of Priestley, had come to Philadelphia, lectured on the "Evidences of Christianity" and printed Unitarian tracts, but, receiving no offer of a church because of orthodox opposition to his theology, he had moved on to Boston.[23] In 1790 or 1791 a preacher who called himself a Unitarian had been forbidden to preach in Philadelphia and had had to flee the city.[24] A potential congregation for such preaching did exist, however, for Vaughan wrote to Priestley in 1791, seeking his aid in finding a Unitarian minister for Philadelphia. Priestley replied that "America itself must find the man, as in due time I doubt not will be the case."[25] Vaughan felt that this man had been found when Priestley arrived in Philadelphia in 1794.

Priestley's gratification over the initial enthusiasm of his reception in Philadelphia did not last long. Very quickly he realized that his welcome came chiefly from scholarly, scientific, and liberal political groups, who saw in him a distinguished philosopher, scientist, and worker in the cause of political freedom. He had declared many times, however, that his primary interest in life was the propagation of Unitarianism and he was deeply chagrined when he found that "Nobody asks me to preach, and I hear there is much jealousy and dread of me."[26] The Rev. William Rogers, pastor of the Baptist meeting in Second Street, had, in fact, worked himself into hysteria, crouching in his pulpit almost doubled in two as he shrieked at his congregation to beware, for "a Priestley had entered the land."[27]

A savage political attack was made by the English journalist, William Cobbett, alias Peter Porcupine, who had come to Philadelphia in 1792 and had appointed himself defender of the English cause in America.[28] Cobbett's tremendous skill as a writer rendered deadly his bitter hatred for Priestley. Filled with rage by the cordial reception given his fellow countryman, whom he considered a traitor to England, Cobbett published a scurrilous pamphlet in August, 1794, entitled *Observations on the Emigration of Doctor Joseph Priestley*. In this work he praised the English mob's action against Priestley, who, he said, had threatened the safety of the British government and the Established Church and would now, in America, add "one more to the partisans of France."[29] Having described those who welcomed Priestley as "several Societies of scoundrels,"[30] and the American Philosophical Society, in particular, as "a nest of such wretches as hardly ever met together before,"[31] Cobbett charged Priestley with using religion as a cloak for political conspiracy in his "inflammatory discourses, called sermons."[32] Other journalists of the same persuasion, led by John Fenno in the *United States Gazette*, joined in the attack, while the liberals, notably Benjamin Franklin Bache in the *Aurora*, with equal bitterness mounted a counter-offensive. Priestley, however, the object of all of this violence, steadfastly held to his resolve not to participate in politics. He wished, in fact, to remain completely aloof from American affairs as such, having "no intention to be naturalized at all, but to live as a peaceable stranger."[33] The latter neither his own temperament nor the times permitted him to do.

The three Priestley sons had set up a homestead for their parents in Northumberland, one hundred and thirty miles northwest of Philadelphia, and according to prearranged plans Priestley and his wife left the city in the middle of July, 1794, for that remote outpost. Before he went, however, Priestley learned that the Universalists were building a church on Lombard Street between Fourth and Fifth, the use of which they proposed to offer for three days a week to any sect of Christians which applied for it. They needed money to finish the project, but Priestley declared that he had friends who were willing to provide the funds if the Universalists would permit his use of the chapel for Sunday mornings. The issue was not yet settled in August, when Priestley wrote to Vaughan from Northumberland: "A place to preach in, so as to lay a foundation for a Unitarian society, I shall be much obliged to you for providing. I am composing some discourses for the purpose."[34]

288   G272

C. 1

Meanwhile the utopian settlement in Northumberland had failed to develop as planned and within a short time after his arrival Priestley seems to have given up the idea of any further sponsorship of the idea. However, he and his family were established in Northumberland, all of his books and apparatus had been transported at great cost to his new home, and he decided to make Northumberland his permanent residence.

In September, Benjamin Rush wrote to Priestley that John Carson, the professor of chemistry at the College in Philadelphia, was dying and Rush thought that Priestley would be invited to fill the vacancy soon to be available if he wanted the post. Priestley was still actively pursuing his research in science and found intriguing the possibilities of this connection with an academic institution of higher learning. An additional and powerful inducement for him to return to Philadelphia was the opportunity it would give him to form a Unitarian congregation in the city, for he was confident that "everything was ripe for the propagation of Unitarianism."[35] The invitation to the professorship actually came early in November but Priestley surprisingly declined to accept.[36] He was much embarrassed, after having assured Rush only a week before that he would accept the offer if it were made, but he gave a number of reasons for his decision. He dreaded the long, hard, expensive trip from Northumberland to Philadelphia, which had to be made by private conveyance. His household goods were now in Northumberland and he did not want to incur the expense and inconvenience of moving them again. He doubted his professional adequacy for the professorship, "For, though I have made discoveries in some branches of chemistry, I never gave much attention to the common routine of it, and know but little of the common processes."[37] On the other hand, he expected Northumberland to have its own college within a year or two, where he would be able to teach while propagating Unitarianism, the project always closest to his heart. Finally, and most important of all, Mrs. Priestley had taken "an unconquerable aversion to Philadelphia and my evil genius having brought her hither, I must give her the choice of a place of residence."[38] The idea of spending four months of every winter in the city, leaving his wife alone in Northumberland, he refused even to consider.

Priestley himself had many times expressed his dislike for Philadelphia as a place of permanent residence. Two weeks after his arrival he had declared:

The expense of living is excessively high. . . . There is no such thing as taking a walk half a mile from the town, or by the river side. Excepting a square, adjoining the State House, there is not, in or near this city, anything like a plantation, or anything else calculated for the pleasure, I may say the health, of the inhabitants. It is only a place for business, and to get money in.[39]

In October he had delivered a capsule criticism: "Philadelphia is unpleasant, unhealthy, and intolerably expensive,"[40] while he had said the final word when he declared flatly, "Indeed, I never saw a town I liked less."[41] This was a harsh judgment of a city reputedly the center of the most refined and elegant society in the United States, the focus of the political life of the nation, at which were gathered the leaders of the state and national governments and the diplomatic representatives of foreign states, the goal of American and foreign travellers, the site of flourishing scientific activities, the home of numerous societies and institutions for advanced learning and scholarship in all fields, most notably the American Philosophical Society and the University of Pennsylvania. One would imagine that such a place would have appealed strongly to a man of Priestley's tastes and accomplishments.

Gossip of the time suggested that Priestley spoke from personal pique, because of having been snubbed by Philadelphia society, when he so castigated the city. This charge, however, his son Joseph indignantly denied and the correspondence of Priestley himself gives no hint that he felt he had been ostracized. Quite possibly he simply could not afford to live in Philadelphia, where the cost of living had doubled in 1790 with the establishment there of the national capital, for he was at this time accepting financial aid from various friends in England. However, his son offered the most logical explanation for his decision to stay in Northumberland. "What had greater weight with him than any thing else was, that my mother, who had been harassed in her mind ever since the riots in Birmingham, thought that by living in the country, at a distance from the cities, she should be more likely to obtain that quiet of which she stood so much in need."[42]

The frenzied state of politics in Philadelphia at the end of the eighteenth century, into which Priestley had immediately been drawn by the violent attacks and counterattacks of the public press, made completely understandable Mrs. Priestley's desire to keep her family far away from the city. The whole pattern of their unhappy English experience seemed to be repeating itself and Mrs. Priestley, her health exceedingly delicate, her nerves badly shaken by events in England, felt that the safest course was to keep her outspoken husband as far as possible from the political temptations of the capital. Having acceded to his wife's wishes, Priestley apparently made up his mind to like his new life. In any case, his enthusiasm for Northumberland had a suspicious ring. He wrote glowingly of the charms of the settlement. The climate was healthful, the situation pleasant, the cost of living half what it was in Philadelphia, and he could pursue his scholarly interests there without the distractions of city life.

There was certainly plenty of quiet if not much else in Northumberland in 1794. The settlement had been laid out in 1762 but had been abandoned during the Revolution. When Priestley arrived there it consisted of one hundred houses. It was to have no post office until the following year, no stage coach service until 1797.[43] Priestley's sense of isolation during this period is reflected in his letters, which he despatched by way of travellers passing through Northumberland, most of his communications being directed to the care of John Vaughan. By May, 1795, he had decided to return to Philadelphia for a visit and so informed Vaughan.

My desire, and I think my duty, is to appear in my proper character, of a minister of the gospel, and I will not make any considerable stay in your city, and be reduced to a disgraceful silence by the bigotry and jealousy of the preachers. I wish particularly to deliver a set of discourses on the evidence of Christianity, and other subjects that may be seasonable and useful, and therefore engage any place in which I can have a hearing and I will come.[44]

Under the benign exterior of the gentle philosopher lived a mettlesome fighter, spoiling with inaction and yearning to get back into the thick of the conflict. The challenge offered by Philadelphia came clear and strong over the one hundred and thirty long and difficult miles separating him from the capital.

Priestley returned to Philadelphia and on February 14, 1796, in the Universalist chapel on Lombard Street preached his first sermon, "to a numerous, respectable, and very attentive audience," including "a great proportion of the members of Congress."[45] Particularly gratifying to him was the presence of John Adams, Vice-President of the United States.

NOTES

CHAPTER I

[1]Presbyterian, 6; Episcopal, 4; Quaker, 4; Methodist, 3; Lutheran, 3; Roman Catholic, 2; and one each for the Baptists, German Catholics, Jews, Moravians, and Universalists. CD, 1796, pp. 64–66.

[2]J. F. Sachse, *The Religious and Social Conditions of Philadelphia during the first decade under the Federal Constitution, 1790–1800* (Philadelphia, 1900), p. 10.

[3]Adams to John Vaughan, November 23, 1813: MSS, APS.

[4]PROC, pp. 1–7.

[5]Ralph Eddowes, "Proceedings on laying the first Corner-Stone of the New Unitarian Church, 10th fronting on Locust Street, Philadelphia, 25th March, 1828, With a Brief Account of the Rise and Progress of the Society," p. 3: CHURCH MSS.

[6]Edgar S. Maclay, ed., *Journal of William Maclay* (New York, 1890), p. 4.

[7]Maclay, p. 329.

[8]Benjamin Henry Latrobe, *The Journal of Latrobe* (New York, 1905), p. 86.

[9]Joseph Priestley, *Memoirs of Dr. Joseph Priestley to the Year 1795* . . . (Northumberland, Penna., 1806), I, 126.

[10]Joseph Priestley to John Vaughan, February 6, 1793: Joseph Priestley Papers, APS. A special study of this project was made by Mary Cathryne Park, "Joseph Priestley and the Problem of Pantisocracy," a Ph.D. dissertation at the University of Pennsylvania, 1947, printed in *Proceedings of the Delaware County Institute of Science*, XI (1947), 1–60.

[11]John Towill Rutt, *Life and Correspondence of Joseph Priestley* (London, 1832), II, 246.

[12]Rutt, II, 261.

[13]George W. Corner, ed., *The Autobiography of Benjamin Rush* (Princeton, 1948), p. 229.

[14]There is no biography of Vaughan. The following manuscript collections at the American Philosophical Society, containing approximately 180 letters written by or to Vaughan or with reference to him, provide the main source of biographical data: Archives, Benjamin Franklin Papers, Miscellaneous Manuscript Collection, another collection called simply "Manuscripts," Joseph Priestley Papers, Benjamin Vaughan Papers. John M. Sheppard, *Reminiscences of the Vaughan Family, and more particularly of Benjamin Vaughan, LL.D.* (Boston, 1865) includes a genealogy of the Vaughan family. There is a brief account of Vaughan in Abraham Ritter, *Philadelphia and Her Merchants* (Philadelphia, 1860), pp. 178–79. There are also innumerable references to Vaughan in the official records of the American Philosophical Society, of which he became a member in 1784 and an officer in 1789, serving continuously thereafter until his death in 1841. An excellent study of a particular aspect of Vaughan's life is Sarah P. Stetson, "The Philadelphia Sojourn of Samuel Vaughan," *Pa. Mag. of Hist. & Biog.*, LXXIII (October 1949), 459–74.

[15]The Franklin Papers, APS, contain over thirty letters relating to the Vaughans. Benjamin Vaughan, John's oldest brother, collected and edited *Political, Miscellaneous and Philosophical Pieces. . . . Written by Benjamin Franklin* (London, 1779) with Franklin's help, the only edition of Franklin's work, other than the scientific, issued during his lifetime. Franklin was also a close friend of Priestley, to whom he was

introduced in London in 1766 (Priestley, *Memoirs*, I, 50). The Franklin Institute of Philadelphia has a small collection of MSS letters exchanged between Franklin, Priestley, and the Vaughans, revealing a close, continuing association between the three families.

[16]Samuel Vaughan to Benjamin Franklin, March 5, 1778: Franklin Papers, VIII, 153.

[17]John Vaughan to William Temple Franklin, September 26, 1778: Franklin Papers, CI, 64.

[18]John Vaughan to Benjamin Franklin, May 19, 1778: Franklin Papers, IX, 183.

[19]John Vaughan to William Temple Franklin, March 10, 1781: Franklin Papers, CIII, 27.

[20]Benjamin Franklin to Robert Morris, January 19, 1782: MSS, APS. Washington refers to this connection in a letter dated June 30, 1784: John C. Fitzpatrick, ed., *The Writings of George Washington, 1745–1799* (Washington, 1938), XXVII, 430.

[21]CD, 1791, p. 134.

[22]Priestley had become acquainted with Samuel Vaughan in Warrington in the 1760's while preaching to a small congregation and tutoring at the Dissenting Academy. Two of Vaughan's children, Benjamin and William, had boarded with the Priestleys then. Two others, Samuel, Jr. and Rebecca, spent five months as students in the Priestley house in Birmingham in 1782. Priestley, *Memoirs*, I, 45, 54.

[23]Earl Morse Wilbur, *A History of Unitarianism* (Cambridge, Mass., 1946–52), II, 391–92.

[24]George Thatcher to James Freeman after hearing Priestley's first sermon, February 14, 1796: Anne Holt, *A Life of Joseph Priestley* (London, 1931), p. 194.

[25]Priestley to Vaughan, October 27, 1791: Priestley Papers.

[26]Priestley to Theophilus Lindsey, June 24, 1794: Rutt, II, 263.

[27]Rutt, II, 363.

[28]William Cobbett, *Porcupine's Works* (London, 1801), I, 121–220; VI, 411–12; VII, 149–50; IX, 224–40, 245–51, 388–410.

[29]Cobbett, I, 121.

[30]Cobbett, I, 121.

[31]Cobbett, I, 138.

[32]Cobbett, I, 153.

[33]Rutt, II, 304.

[34]Priestley to Vaughan, August 1, 1794: Priestley Papers

[35]Priestley to Lindsey, August 5 and September 14, 1794: Rutt, II, 269, 274.

[36]Minutes of the Trustees, University of Pennsylvania, V, 115, 121.

[37]Priestley to Rush, November, 3, 1794: Edgar Fahs Smith, *Chemistry in America* (New York, 1914), pp. 109–10.

[38]Letter dated August 12, 1797, quoted in Holt, p. 187.

[39]Priestley to Lindsey, July 5, 1794: Rutt, II, 269.

[40]Priestley to Lindsey, October 16, 1794: Rutt, II, 276.

[41]Priestley to Samuel Palmer, n.d.: Rutt, II, 287.

[42]Priestley, *Memoirs*, I, 169.

[43]According to John Binns, *Recollections of the Life of John Binns* (Philadelphia, 1854), p. 173, Northumberland was made a post-town by President Adams out of regard for Priestley.

[44]Priestley to Vaughan, May 6, 1795: Priestley Papers.

[45]Priestley to Lindsey, February, 15, 1796: Rutt, II, 333.

JOSEPH PRIESTLEY

Portrait by Rembrandt Peale. Courtesy of the American Philosophical Society.

II

The English Expatriates

ADAMS, WHO HAD KNOWN PRIESTLEY IN LONDON IN 1786, HAD WEL-
comed him on his arrival in the United States with a cordial invitation to visit the Adams family in New England.[1] Priestley resolved
that, when a set of his discourses was printed, he would dedicate it
to Adams as a token of his friendship and admiration, but Adams,
in March, was already repenting of his February enthusiasm. He
was, in fact, thrown into a fit of apprehension by Priestley's goodwill gesture, confiding to Mrs. Adams his fear that "it will give
me the character of a heretic."[2] He bolstered his courage by re-
flecting, hopefully, that "dedicating a book to a man will not imply
that he approves everything in it."

Conservative Philadelphia was actually patronizing Priestley as
much out of curiosity as from any other motive. Priestley acknowledged his awareness of actual hostility in many quarters when he
admitted that there was a doubt, concerning the publication of his
discourses, that "any person will run the risk of printing them."[3]
Certainly no one in Adams' circle was expected to be too friendly
toward the English exile. Undoubtedly, also, Adams had his eye on
the approaching election and did not want any ill-considered friend-
ships outside of the Federalist ranks to prejudice his chances.
Priestley both noted Adams' change of heart and guessed at its
motivation. "When . . . he was near his presidentship, he left
me, making a kind of apology, from the members of the principal
Presbyterian church having offered him a pew there."[4]

Priestley's wounded feelings were somewhat mollified by the

hospitality extended to him by Washington, who received him at tea during this same period and talked with him for two hours, "as in any private family."[5] A copy of a work of Priestley, which survived into the twentieth century and which was said to have belonged to Washington, indicated that the President had been much interested in the English theologian, many passages in the book being underlined and notes written in the margins in Washington's handwriting.[6]

As for the general public, Priestley was "surprised to find to how great a degree the violent prejudice that had been raised against me is overcome. Many of my hearers were those who were the most prejudiced, and great numbers such as never attended any public worship before. I daily hear of the great impression that my discourses make on those who were the most averse to every thing relating to religion."[7]

In May he had finished delivering his series of thirteen discourses and announced that all profits which might arise from their sale would be used for fitting up a place of Unitarian worship. "There is no doubt now of our being able to form a very respectable society of Unitarians, and we are taking measures for the purpose. There is really a noble harvest here. We want nothing but able labourers."[8]

A score of laborers soon presented themselves for the harvesting. While Priestley's lectures were being delivered, this small group of avowed Unitarians held several conversations and meetings, with Priestley present at some of them, and plans were laid to establish a Unitarian church in Philadelphia. However, though Priestley had from the beginning stated and repeated on many occasions that his dearest hope was to establish such a congregation in Philadelphia, when he was asked to accept the pastorate of the proposed society he declined the invitation, giving as his reason his preference for Northumberland as a place of residence. The group nonetheless felt that the procuring of "a proper Minister" was essential and knowing that the Rev. Henry Toulmin, son of the distinguished English Unitarian clergyman, Dr. Joshua Toulmin, a colleague of Priestley, was presently settled in Lexington, Kentucky, and might be available, an offer of the proposed ministry was made to him. Mr. Toulmin declined, however, stating that "he was comfortable in his situation at Lexington, and could not remove except upon a certainty of improving it."[9] This certainty, in all conscience, the Philadelphia group could not offer. So tentative was the whole project at this point, in fact, that Priestley felt it would be best, for the present, to forget the idea of securing an ordained minister and suggested that the group plan to meet quite simply, in their homes if necessary, with lay readers, until their future could be certainly formulated. This they decided to do.

Knowing that Priestley had been promised the use of the Chapel of the University of Pennsylvania when he next visited Philadelphia, James Taylor, as spokesman for the group, wrote to the trustees of the university on June 7, 1796, for leave to occupy one of their smaller rooms on a Sunday morning. The trustees never officially acknowledged this communication, but Taylor approached several of the trustees privately and they assured him that there would be no objection to granting the request. They suggested that he speak to the president of the board, Chief Justice Thomas McKean, who had authority to grant the necessary permission. "The Judge . . . politely assented to the request for a limited time."[10]

A meeting place having been secured, fourteen members of the group on June 12 formally met and pledged themselves to united action by signing a book of record titled "Proceedings": Caleb Alder, William Young Birch, Arthur Blayney, John Bradley, Ralph Eddowes, Joseph Gales, George and John Royston, John and Thomas Shute, Robert Slater, James Taylor, Nathaniel Thomas, and James Tucker.[11] Seven additional names were signed during the summer: George Carter, Samuel Coates, Thomas Gibson, Thomas Housley, William Leishman, Thomas Newnham, and William Russell.[12]

This group of twenty-one men formally organized themselves, in the room made available by the university at Fourth and Arch Streets, on August 21, 1796, taking the name of The Society of Unitarian Christians of Philadelphia. The name "Unitarian" was taken advisedly, for they were fully aware that it bore a great weight of odium, even among the liberal Congregationalists of New England, being equated in the public mind with "deist" or "atheist."[13] Nonetheless, the founders decided to state their position frankly, trusting to their own future efforts to dispel public ignorance of the nature of Unitarianism. Their Society thus became the first permanent Unitarian church in America to bear that name.[14] By the end of the year ten new members had joined: William B. Allport, Samuel Birch, George Blackwell, Joseph Hancox, John Owen, John Roy, John and William Turner, John Wheeler, and William Young.[15] Two had been lost, however. Coates and Tucker dropped out of the society after the organizational meetings.

The new church had no creed to which its members had to subscribe to qualify for membership. They were organized rather under a set of Constitutional Rules, which did, indeed, state their theological position in Rule 1:

In the meetings of this Society for religious purposes, worship shall be paid to the one God & Father of all, & to him only.[16]

Furthermore, Rule 2 went on to state that

none can be considered a permanent member, or entitled to vote in any proceedings of the Society, who do not subscribe the Constitutional Rules.[17]

However, a radical departure from the practice current in other denominations was the provision that in this church no person "of decent behaviour [shall] be excluded from participating in the Celebration of the Lord's Supper."[18] The society celebrated its first Communion service on October 2, 1796.

Services were conducted by lay readers chosen by ballot every six months from among the members of the congregation, to serve for the next half year. Birch, Eddowes, Taylor, Thomas, Leishman, and Gales accepted this responsibility from the beginning and the first four served continuously through the first phase of the society's existence. Leishman served until 1798, with six months out at the beginning of 1797, Gales until he left the city in 1799. John Turner was a reader when he died of yellow fever in September, 1797, and single terms in that same year were served by Allport and Jarvis. The readers were free either to compose their own sermons or read the published works of others but no record has survived to indicate what they actually did. The Constitutional Rules provided for the choice from among their number of a secretary and treasurer. Taylor held the former office during the 1796–1800 period while Russell, Eddowes, and Thomas served at various times as treasurer. Though there is no record that Russell was ever elected a reader, yet his unusual financial talents apparently prompted a by-passing of that requirement in order to secure his services as treasurer between August 28 and October 23 in 1796.

The Philadelphia in which the society was organized was not only the political capital of the United States but its social, cultural, and economic center as well. It was a large city by contemporary standards, numbering approximately 70,000 in population and containing about 9,500 houses in the city proper and its immediately contiguous suburbs, crowded together for a distance of almost four miles along the Delaware River and extending westward less than a mile, to about Eighth Street. Its social life was the most brilliant in America, its social structure an intricate maze of cliques and sets, accepted as a matter of course by Philadelphians but completely baffling to the uninitiated.

It was all very plain to the native sons of Philadelphia. At the top of the social scale was a closely knit oligarchy, membership in which was strictly conditioned, first, on the basis of "proper" family connections and, secondly, on the basis of wealth. While the propriety of one's family was mystically defined in terms either of longevity of residence, or magnitude of services to the government, or excellence of performance in the learned professions— each reaching sufficiently far back into the past—or, ideally, a discreet combination of all three, wealth was the gild on the lily and made even more splendid the glory of lineage. At the other end of the scale were the poor, exceedingly numerous and generally thought at the time to have deserved their fate because of some vaguely innate perversity of manners or morals. In between the two extremes was the middle class, easily definable because it was neither aristocratic nor poverty-stricken. This was the stratum of Philadelphia society in which anything could happen and the period in American history was one in which it could happen rather quickly. A pleasant air of expectancy hung over the United States. The ferment which was to come to a boil in the Age of Jackson had already begun to simmer in the Age of Washington and Adams.

The founders of Philadelphia Unitarianism were certainly not aristocrats, but, aside from their religious unorthodoxy and their erstwhile enthusiasm for the French Revolution, they were to be classified as substantial members of the middle class. Conservatism in morals and conventionality in manners had been outstanding characteristics of Unitarians in England. John Vaughan, upon his arrival in 1782, had been both "surprised" and "alarmed" by the prevalence of "French fashions" and luxury in Philadelphia. "I have in vain sought for the quakers [sic] simplicity which I had imagined," he wrote to William Temple Franklin. "They are full as dressy here as in France."[19] He took consolation, however, from the fact that, though there was "not in this town the least trace of republican manners," nonetheless "the republican Spirit is in its vigour."

The Unitarians in Philadelphia at the end of the eighteenth century had, most of them, but newly escaped from political and religious persecution in England and above all else they sought community acceptance in their new home. While they waited for time to instruct them in the mysteries of "getting on" in Philadelphia they set soberly to work to establish themselves as reliable members of the community. Vitally interested in the struggle being waged in England and on the Continent, with friends and relatives and all the associations of their lifetime left behind them, they watched with deep concern the events in America as they bore upon foreign affairs, and, as thinking human beings, they inevitably formed their own opinions about the battle being waged about them. However, impossible though it seemed to remain aloof from politics, and impossible though Priestley found it, his fellow Unitarians, with one exception, did succeed in standing apart from what Jefferson called the local "frenzy" during the first phase of their American life. Joseph Gales alone made his liberal partisanship sufficiently obvious for him to be invited by a group of North Carolina congressmen to found a Republican newspaper in Raleigh in 1799. The immediate problems of physical survival, however, engrossed all of the members of the new religious society and they could not afford to indulge in any unnecessary activities which might hinder them in their initial struggle with their environment. They apparently soon gave up or at least played down their pro-French sympathies. No wild-eyed reformers were to be found in their group. In the "great propriety and earnestness" with which they conducted themselves in their new life they were in every way "very respectable."[20]

Ralph Eddowes had been a tobacco merchant of some means in the city of Chester in England.[21] Born in Whitechurch in 1751, of an ancestry which on both sides had been Puritan for many generations, he had been taken to Chester at an early age. He had received a good classical education, having been for a while a pupil of Priestley. About 1784 an old controversy which had been waged intermittently for over two centuries between the people and the magistrates of Chester had broken out again. After a study of the charter, which had been granted to the city in 1506, and the subsequent history of the quarrel, Eddowes had championed the popular cause, instituting a suit against two magistrates whom he believed to be holding their offices illegally. The case had been tried three times, while Eddowes carried on an intensive campaign in the press, and had finally been taken up to the House of Lords. Here, in 1790, it had been decided against Eddowes on a technicality. Through an error on the part of his lawyer, Eddowes bore the entire expense of the suit, which amounted to almost £2,000 sterling. Shortly thereafter, new business arrangements had made it necessary for him to remove to Liverpool and it is reported that his departure was recorded in the local history of Chester as the noteworthy event of the year.

Eddowes had welcomed the move to Liverpool as being one step nearer to the realization of a dream which he had begun to find irresistible.

Disappointed . . . in an attempt to restore the ancient free constitution of the city of which he was an inhabitant, . . . harrassed [sic] in his business by the vexatious and oppressive restrictions of the excise laws— exposed as a dissenter to the odium which attached to almost every body of similar principles about the period of the French Revolution, and justly apprehensive of the consequences of that course which public affairs seemed to be taking,[22]

he watched the ships filled with English emigrants departing from Liverpool for America. By June of 1793 he was urging his brother-in-law, Timothy Kenrick: "Let us cast in our lot among them & leave this detestable country which its present corruption & vices of every kind have marked for the object of the divine judgment."[23] It was not until August 1, 1794, however, that he had sailed from Liverpool for Philadelphia, accompanied by his wife and nine children.[24] They had arrived at their destination on November 1. By 1796 Eddowes was listed in the *City Directory* as an ironmonger at 67 North Third Street, but he imported and sold a wide variety of items, from pig and bar lead to shovels, woolen hose to Wilton carpets, pins and buttons to sewing silk, all of which he advertised in the *Independent Gazeteer* of his fellow Unitarian, Gales.

Accustomed by both habit and principle to regular churchgoing, Eddowes experimented with various churches in Philadelphia, particularly the Presbyterian, which he found closest to that which he had attended in England, but, though "he found among them something that occasionally gave satisfaction," he also encountered "so much that excited a contrary sensation, as to render a decided attachment to any of them impossible."[25] He was thus without a church home when he joined the group which was to organize the first Unitarian society.

James Taylor was born in Perth, Scotland, on August 2, 1767.[26] After ten years of schooling, he had, in 1782, been set to learn the weaving business, which purpose took him in 1785 to London. From 1791 to 1794 he lived in Bath, working for a woolen draper. It was during this period that, regularly attending a Presbyterian meeting house, he had decided that he had had too much of Calvinism and began a minute study of the Bible. Before he left England he had become a Unitarian.

On May 9, 1794, Taylor had sailed from London in the brig *Earle*, bound for New York, where he arrived on June 28. With him was a pair of newly-weds, Nathaniel and Mary Thomas, friends with whom Taylor boarded for almost ten years in Philadelphia, and who joined him among the founders of the Philadelphia Unitarian Society. Arriving in Philadelphia on July 11, 1794, Taylor served as a clerk in four different firms successively until, in February, 1795, he was given power of attorney by Daintry and Ryle for the adjustment of a debt due in Philadelphia from a firm declared insolvent. Daintry and Ryle later appointed him their agent in Philadelphia, and "for a word they were the means of his success in this country."[27] In April, 1795, Ralph Mather, agent for the house of Taylor's uncle, David Taylor, in London, and others, proposed that James Taylor enter into partnership of agencies with him. This arrangement was made effective January 1, 1796, and continued until April, 1798. Taylor then accepted various agencies and grew so prosperous that in 1802 he felt that he could afford to relinquish four of the agencies, "wishing to have time for cultivating his mind while pursuing his business."[28] During the period in which he was assisting in the founding of the Unitarian society, his firm, James Taylor and Company, operated the Manchester Store at 28 North Third Street, where textiles and other imports were sold to merchants and storekeepers. Taylor also patronized the advertising columns of Gales's *Independent Gazeteer*.

William Russell came to Philadelphia in August, 1795, specifically to settle near Priestley at Northumberland.[29] Born November

11, 1740, Russell had not become a close friend of Priestley until December, 1780, when the latter moved to Birmingham, but from then on Russell had been one of Priestley's staunchest supporters. "A gentleman of ample means, irreproachable character, and wide intellectual sympathies," Russell seemed, his family's biographer, S. H. Jeyes, notes, "by circumstances as by nature . . . to be marked out for a career of civic usefulness, and perhaps of public distinction. He was a liberal subscriber to such causes as the abolition of slavery, promoted various philanthropic agencies at home, and was on intimate terms with many distinguished Englishmen."[30] Yet within a few years Russell's home had been burned to the ground, he was socially ostracized, and had finally been obliged to leave his native land. Jeyes states unequivocally that "of all these troubles the origin was his friendship with Dr. Joseph Priestley."[31]

Russell's house, Showell Green, had been destroyed by the same mob which had burned Priestley's home, and the two families had fled together to London. Russell, however, had a private fortune and powerful friends in London and he had fought for restitution in the courts, conducting, largely at his own expense, a thorough inquiry into the mob's activities against Priestley and himself, as a result of which investigation a substantial amount of damages was eventually obtained. Russell's continuing sympathies for the French Revolution, however, had finally made it necessary for him to leave England, and he had sailed from Falmouth for America with his son and two daughters on August 18, 1794, four months after the Priestleys had left. The Russells did not arrive at their destination, however, until a year and a day after their departure from England, for their ship was overhauled by a French frigate when only five days out, the Russells were taken prisoners and confined until December 23, first aboard their captor's ship and later upon another French war vessel in the harbor of Brest. After their release they spent the winter in Paris, observing the Revolution at first hand, and then sailed for New York on July 3, arriving on August 19, 1795.

They proceeded to Philadelphia in a coach which they had

brought from Paris, and Russell rented a house in the capital, for which he paid what he considered the exorbitant rate of $400 per annum. Making Philadelphia their headquarters, the family began a leisurely inspection of the American scene which quickly convinced them that they could live more happily elsewhere than in the Philadelphia area. Although at one time they had planned to settle with Priestley in Northumberland, a visit to their old friend clearly revealed that life in the wilderness was not for them and Russell disposed, at a loss, of the property which his agent had bought there for him while he was in Paris. New England finally offered them what they sought, a pleasant, rural setting which would afford father and son an opportunity to indulge in the English gentleman's favorite avocation of amateur farming. They rented in Middletown, Connecticut, a larger house than the one they had in Philadelphia for one half the price and made plans to return there to live in the fall of 1796.

Meanwhile the Russells spent the winter of 1795–96 in Philadelphia, where they were hosts to Dr. and Mrs. Priestley while the former delivered his first series of discourses. Russell's son did not relish the association. "Dr. Priestley is undoubtedly a very virtuous, learned, and agreeable man, and his name will be handed down to posterity . . . yet he is not one with whom one could enjoy the pleasures of domestic intercourse."[32] This clashing of personalities may have had something to do with the family's eventual removal to another section of the country.

Russell was, from the beginning of his life in America, deeply involved in business transactions, which took him up and down the eastern seaboard from Massachusetts to Virginia.[33] A man of wealth and cultivation, he lived in Philadelphia in what his son described as "a vortex of luxury and dissipation,"[34] his friends including such prominent citizens as Samuel Breck, Major Pierce Butler, senator from South Carolina, David Rittenhouse's daughters, Mrs. Sergeant and Mrs. Waters, Benjamin Rush, and Alexander James Dallas, as well as such visiting dignitaries as the Prince de Talleyrand-Périgord and the Duke de La Rochefoucault-

Liancourt. Russell was on terms of great intimacy with Washington, both in Philadelphia and later at Mount Vernon, often visiting him in Virginia and exchanging with him a voluminous correspondence, chiefly as one gentleman farmer to another, concerning such matters as agricultural improvements and stock breeding.[35]

Russell's connection with the Philadelphia Unitarian Society lasted for only a few months but they were the vital, formative months of the society's life and his wealth and prestige must have been of inestimable benefit. Having signed the original agreement binding the group together during the summer of 1796, at the organizational meeting held on August 28 he was chosen treasurer and in September was busily concerned with the problem of finding a larger meeting-place for the society than it then had. At a meeting held on October 23, the society noted the departure of Russell from Philadelphia and James Taylor, the secretary, was also named treasurer pro tem to take his place. For Priestley his friend's departure was "a disappointment of a very sensible kind," but he looked forward to seeing Russell every winter, presumably in Philadelphia.[36]

Joseph Gales was born on February 4, 1761, at Eckington, near Sheffield, England, the son of a village school teacher.[37] At the age of thirteen he had been apprenticed to a printer in Manchester, then to a typographer in Newark-on-Trent, where he had become a master printer and binder. In 1784 he had married Winifred Marshall, a cousin of Lord Melbourne, and had established himself in the printing and publishing business in Sheffield, founding, in 1787, a weekly called the *Sheffield Register*. His home had soon become a center for a circle of radicals and reformers, as he actively advocated the abolition of slavery and imprisonment for debt, the granting of universal manhood suffrage, and the reform of the judiciary system. As a friend of Thomas Paine, he promoted the sale of *The Rights of Man*, while, concerned for the cause of liberal religion, he aided Priestley in the support of Unitarianism. Because of his criticism of the Pitt government, he had finally had to flee England in 1794, going first to Schleswig-Holstein, where his wife and two children joined him, and then to America. He landed in Philadelphia on June 30, 1795. Here he was employed first as a compositor and then as a bookkeeper and reporter for the *American Daily Advertiser*. While he was still in Europe, Gales had learned shorthand and this skill he used in making the first verbatim reports of congressional procedures ever made in America. He shortly bought, published, and edited the *Independent Gazeteer* in Philadelphia at 145 North Second Street, renaming it *Gales's Independent Gazeteer*.[38] His lead article in the first issue, appearing on September 16, 1796, stated that he would

consider it his peculiar duty to notice discoveries in arts and sciences, improvements in agriculture and manufactures, and regulations respecting trade and commerce. These attentions, added to a strictly impartial detail of political measures, and local transactions; a correct abridgement of Congressional debates, original and selected essays, poetical effusions, and biographical and general anecdotes, will, he trusts, form an interesting miscellany.

Among Gales's friends in Congress were some congressmen from North Carolina, who persuaded him to migrate to their new capital at Raleigh for the purpose of establishing a journal. He sold his Philadelphia paper to S. Harrison Smith and on October 22, 1799, founded a weekly in North Carolina, the *Raleigh Register*. Gales became a leading citizen of Raleigh, serving as its mayor for nineteen years. As a Jeffersonian in politics he was elected state printer annually after 1800 until he was ousted by the Jacksonians. Continuing his outstanding career as a liberal journalist and reformer, he was also a missionary of first importance to the Unitarian cause in the South. In Philadelphia he brought all of his talents to bear upon his work for the Unitarian Society, serving in various important capacities until his removal from the city in 1799. His historical sketch of the society's origin and progress, written at the group's request, was the first entry made in its first record book. He was elected one of six lay readers in August, 1796, and was re-elected five times, serving continuously until he left the city. He served on a committee editing the Hymn Book and helped to plan the religious education of the society's children.

Little is known of the pre-American life of the other founders of the society.

William Young Birch had come to the United States from Manchester in 1793 and set himself up as a bookseller and stationer.[39] His establishment at 17 South Second Street has been declared the first Unitarian propaganda center in the United States, though Birch had, for non-Unitarian Philadelphians, other claims to public attention. In 1800 he entered into partnership with Abraham Small and their publishing business became one of the city's most prosperous concerns. Among the firm's accomplishments were the first *Gentleman's Annual Pocket Remembrancer* and *The American Lady's Pocket Book*.

William Turner had suffered bankruptcy in England and came to America to retrieve his fortunes.[40] He eventually paid all his debts, a feat which led his creditors to present him with a silver cup, although he kept the latter a secret even from his family. His daughter was not aware of the cup's existence until she found it among his effects after his death.

Of the others who signed the records in the first few months of the society's existence, it is known that Wheeler was a painter, Owen a shoemaker, George Royston and Young "taylors," Newnham a silk dyer, Thomas a scrivener, Blayney a physician, Blackwell, Carter, John Shute, and Tucker merchants, and Alder an upholsterer and paper-hanger, who was also a merchant on the side, importing such disparate items as feathers, lace, and carpets. Newnham and Blayney were active in August, 1794, in the formation of the Philadelphia Society for the Information and Assistance of Persons Emigrating from Foreign Countries, Newnham being elected the treasurer and Blayney the physician of the society.[41] In 1796 both were still holding these offices and also serving on the society's Committee of Conference and Correspondence, as was their fellow Unitarian, William Y. Birch.[42] Many of the early members tragically formed a part of the ghastly mortality statistics of the yellow fever epidemics which ravaged Philadelphia at the end of the eighteenth century and the beginning of the nineteenth. John Turner died on September 18, 1797, John and George Royston, John Roy, and William Allport in October, 1798, and Thomas Newnham in October, 1799.[43]

These were the founders of the Philadelphia Unitarian Society.

Although Priestley had been a primary source of inspiration, he was never active in the daily affairs of the group. This was probably not an unalloyed tragedy for the society, however. Although Priestley won many friends among the intellectual elite, he was a symbol of political and religious unorthodoxy to the generality, whose reactions to him ranged from suspicion to hatred. His fame made it impossible for him to work inconspicuously, if, indeed, such had been his wish, which seems unlikely, so that he was always a storm center. Gentle and courteous though he was in person, he fought religious orthodoxy with ruthless and devastating force, and inevitably made enemies in the process.

The society was formally organized after Priestley's return to Northumberland in the spring of 1796 and it was six months before he visited Philadelphia again. On January 8, 1797, when he was in the city to give his second set of Discourses, he signed the records as a member of the society.[44] Whenever he visited Philadelphia, which he did four times,[45] he preached to the group and administered the Lord's Supper. He advised them from time to time on such subjects as their choice of psalms and hymns, and their affairs, in general, were always very close to his heart. His pride in the society was expressed in a letter to his friend, the Rev. Theophilus Lindsey, in England, on September 11, 1796, in which he declared: "I do not know that I have more satisfaction from any thing I ever did, than from the lay Unitarian congregation I have been the means of establishing in Philadelphia."[46] The tablet erected to Priestley's memory in the church building describes his actual relationship to the society: "This church was founded under his encouragement."[47]

For some unexplained reason, John Vaughan was apparently not active in the formal affairs of the society during this early period. He came of a staunchly Unitarian family and had been interested in the progress of Philadelphia Unitarianism as early as 1791, yet he did not sign the society's records until June 3, 1798, being elected a member the next day,[48] and there is no further mention of him in the "Proceedings" until 1807. He could not have ignored the infant society. His close connection with Priestley, for whom he acted as Philadelphia agent, would have made that impossible. Still it is curious to find his name so conspicuously absent from the recorded activities of the society at this time, beyond his formal admission as a member.

So severe were the recurring outbreaks of yellow fever in Philadelphia that the society cancelled its meetings from August to November in 1797, 1798, and 1799, but with these exceptions it continued to meet every Sunday in the room provided by the University until permission was withdrawn by the trustees, who decided that no outside organizations should meet on university property after January, 1798.[49] The society then began a series of peregrinations, meeting in a succession of locations in the same general area. From January 7, 1798, to August 17, 1799, they met in Mr. Moon's schoolroom in Church Alley. That site having failed, they met at 24 Market Street on October 24, 1799, and decided to appeal again to the trustees of the university, who again gave them permission to meet at Fourth and Arch Streets.[50]

Nine new members had been added: Edmond and Samuel Darch; Matthew Falkner; Thomas Whitney; William Woodman; William Davy, a merchant; John Jarvis, a scrivener; John Miles and his son, John, Jr., gunmakers.[51] Of the entire membership before 1800, Priestley said: "They were all English families. Not a single native American had joined them."[52]

Not only nationality, however, but actual blood ties linked them together, with at least twelve members related to each other in six family groups: William and Samuel Birch, Edmund and Samuel Darch, John Miles and his son, John, Jr., George and John Royston, John and Thomas Shute, and John and William Turner. They all lived in close proximity to each other, concentrated, with few exceptions, at the center of the city's trade, between Front and Fourth Streets and a few blocks north and south of High. The Birches lived together, as did the Darches, and the Roystons. The Turners shared a house with Newnham; Taylor lived with the Thomas family. The predominance of business among the concerns of the society was evident from the start. Of the twenty-three members whose occupations are known, ten were merchants, seven were artisans, two were scriveners, one was a teacher, one a journalist, one a physician, one a "gentleman."[53] According to Priestley the members showed "an attachment to each other similar to that of the primitive Christians . . . and many who do not openly join them, respect them."[54]

While the members of the society met for religious worship and quietly went about their daily concerns without fuss or fanfare, for the rest of Philadelphia, Unitarianism was summed up in the person of the much publicized Priestley. His fame as a liberal in politics and theology made him a natural target for attack and defense in the bitterly controversial decade of his residence in America, and through the highly vocal public reaction to him one obtains an excellent idea of Philadelphia's attitude toward Unitarianism in general. For Philadelphians, Priestley *was* Unitarianism.

In the course of his American residence, Priestley did much to allay the "fear and dread" with which he had originally been regarded by many of the orthodox church leaders in the city. From the beginning he had been treated with understanding and respect by such clergymen as the Episcopal bishop, Dr. William White, and the Presbyterian Drs. John Ewing and John Andrews, provost and vice-provost, respectively, of the University of Pennsylvania. Priestley found this "the more extraordinary as the bishop is orthodox, and [he and Andrews] are both Federalists, and Dr. Andrews, they say, very violent."[55] Bird Wilson in a *Memoir* of Bishop White written in 1839 described White's friendship with Priestley as "a very pleasing proof of the bishop's liberal and truly Christian temper."[56] Many, however, who had been hostile, were won over, often to terms of close friendship, by the considerable personal charm which Priestley could exercise when he chose. Perhaps one of his most notable conquests was Dr. Rogers, the pastor of the Baptist meeting in Second Street, whose initial aversion to Priestley had bordered on the ludicrous. He soon became a good friend, not only to Priestley but to the society itself, to which he gave his permission to meet in his room at the University in 1797 and again in 1799, subject to the approval of the trustees.[57]

One young clergyman, Dr. John Blair Linn, pastor of the First Presbyterian Church, engaged the veteran Priestley in a pamphlet "war" in 1803. Linn, only twenty-nine years of age, was considered a brilliant young man, to whom even Priestley originally ascribed "considerable ability."[58] Priestley's pamphlet entitled *Socrates and Jesus Compared*, recently published, was the cause of the exchange, with each man delivering two blows, but the honors apparently going to Priestley.[59] This was a very polite contest, however, with each man "very respectful" to the other, and Priestley seemed to enjoy it thoroughly. In fact, he felt that his defense was more interesting than his original pamphlet, and it happily led to "a public discussion, so much wanted here, of the doctrine of the Divine Unity."[60]

Though he was personally well received by many of his fellow clergymen, Priestley was greatly disappointed that he was not invited to occupy any pulpit other than that of the Rev. Elhanan Winchester of the Universalist Church. Winchester had had troubles of his own and was able to sympathize with Priestley from bitter personal experience, for in 1781, then a Baptist minister, he had been excluded from his church because of preaching the doctrine of universal salvation.[61] Those who still operated safely within the orthodox ranks, however, were shocked by Priestley's heterodoxy, whatever they thought of him otherwise, and "shuddered while they contemplated the imminent danger of his soul."[62] On one occasion, when he and Ewing were dinner guests at the home of Professor Davidson of the university, Priestley pointedly referred to the appropriateness of his preaching a funeral sermon in Ewing's church for a man who had been one of Priestley's hearers in England, but Ewing dared not issue such an invitation, "for he well knew that it might cost him his living."[63]

Priestley tried to be tolerant of the intolerance directed against him, for he felt that "The extreme bigotry of some, affords a better prospect than the total indifference of others,"[64] yet he often displayed a most un-Christian contempt for what he regarded as shortcomings in others. He found indifference to religion greater in America than it had been in England, "and those with whom it is any object, are mere enthusiasts, without any knowledge. I have attended some of their places of worship; but I have not found one that a man of sense can hear with any satisfaction; except Bishop White."[65]

Of thirteen denominations organized in Philadelphia in 1796, he declared the Episcopalians the most liberal, while even the Roman Catholics were "not more bigoted than the Presbyterians."[66] His remarks about the neighboring Protestant churches, delivered in his address to the Unitarian congregation on March 5, 1797, certainly did nothing to foster interfaith relationships, as he congratulated his fellow Unitarians upon their independent establishment and told them, "From churches so fundamentally corrupt, though nominally Christian, you do well to separate yourselves."[67]

Priestley was greatly concerned over the "progress of infidelity" in America, which he found "independent of all reasoning."[68] Lack of religion he believed to be the common enemy and it was against this that he felt called to exert all his strength. The general public knew little, if anything, about the nature of Unitarianism. Priestley himself was inextricably bound up in the public mind with the cause of the French Revolution and hence inevitably with atheism, yet even a cursory examination of the titles of his theological works would have demonstrated his deep religiosity and his Christian conviction. In *Unitarianism explained and defended . . .* published in Philadelphia in 1796, he declared: "To the people of this country I must suppose that, like Paul, I have been represented either as a setter forth of strange gods, or some strange and dangerous doctrine concerning God. . . . But, in reality, like Paul I only preach *Jesus and his resurrection.*"[69]

In January, 1797, Priestley issued a pamphlet, *Observations on the Increase of Infidelity,* subtitled, "To which are added, Animadversions on the Writings of several Modern Unbelievers, and especially the Ruins of Mr. Volney." He hoped, primarily, to provoke Volney into a prolonged verbal contest in which he, Priestley, could annihilate Volney, then in Philadelphia "and much looked up to by unbelievers here."[70] Also, he admitted, he hoped "that my animadversions on his work may excite some attention."[71] In a subsequent exchange of letters, however, Volney refused to accommodate Priestley. "The question between us," he told Priestley, "is not of a very urgent nature: the world would not go on less well with or without my answer as with or without your book."[72]

Adams, in some way not made too clear, interested himself in Priestley's favor against Volney,[73] but he attended only once at the second series of Discourses which Priestley gave in Philadelphia from January to March, 1797. Nor did he ever subscribe to Priestley's *Church History.* Had he done so and recommended the subcriptions, Priestley declared, "it would have succeeded, I doubt not."[74] Adams had definitely abandoned his old friend, to all practical intents and purposes.[75]

Though losing the sponsorship of the President, however, Priestley was gaining the friendship of a Vice-President who was soon to be President. The second series of lectures was in general not so well attended as had been the first, but Jefferson came to hear them and Priestley saw a great deal of him at this time.[76] The friendship between the two had not been of quick growth. Though they could hardly have been unaware of each other's reputation in science, philosophy, and governmental theory, and would, by their very natures, have respected each other, there is no record of any close relationship between them until 1797, from which time forward their friendship developed steadily until Priestley's death in 1804. Priestley had one worry about his new friend in 1797, however. "I hope he is not an unbeliever, as he has been represented."[77]

He soon discovered, to his great satisfaction, that Jefferson "cannot be far from us, and I hope in the way to be not only *almost*, but *altogether*, what we are."[78]

There had been such a lessening of interest in Priestley's discourses in 1797 that he decided not to go down to Philadelphia any more for that purpose. "The state of politics had, I believe, contributed something to this. I am considered as a citizen of France, and the rage against everything relating to France and French principles, as they say, is not to be described. . . . I have nothing to do with their politics, and have taken no part whatever; but this does not exempt me from the most rancorous abuse."[79]

Some of the bitterest attacks were made by his fellow Englishman, Cobbett. In *Porcupine's Gazette* in September, 1798, Cobbett published a copy of a letter dated February 12, 1798, written to Priestley by John Stone, then in Paris, enclosing a letter for Benjamin Vaughan.[80] These two letters had been seized in a neutral vessel by the English and had been used in the High Court of Admiralty as part of the proceedings against the ship. Stone hinted in his letter to Priestley of a future revolution in England and Cobbett tried to attach this treasonable intention to Priestley, whom he called "this Apostle of Sedition."[81] Priestley replied quite simply to Cobbett on September 3 that he was "not answerable for what Stone or any other person may think proper to write to me."[82] Cobbett insisted on believing that he had vanquished Priestley, however, dismissing him as "a political viper but a viper without a sting," for whom he had "unqualified contempt."[83]

Priestley's friend Lindsey in England asked why President Adams did not silence Cobbett. Priestley's answer revealed Adams in a very unflattering light. "He said once to me, 'I wonder why the man abuses you,' when a hint from him would have prevented it all. But he is too useful to the party, on the whole, and it answers their purpose to cry down all who are supposed to favour French principles."[84]

Priestley was finally provoked into writing his one political article to be published in America, "Maxims of Political Arith-

metic," signed "A Quaker in Politics," which appeared in the
Aurora on February 26 and 27, 1798. Though he never became an
American citizen and was hence unable to vote, there is no doubt
that had he had the privilege he would have cast his ballot for
Jefferson.

In 1799 Priestley became involved in serious trouble through
his friend, Thomas Cooper. Cooper had been closely associated
with him in England and had planned the Northumberland project
with Priestley's sons. He had made a preliminary trip to Northumberland in 1793 and then returned home for his family, sailing back
to the United States again the following year. Settling in Northumberland, he had resumed his close relationship with Priestley,
although Cooper's disbelief in religion must have been hard for
Priestley to bear. Benjamin Vaughan had feared that Cooper would
get Priestley into trouble because of his natural talent for stirring
up political hornets' nests[85] and Vaughan was right.

Cooper needed a job and there was a political post in the
federal service which Priestley thought admirably suited to his
friend's abilities. He recommended Cooper to Adams, but Adams
had no intention of appointing a foreigner. Unfortunately, he had
the custom of never acknowledging letters of application for positions and he never replied to Priestley. This, he felt later, might
have offended Priestley. In any case, when Cooper, two years later,
published at Northumberland his *Political Essays*, criticising the
Federalist administration, an open controversy ensued, in the
course of which Cooper expressed his disapproval of the Federalist
party in general and Adams in particular. By 1800 Cooper had
become involved in the battle between William Duane, editor of
the *Aurora*, and the United States Senate, and his political importance was recognized. It was then, five months after his published
criticism of Adams, that the Federalists chose to remember the
earlier incident of 1797 and made of Cooper's political views a
calculated insult to the President, based on disappointment at not
having been given the appointment he sought. Cooper was tried
under the Sedition Act on April 19, 1800, and convicted on May 1,

subsequently serving six months in prison, while his friends paid his fine of $400. It was obvious that Cooper had deliberately courted his fate in order to publicize the hateful character of the Alien and Sedition Acts, and he went to prison cheerfully as a political martyr. Actually, the case made his name famous and greatly increased his political effectiveness.

Priestley, however, was worried about the whole proceeding. Although Cooper had been living in his house when he published the *Political Essays*, Priestley's son denied that his father had had any connection with their publication. "In truth he saw none of the essays until they were printed, nor was he consulted by Mr. Cooper upon any part of them."[86] Adams had asked Priestley to abstain from any talk of politics, for he knew that the Federalists would be only too happy to indict him under the Alien Act. Timothy Pickering, his secretary of state, wrote to Adams on August 1, 1799, stating his belief that Priestley had helped Cooper to print and distribute his *Essays*, which, he felt, "demonstrates the Doctor's want of decency, being an alien, his discontented and turbulent spirit, that will never be quiet under the freest government on earth."[87] Pickering was sorry that Cooper had become a citizen, "for those who are desirous of maintaining our internal tranquillity must wish them both removed from the United States." Fortunately, Adams felt disposed to be lenient to his old friend and had declined to forward Pickering's plan to indict Priestley on the basis of "guilt by association." He replied to Pickering on August 13: "I do not think it wise to execute the alien law against poor Priestley at present. He is as weak as water, as unstable as Reuben, or the wind. His influence is not an atom in the world."[88]

While Cooper was enjoying the pleasures of political martyrdom in jail, Priestley, though at liberty, was not happy. He had written his *Letters to the Inhabitants of Northumberland* in 1799 to make clear his innocence of any intention to interfere in American politics. Newspaper attacks against him continued, however. They were "coarse and low," and "nothing in an English paper was half so malignant."[89] In 1799 Cobbett had left Philadelphia after

Benjamin Rush had been awarded the crushing sum of $5,000 in damages in a successful libel suit against the English journalist, but others continued his campaign against Priestley. Jefferson expressed deep concern for his friend:

How deeply have I been chagrined and mortified at the persecutions which fanaticism and monarchy have excited against you, even here! At first, I believed it was merely a continuance of the English persecution; but I observe that, on the demise of Porcupine, and the division of his inheritance between Fenno and Brown, the latter . . . serves up for the palate of his sect dishes of abuse against you as high-seasoned as Porcupine's ever were. You have sinned against Church and King, and therefore can never be forgiven.[90]

Priestley had other cause for concern. "The society of our Unitarians at Philadelphia, I understand, does not increase. . . . They have had some differences among themselves, and they want a sufficient number of good readers. . . . They have also lost many valuable men lately by the yellow fever."[91]

On August 24, 1800, the society decided to suspend its meetings. Priestley's analysis of the situation was tinged with bitterness:

My greatest mortification is that the Unitarian Society is wholly dispersed, and the few that remain, so dispirited, that I cannot bring them together, I fear, even to hear a few discourses that I had prepared, principally for them. I shall, however, see what farther can be done. Several of the most zealous died of the yellow fever, and most of the rest have left the place. There were not half a dozen at their last meeting. . . . The more opulent of their society, as Mr.—left them, evidently because they made no figure, and it was disreputable to belong to it.[92]

Of the forty-two names inscribed on the records from June, 1796, to August, 1800, six are known to have died of yellow fever,[93] at least three had left the city, [94] eight others were dropped from the *City Directory* in 1798,[95] twelve had never been listed in the *City Directory*,[96] while twelve were still in the city.[97]

Little of permanent importance had been accomplished by the society beyond the registering of its existence in the city. The small group of expatriate Englishmen had been made aware of each other's presence and had made a mutual declaration of Unitarian principles of religion. For a period of seven years, however, the pressures applied by the necessity of establishing themselves in new homes and businesses were to make it impossible for them to maintain the Unitarian Society. Perhaps the same thing could be said of the group, collectively, as was said of its most illustrious member, Priestley. "In his feelings he was still an Englishman."[98] The Philadelphia Unitarians were, at least, Englishmen who were determined to make a success of themselves in the New World.

NOTES

CHAPTER II

[1] Adams first met Priestley in April, 1786. Noted in his diary, April 19, 1786, in Charles Francis Adams, ed., *The Works of John Adams* (Boston, 1856), III, 396. He heard Priestley preach in the Essex Street Chapel on April 23 (p.397). He thought Boston the best place for Priestley to settle in America (Rutt, II, 234).

[2] Adams, I, 488.

[3] Priestley to Lindsey, April 8, 1796: Rutt, II, 336.

[4] Priestley to Thomas Belsham, January 11, 1798: Rutt, II, 391.

[5] Priestley to Lindsey, February 15, 1796: Rutt, II, 332.

[6] Dr. Charles L. Chandler, professor emeritus at Ursinus College, was told by Miss Frances A. Wister, a member of the First Unitarian Church of Philadelphia, that A. W. S. Rosenbach had once offered this volume to her for purchase.

[7] Priestley to Lindsey, April 8, 1796: Rutt, II, 336.

[8] Rutt, II, 336.

[9] PROC, pp. 1–2.

[10] PROC, p. 4. By the terms of the Whitefield trust, the unversity was obligated to provide a meeting-place for the use of religious groups which for various reasons might be temporarily without lodging. However, the deed required that a very strict Calvinistic creed be subscribed. Edward Potts Cheyney, *History of the University of Pennsylvania, 1740–1940* (Philadelphia, 1940), pp. 35–36. Priestley commented that such subscription "has never been actually required, except when, for other reasons, the Trustees wished to exclude a preacher. It was apprehended by some, that I should have been excluded on this pretence . . . but my discourses having been popular, and altogether unobjectionable, not one of the board chose to make any objection." Priestley to Lindsey, May 3, 1796: Rutt, II, 339.

[11] PROC, p. 5. Following listed in CD, 1796:
    Caleb Alder, upholsterer, 119 S. 3rd St.
    Arthur Blayney, M.D., 158 S. 2nd St.
    John Shute, merchant, 106 High St.
    Nathaniel Thomas, scrivener, 186 S. 3rd St.
Following listed in CD, 1797:
    William Young Birch, stationer, 17 S. 2nd St.
    Ralph Eddowes, ironmonger, 67 N. 3rd St.
    Joseph Gales, editor of *The Independent Gazeteer*, 145 S. 2nd St.
    George Royston, taylor [*sic*], John S. between Broad and Coates
    James Taylor (and Co.), Manchester Store, 28 N. 3rd St.
    James Tucker, grocer, cor. South and 4th Sts.
Not listed in CD, 1796 or 1797; address given in PROC:
    John Bradley, 33 N. 7th St.
    John Royston, John St.
    Robert Slater, 145 N. 2nd St.
Not listed in CD, 1796, 1797; no address given in PROC:
    Thomas Shute

[12] PROC, pp. 5, 10–11. Following listed in CD as indicated:
    George Carter, dry goods store, 55 N. Front St. (1797)

Thomas Newnham, silk dyer, near 232 N. 2nd St. (1796)
William Russell, gentleman, 319 High St. (1797)
Not listed in CD 1796 or 1797; address given in PROC:
Thomas Gibson, 103 Market St.
Thomas Housley, near 141 N. 3rd St.
William Leishman, German Court
Samuel Coates, who signed PROC without giving an address, is of doubtful identity. The only man of that name listed in CD, 1796 and 1797, was a merchant at 82 S. Front Street. This was probably the eminent Quaker, who is not known to have espoused the Unitarian cause at any time.

[13]In 1813 Samuel Carey, Freeman's assistant at the liberal King's Chapel, Boston, advised against the use of the name "Unitarian" because of its unpopular connotation. W. H. Furness, *Address at the Installation of the Rev. Joseph May . . . January 12, 1876* (Philadelphia, 1876), pp. 62–63. When the orthodox Jedidiah Morse in 1815 attempted to fasten upon the New England liberals the name of "Unitarian" the charge was refuted by William Ellery Channing, who declared the liberals were Arians. Wilbur, II, 417–19. The same point is made by Conrad Wright, *Beginnings of Unitarianism in America* (Boston, 1955), p. 217.

[14]A Unitarian society had been formed at Portland, Maine, in 1792, led by Thomas Oxnard, an Episcopal layman, but it survived only a few years. Oxnard died in 1799 and, no successor being found for him, the congregation gradually drifted back into other denominational groups. Wilbur, II, 394–95.

[15]PROC, September 11, pp. 10–11:
John Turner, lived with Thomas Newnham
William Turner, lived with Thomas Newnham
John Wheeler, painter, 12 Combs Alley (CD, 1796)
William Young, taylor [*sic*], 153 South St. (CD,1797)
PROC, October 30, p. 11:
William B. Allport, 145 N. 2nd. St (Not in CD, 1796, 1797; given in PROC)
Samuel Birch, 17 S. 2nd St. (Not in CD, 1796, 1797; given in PROC)
PROC, November 6, p. 11:
John Owen, shoemaker, 12 Pear St. (CD, 1797)
PROC, December 18, p, 11.
George Blackwell, china merchant, 206 N. 2nd St. (CD, 1797)
Joseph Hancox, 108 Market St. (Not in CD, 1796, 1797; given in PROC)
PROC, December 25, p. 11:
John Roy, 25 Walnut St. (Not in CD, 1796, 1797; given in PROC)
[16]PROC, p. 7.
[17]PROC, p. 7.
[18]PROC, p. 7. Because of the informality of the society's Communion arrangements this was facetiously referred to by Thomas Bradford as "John Vaughan's supper." J. Thomas Scharf and Thompson Westcott, *History of Philadelphia, 1609–1884.* (Philadelphia, 1884), II, 1405.
[19]Vaughan to William Temple Franklin, May 18, 1782: Franklin Papers, CIV, 41.
[20]Priestley to Lindsey, January 13, 1797: Rutt II, 369.
[21]Eddowes gives a brief account of his pre-American life in the Preface to his *Sermons* (Philadelphia, 1817), pp. vi–vii.
[22]Eddowes, *Sermons*, pp. vi–vii.
[23]Eddowes to Kenrick, June 16, 1793, in Mrs. W. Byn Kendrick, ed., *Chronicles of a Nonconformist Family, the Kenricks of WynneHall, Exeter and Birmingham* (Birmingham, England, 1932), p. 73. Eddowes had married Kenricks' sister Sarah in 1777.

[24]Eddowes wrote a full account of this voyage, entitled "Occurrences During a passage from Liverpool to Philadelphia from 1st August to 1st Novr. 1794," CHURCH MSS. In the back of this journal, Charles J. Staples, a great-grandson, in 1927 listed the names of the children accompanying Eddowes, together with miscellaneous data about them. They were: Ralph, Jr., John, Roger, Sarah, Catherine, Mary, Anna, Eleanor, and Martha.

[25]Eddowes, *Sermons*, p. vii.

[26]MS extracts from a Memoir written by Taylor supply the following data. CHURCH MSS.

[27]Taylor, Memoir.

[28]Taylor, Memoir.

[29]S. H. Jeyes, *The Russells of Birmingham* (London, 1911) provides an excellent biographical account of Russell.

[30]Jeyes, p. 8.

[31]Jeyes, p. 9.

[32]Jeyes, p. 208.

[33]The William Russell Papers, HSP, including Russell's Docket Book, 1795–1799, his Journal, 1795–1802, his Waste Book, 1795–1802, and a Ledger, 1794–1815, in addition to an extensive collection of letters, indicate the complexity and variety of his family and business concerns.

[34]Jeyes, p. 203.

[35]Jeyes, pp. 203, 262–65. Letters from Washington to Russell in Fitzpatrick, XXXVI, 469, and XXXVII, 85 and 216, are filled with details concerning farm machinery, exchange of sheep and swine for breeding purposes, etc.

[36]Priestley to Russell, December 30, 1795: Rutt, II, 330. "If I was undetermined, I would certainly choose to fix wherever you should be," he told Russell, somewhat reproachfully, but he was "so fixed in Northumberland as never to think of removing."

[37]DAB, VII, 99–100; Clement Eaton, "Winifred and Joseph Gales, Liberals in the Old South," *Jour. South.Hist.* X (November 1944), 461–74.

[38]Gales was generously supported in his journalistic enterprise by his fellow Unitarians, several of whom took large advertisements in the paper, including Alder, Birch, Davy, Eddowes, Newnham, Taylor, Thomas, and Woodman.

[39]A biographical sketch of Birch is given in Henry Simpson, *The Lives of Eminent Philadelphians Now Deceased* (Philadelphia, 1859), pp. 90–91.

[40]*Christian Examiner*, March and April, 1828, p. 172.

[41]Scharf and Westcott, I, 480.

[42]CD, 1796, p. 19.

[43]PROC, pp. 10–11.

[44]PROC, p. 11.

[45]February–May, 1796; January–March, 1797; January–April, 1801; February–March, 1803.

[46]Rutt, II, 352.

[47]*Church Memorials*, a pamphlet printed by the First Unitarian Church (Philadelphia, n.d.), p. 11.

[48]PROC, pp. 11, 51.

[49]Minutes of the Trustees, V, 176.

[50]Minutes of the Trustees, V, 198.

[51]Edmund and Samuel Darch, 140 S. 2nd St. (PROC, p. 11; not in CD, 1796, 1797)

Matthew Falkner, 33 N. 10th St. (CD, 1797)

Thomas Whitney, 74 S. Front St. (PROC, p. 12; not in CD, 1800)

William Woodman, Cooper's Court (PROC, p. 11; not in CD, 1797, 1798)
Woodman advertised in *Gales's Independent Gazeteer* on October 5, 1796, that he would conduct an evening school during the winter to teach reading, writing, and arithmetic, every evening from six to nine, and from two to five every afternoon would teach the same, plus the French language, to both young ladies and young gentlemen.

William Davy, merchant, 59 S. Water St. (CD, 1798)

John Jarvis, scrivener, 126 N. 3rd St. (CD, 1797)

John Miles and John Miles, Jr., gun-makers, 500 N. 2nd St., Northern Liberties (CD, 1798)

[52]Priestley to Lindsey, n.d., "Received March 16, 1810:" Rutt, II, 453.

[53]*Merchants:* William Y. Birch, Blackwell, Carter, Davy, Eddowes, Newnham, John Shute, Taylor, Tucker, Vaughan; *artisans:* Alder, Miles, Sr. and Jr., Owen, George Royston, Wheeler, Young; *scriveners:* Jarvis, Thomas; *teacher:* Woodman; *journalist:* Gales; *physician:* Blayney; *gentleman:* Russell.

[54]Priestley to Lindsey, April 3, 1797: Rutt, II, 375.

[55]Priestley to Lindsey, n.d. "Received March 16, 1801:" Rutt, II, 453.

[56]Bird Wilson, *Memoir of the Life of the Right Reverend William White, D.D.* (Philadelphia, 1839), p. 170.

[57]PROC, pp. 47–48, 54.

[58]Linn's epic poem, *Valerian*, was edited by Charles Brockden Brown, an intimate friend, after Linn's death in August, 1804. Brown married Linn's sister in November. Ellis Paxson Oberholtzer, *The Literary History of Philadelphia* (Philadelphia, 1906), p. 170. Cited hereafter as Oberholtzer, *Literary History.*

[59]Priestley wrote to Lindsey, September 12, 1803: "I am informed that all his friends wished he had never provoked the controversy." Rutt, II, 516. He later wrote to Belsham, December 23, 1803: "My controversy with Dr. Linn has had all the effect that the most sanguine friends of Unitarianism could wish. . . . [A]ll his friends are mortified and ashamed for him." Rutt, II, 521.

[60]Priestley to Lindsey, September 12, 1803: Rutt, II, 516.

[61]Abel C. Thomas, *A Century of Universalism in Philadelphia and New-York . . .* (Philadelphia, 1872), pp. 27–28.

[62]James Taylor's "Recollections:" Rutt, II, 342.

[63]Rutt, II, 342.

[64]Priestley to Lindsey, May 17, 1798: Rutt, II, 400.

[65]Priestley to Lindsey, n.d., "Received March 16, 1801:" Rutt, II, 453.

[66]Priestley to Belsham, May 29, 1797: Rutt, II, 379.

[67]Joseph Priestley, *An Address to the Unitarian Congregation at Philadelphia. Delivered Sunday, March 5, 1797* (Philadelphia, 1797), p. 7.

[68]Priestley to S. Palmer, February 22, 1797: Rutt II, 372.

[69]Joseph Priestley, *Unitarianism explained and defended . . .* (Philadelphia, 1796), p. 3.

[70]Priestley to Palmer, February 22, 1797: Rutt, II, 371.

[71]Priestley to Lindsey, January 13, 1797: Rutt, II, 369.

[72]*Volney's Answer to Dr. Priestley* (Philadelphia, 1797), p. 3.

[73]Priestley to Lindsey, April 3, 1797: Rutt, II, 374.

[74]Priestley to Belsham, January 11, 1798: Rutt, II, 391.

[75]When Foster, the British ambassador, visited Adams in 1810 or 1811, he got the impression that Adams held Priestley at least partly responsible for his failure to win re-election in 1800, believing that Priestley had worked against him politically because of Adams' failure to give Thomas Cooper a government appointment for which

Priestley had recommended him. Richard Beale Davis, ed., *Jeffersonian America* . . . (San Marino, Calif., 1954), pp. 329–30. Yet Adams wrote to Jefferson on July 18, 1813, about Priestley: "This great and extraordinary man, whom I sincerely loved, esteemed and respected, was really a phenomenon; a comet in the system, like Voltaire, Bolingbroke, and Hume." Adams, X, 57. When he wrote to John Vaughan on November 23, 1813, however, he revealed mixed feelings. "I never recollect Dr. Priestley, but with tenderness of Sentiment. Certainly one of the greatest Men in the World, and certainly one of the weakest." MSS, APS.

[76]Priestley to Belsham, March 14, 1797: Rutt, II, 373.

[77]Priestley to Lindsey, April 23, 1803: Rutt, II, 511.

[78]Priestley to Lindsey, April 23, 1803: Rutt, II, 511.

[79]Priestley to Dr. Joshua Toulmin, January 9, 1799: Rutt, II, 413.

[80]Cobbett, IX, 224–40, 245–51.

[81]Cobbett, IX, 246.

[82]Priestley to Cobbett, September 4, 1798: Rutt, II, 406.

[83]Cobbett, IX, 250–51.

[84]Rutt, II, 418.

[85]During a visit to the Adams home in Quincy, Vaughan told Mrs. Adams that "Mr. Cooper was a rash man, and had led Dr. Priestley into all his errors in England and he feared would lead him into others in America." Adams to Timothy Pickering, August 13, 1799, in Adams, IX, 13.

[86]Priestley, *Memoirs*, I, 201.

[87]Adams, IX, 5–6.

[88]Adams, IX, 14.

[89]Priestley to Lindsey, January 16, 1800: Rutt, II, 427.

[90]Jefferson to Priestley, January 18, 1800: Rutt, II, 435.

[91]Priestley to Belsham, March 30, 1800: Rutt, II, 429.

[92]Priestley to Lindsey, n.d., "Received March 16, 1801:" Rutt, II, 453.

[93]Allport, Newnham, Roy, John and George Royston, John Turner.

[94]Alder had gone to New York, Gales to North Carolina, Russell to Connecticut.

[95]Carter, Falkner, Jarvis, Owen, John Shute, Tucker, Wheeler, Young.

[96]Samuel Birch, Coates, Edmund and Samuel Darch, Gibson, Hancox, Housley, Thomas Shute, Slater, William Turner, Whitney, Woodman.

[97]William Y. Birch, Blackwell, Blayney, Bradley, Davy, Eddowes, John Miles, Sr. and Jr., Priestley (on visits), Taylor, Thomas, Vaughan.

[98]Priestley, *Memoirs*, I, 198.

III

Brisk Young Americans

CONGRESS MET IN PHILADELPHIA FOR THE LAST TIME ON MAY 14, 1800, its next session, in November, to be opened in the new capitol being built at Washington. The state government, discouraged, as was the Unitarian Society, by the prevalence of yellow fever, and yielding also to the demands of the western counties for a more central location, had left Philadelphia the year before for Lancaster. Even though it was no longer the seat of the national or state governments, the city still offered, however, much to make life interesting.

Philadelphia continued to be the largest city in the United States. The population of the city and surrounding suburbs was a little over 70,000 in 1800. By 1810 it had grown to 96,664, half of which increase had taken place beyond the original limits of the city. There began to be considerable growth westward, with High Street paved as far out as Ninth Street in 1806, and in 1807 the paving was ordered to be continued as far as Twelfth. However, the main shipping center was still on Front and Water Streets, the main retail stores on Second Street between Arch and Walnut. The only way to travel within the city being by foot, horse, private carriage, or hired coach,[1] there was naturally resistance to the dispersal made necessary by sheer force of accumulating numbers, but the dread of yellow fever, which had been brought to the city on incoming ships, acted as a strong persuader to many to leave the water-front area. Merchants began moving their households from their business locations to fine new dwellings on High Street as

61

far west as Seventh, though it was still "considered a wonder how they could encounter such fatiguing walks from their counting-houses and business."[2] William Sansom, having the first units of the first large-scale housing development in America ready for occupancy in 1800, had to wait a long while for customers, for, with Walnut Street unpaved beyond Sixth, Sansom's Row, between Seventh and Eighth Streets, was considered "too remote and lonely."[3]

Political activity flourished, even though state and federal affairs had to be carried on from a distance. The "revolutionary tide" of Jeffersonianism engulfed Philadelphia on October 21, 1800, when John Inskeep was elected mayor, the first Democrat ever to hold that post. Mayor Inskeep ordered appropriate festivities for the announcement of Jefferson's election on February 17, 1801, and again on the day of his inauguration there was a great celebration. Jefferson's coup in the acquisition of the Louisiana Territory occasioned further public rejoicing at the beginning of 1804. However, despite the Democratic mayor in City Hall from 1800 to 1805, in 1808 and 1809, and from 1811 to 1813, the Federalists still retained a goodly measure of strength and returned Robert Wharton to the mayor's office fifteen times between 1798 and 1824.

The press did its best to keep the fires of partisanship burning brightly. Benjamin Franklin Bache had been a victim of yellow fever in 1798 but his *Aurora* continued the defense of the liberal cause under the direction of William Duane, who had joined its staff in 1795, and, after Bache's death, married his widow and took over the ownership of the paper. Duane happily reported in July, 1805, that there were sixty or seventy libel suits pending against him, a fair total even in an age partial to such litigation.

The Federalists had also lost their editor, John Fenno, by yellow fever, in 1798, and Cobbett had left the city in 1799 after Rush had won his libel suit against him. The conservatives gained a new champion, however, when Joseph Dennie came to Philadelphia from Massachusetts in 1799 at the request of Timothy Pickering, then secretary of state in Adams' cabinet. Dennie began publishing *The Port Folio* in 1801, first as a weekly, later as a monthly. Strictly following the party line, he took up the attack on Priestley when the latter made his fourth visit to Philadelphia in that year, declaring: "The tricks of Dr. Priestley to embroil the government, and disturb the religion of his own country, have not the merit of novelty."⁴ The *Aurora* replied: "Dennie is only Porcupine with a little more tinsel to cover his dirt." Actually, Dennie's Tuesday Club, formed by contributors to *The Port Folio*, was a gathering point for elegant and aristocratic young lawyers and doctors like Nicholas Biddle, Charles Jared Ingersoll, Joseph Hopkinson, and Dr. Nathaniel Chapman, dilettanti of the arts, who liked to spend their spare time in the cultivation of "polite and elegant literature."⁵ Thomas Moore, the Irish poet, after a visit to the United States in the summer of 1804, said, "In the society of Mr. Dennie and his friends at Philadelphia I passed the only agreeable moments which my tour through the States afforded me."⁶

An Irish friend of Priestley entered the battle of the newspapers in 1807 on the Democratic side. John Binns had come to the United States from Ireland in 1801 and had gone to Northumberland to be near Priestley. There he had published the *Northumberland Argus* and plunged into active politics in the Democratic party. In March, 1807, he came to Philadelphia at the invitation of friends of Simon Snyder and in May started, in support of Snyder's candidacy for the governorship, the publication of the *Democratic Press* as a tri-weekly and soon as a daily, the first newspaper in the United States to bear the name of "Democratic."

Very different from Philadelphia's strident and often vituperative newspapermen were its leaders in the practice of law and medicine. Both professions had had a long and honorable history in the city. Both were bound up in proud family traditions of gentility, learning, and public service. Both added to their historic accomplishment during the early years of the nineteenth century.

Although the Quaker founders of the city had frowned upon lawyers and preferred to settle all differences simply between themselves, the legal profession had flourished in the city which had the largest population in the country, was the center of trade and commerce, and, for a quarter of a century, the political heart of the new nation. From the beginning the bench and bar had called forth the finest of the city's talents and had operated at the highest possible level of honesty and decency as well as professional competence, so that, as Peter Stephen Du Ponceau, one of the greatest of them, said, "It was really a proud thing in that day to be a Philadelphia lawyer."[7]

The old Philadelphia families contributed largely to the carrying on of the legal tradition, with such men as Joseph Hopkinson, John Sergeant, and Richard Peters, Jr. Brilliant new strains were added by men like Peter Stephen Du Ponceau, a native of France, who practiced with distinction at both state and federal levels, but was especially active in raising the standards of legal education to new heights; and Alexander James Dallas, born in Jamaica of Scottish parents, who combined the practice of law with a political career of distinguished attainments. Another newcomer to Philadelphia, although he had journeyed only from Connecticut, was Jared Ingersoll, who exercised his remarkable gifts for both the law and politics with the same restraint and dignity which characterized his colleagues.

Philadelphia had always been the most important center for medical education in America, the first medical college in the colonies having been established there in 1765, and the early years of the nineteenth century were marked by further outstanding accomplishments. The yellow fever epidemics at the end of the eighteenth century, which had decimated the city's population, had focused the nation's attention upon Philadelphia's doctors, who had heroically fought, against overwhelming odds, an enemy whose nature they did not understand. As soon as it was considered safe, students began to flock to Philadelphia, to the Medical School of the University of Pennsylvania where these men taught. In 1784 there had been sixty students. In 1802 there were one hundred and twenty-five, and by 1810 more than four hundred, which number remained relatively constant thereafter, with never less than three hundred and fifty.

Teaching in the Medical School were brilliant leaders in every branch of the medical sciences: William Shippen in anatomy and midwifery, Benjamin Rush in the theory and practice of physic and of clinical medicine, Caspar Wistar in anatomy and midwifery, James Woodhouse in chemistry, Benjamin S. Barton in materia medica, botany, and natural history, Philip S. Physick in surgery. Physick began lecturing on surgery in 1800, so successfully that in 1805 a separate chair was created for this specialty, with Physick as its first occupant, "the Father of American Surgery." In 1809, Wistar requested the establishment of a chair in obstetrics and in 1813 this was finally accomplished, with Thomas C. James as the first professor. James Woodhouse had succeeded to the chair of chemistry in 1795 after Priestley had declined it, and served with great distinction until 1809, when he was succeeded by John Redman Coxe. Coxe in 1804 had founded a quarterly, *The Medical Museum*, a pioneer effort in medical journalism. In the same year a second journal had been launched by Benjamin S. Barton, the first teacher of natural science in America.

There had been one physician, Arthur Blayney, among the founders of the Unitarian Society, but he did not reappear in the society's recorded affairs after 1800 and no other known Unitarian practiced medicine at this time. However, the society had from the beginning been closely drawn into the scientific life of the University of Pennsylvania through the hospitality extended by its professors to their fellow scientist, the Unitarian Priestley, who was always welcome in their laboratories and lecture-halls. In 1802 Priestley was given to understand that the provostship of the university, left vacant by the death of Ewing, could be his if he wanted it, but he declined for reasons of health. [8]

As men devoted to the cultivation of reason, Unitarians had always been concerned with books, Birch among the founders of the society being a printer and bookseller, Gales a journalist who promoted the sale of literature. In Philadelphia they had found a receptive climate for their activities. By the beginning of the nineteenth century, fifty-one printing houses in the city with a total of one hundred and fifty-three presses annually printed an estimated 500,000 volumes. Mathew Carey, founder and head of the leading publishing firm, in 1802 organized the American Literary Fair, which brought to Philadelphia a tremendous amount of book business and added still further to the city's fame as a center of the book trade. Birch and his partner, Abraham Small, who was later to join the Unitarian Society, were two of the five Philadelphia representatives at this fair, the others being Samuel F. Bradford, William Duane, and Carey himself.

With the state and federal governments and their attendant entourages removed from the local scene, Philadelphia tended to concentrate more on its commerce and industry and it was in this activity that the Unitarians chiefly concerned themselves. The city had always been a busy port. At the beginning of the nineteenth century its ships were trading with every part of the world, while its harbor offered facilities annually to approximately seven hundred foreign ships and almost thirteen hundred coastal vessels. Its shipping merchants were among its leading citizens, amassing tremendous wealth and exercising great power in the city's affairs. Vaughan, Taylor, and many other Unitarians followed this calling. The merchants formed a Chamber of Commerce in 1801 to promote the development of trade and regulate their mercantile affairs among themselves. Vaughan was secretary in this organization in 1813 and held that office or the post of treasurer at various times thereafter. Shipbuilding continued to be one of the city's principal industries, and the manufacturing of consumers' goods showed remarkable development under the stimulus of a determined "Buy American" campaign. Birch and Small interested themselves in this. Philadelphia eventually became the headquarters of protectionism and already this theory was beginning to take form, with Mathew Carey prepared to initiate the program while growing up in his household was his son Henry, who was to make it his life work. A Scottish exponent of protectionism, John Melish, resident in Philadelphia during the early years of the century, later came to be connected with the Unitarian Society.

New banks were needed to take care of the increasing business and the Bank of Philadelphia, with a capital of $2,000,000, was established in 1803, the Farmers' and Mechanics' Bank in 1807, with its capital fixed at $1,250,000. Four new insurance companies were incorporated in 1804—the Union, the Phoenix, the Philadelphia, and the Delaware—to which were added the Marine Insurance Company in 1809, the United States Insurance Company and the American Fire Insurance Company in 1810. New arteries of transportation were needed to carry the growing trade and the beginning of the century saw a brisk development in the construction of turnpikes, canals, and bridges. By 1810 Philadelphia was the center of a considerable network of stage coaches and packets, which daily brought it news and trade from the rest of the world.

In the midst of all this activity the Philadelphia Unitarian Society, as an organization, spent the years from 1800 to 1807 in a state of dignified silence.[9] Many of the original members had died from yellow fever and several had moved from the city, yet several were still resident in the city and exceedingly active in its temporal concerns. Their unbroken silence, as far as their organized life as a denomination was concerned, for a period of almost seven years, is one of the unexplained mysteries of their past. One possible explanation is that their absorption in business and civic affairs left no time or energy for the affairs of the society, but their previous history in the life of the denomination and their intense moral earnestness make this seem unlikely. They were men of serious aim and purpose and would certainly not have let the important matter of religious worship go by default. Their conduct must necessarily have represented a conscious choice, and one could understand in such a choice the dictation of expediency. It was an age which had produced the Alien and Sedition Laws, under which the threat of prosecution had been directed at their most distinguished member, Priestley. For a group composed of newly naturalized citizens and, in many cases, men who were still English aliens, discretion was certainly the order of the day. The active promulgation of religious beliefs looked upon by many in the Philadelphia community even forty years later with "holy horror,"[10] could not have been either discreet or advisable.

Priestley was now struggling to bring to completion his monumental *History of the Christian Church* and the first volume was dedicated in June, 1802, to Jefferson, who "is everything that the friends of liberty can wish."[11] He delivered his third and last series of lectures in Philadelphia in 1803. His health was deteriorating rapidly but he was still filled with self-confidence. He wrote to Lindsey on March 1, 1803: "I am hardly able to speak loud enough for a large audience or I am persuaded I should now have many hearers in this place."[12] In the same letter he remarked that he was to administer the Lord's Supper on Sunday in a house where some Unitarians were meeting every Sunday morning. "They are the remains of the society of lay-unitarians, and I am not without hopes that it may revive." He was not to live to see the fulfillment of his hopes. He died in Northumberland on February 6, 1804.

Priestley spent only ten years of his life in America, the last two of them in very poor health, yet in this decade he had produced some of his most important theological writings, while, continuing his scientific experiments, he had made a significant contribution to the world of chemistry. It has been said that though he discovered oxygen he never understood what it was, calling it "dephlogisticated air," and certainly he spent many years defending the phlogiston theory, which was even then being disproved.[13] It was as a source of inspiration to others that Priestley made his most important contribution to American life. Though he spent comparatively little time in Philadelphia, when he was there he was a regular visitor in the classrooms and laboratories of the University, and, even when he was absent, his letters and scientific articles stimulated his Philadelphia colleagues to greater efforts. Until the day he died, Priestley was an untiring dynamo of activity in the fields of theology, philosophy, and science. One of his last thoughts was for his great friend, Jefferson, expressed in a letter to Dr.

George Logan a few days before his death: "Tell Mr. Jefferson that I think myself happy to have lived so long under his excellent administration and that I have a prospect of dying in it. It is, I am confident, the best on the face of the earth, and yet, I hope, to rise to something more excellent still."[14]

In 1803 Priestley had admitted to Lindsey that he felt he had been wrong in advising the Philadelphia society to continue operating under lay leadership only. He finally saw that it was necessary to have a professed minister at the head of the group to give it coherence and direction, which he had not realized before. The force of his observation seemed to be borne out when, in 1807, the availability of an ordained Unitarian minister stimulated the Philadelphia Unitarians into taking group action, such as they had initially taken under the stimulus of Priestley's arrival.

The Rev. William Christie had been a merchant in Scotland when, self-converted by his theological studies, he had become a Unitarian and gathered together a Unitarian society in Montrose in 1782.[15] In 1794 he had a charge in Glasgow and had acquired a measure of fame for his "Dissertations on the Unity of God." In August, 1795, he left Scotland for the United States, arriving in New York with his family in October. After a few months in Philadelphia, he went on, in February, 1796, to Winchester, Virginia, where he taught school and preached Unitarianism, but with little success. According to Eddowes, he had an "unhappy singularity of disposition,"[16] and even Priestley, who had been his friend and admirer since 1782, admitted that "he injured himself materially, by his zeal in the cause, without gaining, as he says, a single convert."[17] His wife was apparently an exception, for, in Christie's own words, when she listened to his expounding of the Unitarian faith, she was "quite overcome by Truth's superior ray."[18]

In 1801 Christie moved to Northumberland to be near Priestley, and shortly began to preach there, about once every fortnight, from Christmas Day, 1801, to February, 1806. When Priestley died, Christie delivered a funeral oration at his grave and shortly thereafter wrote a review of Priestley's theological works, which Priestley's son included in his father's *Memoirs*. Christie moved to Pottsgrove in February, 1806, where he was, again unsuccessfully, attempting to establish himself as a schoolteacher when the Philadelphia Unitarians invited him to come to Philadelphia and be their minister. Christie accepted the invitation and arrived in Philadelphia on February 26, 1807. The Universalist Church which had offered its pulpit to Priestley did the same for Christie, and the Philadelphia Unitarian Society resumed its regular Sunday morning and evening meetings in March. Christie continued to preach at the Universalist Chapel until May 3, when, "in consequence of leave from the Carpenter's [*sic*] company, he now preached in their hall for the first time."[19] The leave did not long endure, unfortunately, for, in a letter dated July 1, 1807, the Managing Committee of the Carpenters' Company felt obliged to ask the society to discontinue meeting in their hall, "finding it has caused some uneasiness."[20]

On July 9, the society held what might be called a reorganizational meeting in the schoolroom of Thomas Trendel at 229 Arch Street. Thirteen men signed the roll-call.[21] Of those who had been members before 1800 only five were present: Eddowes, Leishman, Owen, Vaughan, and Young. Christie attended as the new pastor, and there were seven additional newcomers.[22] Three days later the society met for public worship in Mr. Correy's room in Church Alley, the only place they had been able to obtain "after much inquiry and many refusals."[23] This had been a music-room. The society took a lease for seven years and furnished the room with a reading desk and benches. Fifteen new members were formally admitted on July 12, Christie and the other seven who had attended for the first time on July 9 and seven more.[24]

At this meeting, James Taylor, prominent among the founders, reappeared in the affairs of the society. Four others of the early group, however, though still active in the city, did not return when the group reorganized itself. Of these four, William Y. Birch contributed $25 to the society in 1811,[25] so it is possible that he continued to participate in its activities, although he was not formally re-elected a member until February 16, 1817. Nathaniel Thomas, with whom Taylor had come to the United States and with whom he had boarded until 1805, was not mentioned in the affairs of the reorganized society, though he was registered in the *City Directory* for 1807 as the proprietor of a tea warehouse at 24 High Street. He died in 1810.[26] Blayney, who had been one of the original founders, was listed in the same *Directory* as a physician at 165 Sassafras Street. Davy, who had been very active with Russell in the early years of the society's existence, and who had been closely attached to Priestley, appears to have been busy with the world's affairs in 1807, as the head of the firm of William Davy and Son, merchants, 112 Spruce Street, where he was also listed as "principal Indian factor," and as a director of the United States Insurance Company and of the Germantown and Perkiomen Turnpike Company. His activities no longer included, however, the Unitarian Society.

By August, 1807, "the present circumstances of the Society were so considerably different from what they were at the time the old constitution was adopted," that a committee was appointed to revise the Rules of the church.[27] "Considerations of peculiar delicacy" relative to the pastoral office seem to have been the real reason for taking this action. With rather elaborate circumlocution, the committee stated:

In these days of light & liberty, they are sure that no person who undertook that function in an Unitarian Society would assume or wish to be invested with, powers inconsistent with its proper nature & duties, & which must be acknowledged to belong exclusively to the Society, who may exercise them or delegate their exercise, in such manner as they deem most expedient.[28]

Mr. Christie found that he had "insuperable objections" to the new constitution, which was approved by the society on August 23, and, according to Eddowes, "left us abruptly."[29] Christie published his version of the breach in two pamphlets, *Remarks on The Constitution, Framed by Three Leading Members, and lately Adopted by A Majority of the Society of Unitarian Christians, Who Assemble*

71

in Church Alley . . . and *A Sequel to the Remarks on the Constitution* . . . *Containing a Defence of The Remarks and Their Author.*[30] He not only left himself, however, but also took a dissident minority of the already small congregation with him, and organized the Independent Society of Unitarian Christians.[31] This group began their meetings at 26 N. Sixth Street on September, 1807, where they survived for nine months, listening to Christie read his dissertations and apparently quarreling among themselves as to the respective responsibilities of the Elder, as Christie called himself, and the two deacons, who were supposed to share the burdens of management with him. The Independent Society gave up the struggle on May 22, 1808.

Although this schism must have been a hard blow to the struggling parent society, it wished Christie well, assuring him that, though he could be neither its pastor nor a member, since he did not wish to subscribe to the constitution, yet it would "always welcome him as a Christian brother and he could take his place at our Communion table."[32] In 1808, Christie decided he would give up trying to preach to "a very small congregation, most of whom as they are pious and moral people, stand in little need of my instruction or admonition."[33] Though he had undoubtedly suffered chagrin and humiliation as a result of the failure of his "secession," as the society called it, he was afterward "thoroughly reconciled and frequently attended our ordinary and communion services."[34] He was elected a member again on December 20, 1812, presumably having overcome his formerly "insuperable objections" to the constitution.[35]

The revised constitution was signed on August 23, 1807, by fifteen members.[36] The occupations of twelve are known: six were merchants, one was a broker, one a coachmaker, one a plasterer, one a shoemaker, one a wire fender and cagemaker, and one a teacher.[37] There were no politicians, no journalists, no lawyers, no doctors, no artists. Nor were there any social leaders. The Unitarians definitely belonged to the middle class.

The new constitution stated flatly: "The general rule, applicable at all times and upon all occasions is, 'Let all things be done decently and in order.'"[38] Charged with the responsibility to see that they were, was the newly established Committee of Management, consisting of five members of the society, to be chosen annually by ballot each December. The first committee was composed of four merchants—Peter Boult, Ralph Eddowes, James Taylor, and John Vaughan—and a teacher, Thomas Trendel. In 1808, however, Trendel was replaced by the merchant Thomas Astley, who was elected a member of the society on Christmas Day and a member of the committee the next day, thus making the governing body of the society completely mercantile, which it continued to be for the next decade. When Vaughan withdrew from membership on the committee for one year from 1809 to 1810, he was replaced during that interval by another merchant, William Turner, but with this single exception the membership of the Committee of Management continued unchanged—Astley, Boult, Eddowes, Taylor, Vaughan—until, under the new constitution adopted December 11, 1811, it was succeeded by the Committee of Order in January, 1812. At that time Boult ceased his service as an officer of the society, Taylor was not re-elected for two years, Turner continued serving, and John Eddowes was added for two years.

Although all members of the society had originally been eligible to do lay preaching for the group, and in the beginning six members were formally elected every six months to perform such services for the following half year, this practice was dropped in 1800 and was not resumed when the society began meeting again in 1807. Christie was the official preacher from March until August in that year, but after his departure the preaching was done exclusively by Vaughan, Eddowes, and Taylor, relieved occasionally by ministers from New England. Vaughan read published works from various sources, but Eddowes and Taylor composed their own sermons and Taylor began listing himself as "Unitarian minister" in the *City Directory* in 1807, prefixing "the Rev." to his name. All three men were highly successful merchants, whose generous financial contributions to the work of the society were the mainstay of its support. Though the new constitution required a contribution of only four dollars per annum as a qualification for membership in the society, on August 23, 1807, Taylor pledged himself to one hundred dollars per annum, Vaughan to forty dollars and Eddowes to twenty. Their business acumen was no less an asset to the group and all three gave freely of their time and energy to the church's activities.

Taylor and Vaughan were both unmarried in 1807,[39] but Eddowes added to the society the active presence of a large and growing family. Of the nine children he brought with him from England, six married and began to raise families of their own. His daughter Sarah married Peter Boult, who became a member of the society in July, 1807. The registration of the births of their four children, born between 1806 and 1812, provided the first entries made in the new Register of the society's vital statistics, opened in 1814. Two of Eddowes' sons, Ralph, Jr. and John, became china merchants and joined the society in 1807. Eddowes, Sr., an only child himself, left nearly forty living descendants to mourn him when he died.[40]

Vaughan was undoubtedly the outstanding member of the group from the viewpoint of his impact upon the life of Philadelphia. Born of a wealthy mercantile family in which public service had long been a tradition, he followed in the steps of his forebears. He made his living, first of all, in one of the most highly regarded callings in the city, that of merchant-shipper. His natural amiability of disposition had at first seemed to threaten his success. Benjamin, his older brother, had berated him for his laxness in business matters and had urged him, in particular, to pursue debtors strongly, for American credit was bad enough without making it worse. "You are I fear too lenient," he had written in 1784.[41] "You must be decisive and force people. . . . Correct your generous turn for attachments. In business you must try to be safe, which will often lead you to seem neither polite nor merciful." This advice John was temperamentally incapable of following. He happily managed to be both generous and successful. In 1794 he

JOHN VAUGHAN
Portrait by Thomas Sully. Courtesy of the American Philosophical
Society.

was importing and selling wines at 109 and 111 South Front Street, numbering among his customers President Washington.[42] In the same year he was also a director of the Insurance Company of North America, which had been founded by merchants in 1792, and incorporated in 1794, to insure vessels and their cargoes.[43]

Before coming to America, Vaughan had worked and traveled extensively in the West Indies and on the Continent, and he knew the French and Spanish languages, which added greatly to the ease with which he maintained contact with men all along the trade lines of the world. Philadelphia was a center, in the last two decades of the eighteenth century, for agents for and sympathizers with the revolutionists who were trying to wrest Latin America from Spanish control. Vaughan was prominent among the Philadelphia merchants who, carrying on a brisk trade with New Orleans, broke the Spanish commercial monopoly and led eventually to the achievement of political freedom in Spain's American empire. As an intermediary between his fellow merchants and the representatives of South American interests, he was one of the "advance agents" who, by the relatively peaceful means of commercial expansion, extended the territory of the United States toward the fulfillment of its Manifest Destiny.[44]

At the same time Vaughan's connections with the American Philosophical Society kept him in constant touch with scientists, scholars, and men of affairs, both at home and abroad.[45] In 1784 he had been elected a member of the society. In 1789 he was elected its secretary, its treasurer in 1791, and its librarian in 1804, both of which latter posts he held until his death in 1841. He lived in the society's building at the corner of Fifth and Chestnut Streets from 1822 until he died. It was a connection exactly suited to Vaughan's natural genius for making friends and he became famous all over the world as an outstanding host in a city famous for its hospitality. His breakfasts were his unique contribution to the social life of the city, large and distinguished gatherings of local and visiting celebrities in sessions often lasting five hours.[46]

Although Philadelphia was torn by political animosities into two warring camps, Vaughan, a professed Federalist, succeeded in remaining on friendly terms with both sides. His father was a close friend of Washington and John was cordially received by the great man, first as his father's son but soon on his own merits as well.[47] Washington dined with him on May 30, 1787, during the Constitutional Convention.[48] Vaughan persuaded John Dickinson to write a series of articles supporting the ratification of the Constitution, which Dickinson produced under the signature of "Fabius," "the condition was, that no person but Mr. Vaughan should know the author, and nearly all the essays were taken by him from Dickinson at Wilmington, and were first published in an obscure paper in Philadelphia to insure secrecy."[49] Vaughan joined Washington's forces sent to suppress the Whiskey Rebellion in 1794.[50]

At the same time Vaughan was closely connected and on friendly terms with Jefferson through the American Philosophical Society, of which the latter was president from January 6, 1797 to November 23, 1814. Vaughan always maintained his own independence, however. Once, when he and Jefferson were riding together, Vaughan's horse became restive and he burst out, without thinking, that it was "unruly as a democrat." Jefferson mildly answered, "If he had been he would have thrown his rider."[51]

Vaughan was a many-sided man. The Rev. Jared Sparks, Unitarian clergyman, then editor of the *North American Review*, visiting Philadelphia in 1818, expressed the generally felt amazement at the number and diversity of Vaughan's interests.

I called on Mr. V. . . . and found him in the character of Portugese Consul. In addition to this he is merchant agent for Dupont's famous powder factory, librarian and the most active member of the Philosophical Society, cicerone and friend to all the strangers who visit the city, occasional preacher in the Unitarian Church and parish minister to all the poor of that society . . . recommender-general of all schoolmasters, inventors, young men just entering on their professions, and every sort of personage, whose characters are good, and who can be benefitted by his aid.[52]

As a merchant Vaughan was interested in the Chamber of Commerce, of which he began serving as secretary in 1813, continuing in that capacity or as treasurer for many years. His interest in science engaged him in the activities of the Society for the Promotion of Agriculture, of which he was one of the earliest members, having been admitted on April 5, 1785. When the society reorganized in 1808, after "a long sleep" of several years, he was again among the members. The Company for the Improvement of the Vine, long discussed by Philadelphia horticulturalists, was finally organized in 1802, with Vaughan among the managers, and he was later to be one of the organizers of the Pennsylvania Horticultural Society in 1827. From 1794 to 1798 he acted as a director of the Insurance Company of North America, and in 1812 was a director of the Delaware Insurance Company. Having heard of Jefferson's successful vaccination experiments in Virginia, Vaughan wrote to him, asking his help in carrying on this work in Philadelphia, and in 1801, with the aid of Jefferson, he was directly responsible for introducing smallpox vaccination into the city, eventually leading to the establishment of the Society for Promoting Vaccination in 1809.[53] He was among the "liberal patrons of the drama" who took a share of stock in the new theatre which opened on Chestnut Street above Sixth in 1794.[54]

Mathew Carey paid tribute to Vaughan in a work called the *Annals of Benevolence*:

Throughout his whole life, a large portion of his time has been employed in active beneficence. . . .To needy strangers, particularly his countrymen, destitute of money and friends, and, though industrious and desirous to work, destitute of employment, his services have been invaluable. For hundreds of persons, thus circumstanced, he has found advantageous situations; many of whom are now in independent circumstances, the foundation of which was laid by his interference.[55]

Vaughan's beneficence toward his fellow Englishmen was undoubtedly channeled through his activities with the Society of the Sons of St. George, an organization "for the advice and assistance of Englishmen in distress," founded in 1772.[56] The society had been inactive from 1776 to 1787, because of "the peculiar situation of its members,"[57] had been active again for five years and again inactive for two years, but had finally decided to apply for a charter from the Commonwealth in 1808. Vaughan was a member of the charter committee appointed on December 15, 1808, which finally secured a charter on January 16, 1813. Having become a member of the society on April 23, 1789, Vaughan served it in many capacities, as a steward from 1791 to 1799 and president in 1840 and 1841.

Vaughan's personal popularity and influence, exercised through both his wide commercial connections and his absorbing avocation, the American Philosophical Society, undoubtedly played a large part in the growth of the Unitarian Society after 1807. In that year a course of evening lectures was added to the group's activities, an effort being made "to render them applicable to the circumstances of the society and the relation in which it stood to the rest of the community."[58] It was reported:

This created a new interest and the attendance became regular and was gradually increased. We have reason to believe that the religious services at this period were attended with pleasure and gratification. The sacred music was particularly excellent, and the audience was brought together by no habits of listless conformity, but a real interest in the great topics of religion.[59]

So much interest had developed, in fact, that by the end of 1810 the society was able to entertain the thought of building its own edifice for the purposes of religious worship. A committee was appointed to investigate the possibilities of purchasing a suitable piece of ground, and in August, 1811, another committee was asked to draw up plans for a place of worship. A lot on the northeast corner of Tenth and Locust Streets, then on the outskirts of the city,[60] was acquired in November and a building plan approved. On December 27, 1811, the society applied to the Commonwealth of Pennsylvania for a charter of incorporation as "The First Society of Unitarian Christians in the City of Philadelphia," which was granted to them on January 7, 1813.

In March, 1812, the cornerstone of the new building was laid, and on February 14, 1813, it was formally dedicated. The new church was an octagonal brick structure, seating about three hun-

dred persons, the design of Robert Mills, who is claimed to have
been the first native American to be trained primarily as a professional architect. [61] Although unconventional in shape among Philadelphia churches, it followed the pattern of many Unitarian churches
in England, the design of the octagon in place of the cross probably having a symbolic significance in marking the ideological
departure of the Unitarians from the conventional cross of orthodox
Christian theology.

The new church cost approximately $25,000, an expensive pro-
ject, all things considered. Actually only a few persons had been
formally admitted to membership between 1807 and 1813, in
addition to the sixteen already mentioned, fifteen others having
signed the records. [62] Of these fifteen, five are known to have been
merchants, one a broker, one a translator, one a gilder and japanner, one a tanner and currier, and one a "gentleman."

At least one distinguished native Philadelphian joined the
society during this period. William Empson Hulings, born in
Philadelphia, had made "a decent fortune" in New Orleans before
his appointment as vice-consul there in March, 1798, by President
Adams, acting upon the recommendation of Timothy Pickering,
secretary of state, a friend of the Hulings family. [63] The Royal
Government of Spain never accepted his commission but Hulings
had continued to function nonetheless, at first by himself and after
January, 1802, under Daniel Clark, who had been appointed consul.
After the cession of New Orleans to the United States, Hulings
had remained there for a time in an unofficial capacity, being regarded in 1804 by Governor Claiborne "among the Inhabitants
of this place who stand highest in Public estimation." [64] By 1807
he was back in Philadelphia and in July of that year notified
Vaughan that he wished to be recorded a subscriber to the Unitarian Society for twenty dollars a year. [65]

Two of the new members of the society died before 1813 and
one membership was declared void, [66] so that on the eve of the
group's entrance into its new quarters it numbered only twenty-
eight persons. Membership was limited to those who had been in

regular attendance for twelve months, were recommended by two members, subscribed to the Constitutional Rules, were formally admitted to membership, and paid not less than four dollars per annum toward the church's support. By contributing regularly for twelve months, one could be considered a "contributor," entitled to vote only in the choice of a pastor.

The subscription list for the new building, however, contains two hundred and fifty-eight names. Attesting to Vaughan's importance in the building fund campaign is a list of contributions made personally to him which reads like an excerpt from *Who Was Who in Philadelphia*. Included were the prominent physicians: Benjamin S. Barton, Nathaniel Chapman, J. Redman Coxe, and George Logan; lawyers: Nicholas Biddle (then state senator), Thomas Cadwallader, Joseph Reed (then recorder of the city of Philadelphia), and Sampson Levy; merchants: Joseph Carson, Godfrey Haga, Alexander Balch of Balch and Ridgway, Simon Gratz, John Markoe, James McMurtrie, Condy Raguet, Joseph Sims, and Jacob S. Waln; the publishers, Zachariah Poulson and Mathew Carey; the artists, Charles Willson Peale and his son Rubens.

Another highly influential group of prominent Philadelphians made their contributions to James Taylor. Heading his list were Robert Wharton, then serving his fifth term as mayor of Philadelphia, William Tilghman, chief justice of the Supreme Court of Pennsylvania, Richard Rush, attorney general of Pennsylvania, Alexander J. Dallas, United States district attorney for Philadelphia, Richard Bache, clerk of the Court of Quarter Sessions, and such other distinguished lawyers as Horace Binney, Charles Chauncey, Joseph Hopkinson, and Moses Levy.

These were but the most outstanding names in a large collection of famous contributors. None of these men was ever formally connected with the Unitarian Society, yet by their contributions toward the building of the society's first church they indicated that the Philadelphia Unitarians had won at least a measure of public approval. This was largely, to be sure, a tribute by liberally minded individuals to others of similar propensities, centered strongly within the same circle of intellectuals which had welcomed Priestley. Connections with the American Philosophical Society and with the University of Pennsylvania were notable. Yet many others as well, substantial citizens, prominent in business and commerce as well as in the learned professions, the arts and sciences, lent their names and their financial support to the endeavor. Of the group of over two hundred and fifty subscribers at least sixty were merchants, with at least twenty-three lawyers, nine printers and book-sellers, eight physicians, and nine "gentlemen," and a representation also from a wide range of trades and crafts, including cabinet makers, painters, bricklayers, silverplaters, coachmakers, tailors, etc.

The approval and support of wealthy and powerful non- Unitarians were of obvious benefit to the society, but the more significant factor, for the future of the group, was the new strength gained from many persons who, while not formally admitted members at this time, were contributors to its new building and were to become active members of the congregation in the near future. On the subscription list for the 1813 building appeared for the first time in the society's brief history the names of such men as Guy Bryan, Robert Desilver, Isaac Heylin, James Mease, Thomas Natt, and William Renshaw, all of whom, and many more who appeared on the list, were to form a potent nucleus of new and continuing growth.

The basic character of the society continued to be what it had been from the beginning—predominantly English in national origin, mercantile in occupation, middle class socially, economically substantial, eager for self-improvement, zealous in good works. Eight of the twelve men who signed the charter application in December, 1811, were merchants.[67] Their English birth called many of the members to the work of the Society of the Sons of St. George, Vaughan having become a member in 1789, Taylor in 1796, joined in 1801 by Thomas Astley, who served as a steward from 1812 to 1822, and by Samuel Darch and Peter Harvy in 1810.

When the committee of which Vaughan was a member prepared the new charter which was finally approved in 1813, Astley, Darch, and Harvy, as well as Vaughan, were among the signers. The Unitarians also continued their interest in the Society for the Propagation of Agriculture, of which Vaughan's father had been one of the founders, Thomas Harper becoming a member in 1806, Ralph Eddowes in 1809, his son, Ralph, Jr., and Dr. Thomas P. Jones in 1813. The Society for the Institution and Support of First-Day or Sunday Schools in the City of Philadelphia and the Districts of Southwark and the Northern Liberties had been founded in 1791 to provide educational opportunities for the "offspring of indigent parents" who did not have such advantages during the week because of their apprenticeship to various trades.[68] Taylor served as vice-president of this society in 1807 and 1808, while John Eddowes was secretary from 1810 to 1814.

Philadelphia's industry, after a slow beginning, was forced into quicker growth by the pressures of the Embargo of 1807. Cut off from its foreign suppliers, the city had to learn to produce its own goods and the capital it normally invested in foreign shipping found its way into domestic manufacturing. This inevitably involved a serious derangement of the city's economy, but, even while the War of 1812 was being fought, "recovery" was under way, prodded along by a number of public-spirited and economically far-sighted citizens. Birch, erstwhile of the Unitarian Society, was one of these. Although he was listed in the *City Directories* as a stationer and bookseller, Birch actually sold, in addition to stationers' supplies and books, a wide variety of items, ranging from soap, toothbrushes and razors to glass, Wedgwood, and mahogany writing desks, all imported from England.[69] When the Philadelphia Manufacturing Society was founded in 1808, however, Birch was one of the nine members of the managing and subscription committee who announced their intention of erecting buildings and equipping them with machinery to use water power in the manufacture of cotton, woolen, and linen textiles and other goods.[70] In 1813 he was a manager of the Premium Society, which offered cash bounties for the best American textiles produced and for the first threadmill to be established. [71]

The years between the resumption of the society's meetings in 1807 and the dedication of its first church edifice on February 14, 1813, were marked by a slow but steady growth in numbers and financial stability. In view of the fact that most of the leaders of the society were not only English by birth but shipping merchants by occupation, the prospering of the society during the period leading up to the War of 1812 and through the war itself is somewhat surprising. Ever since the Napoleonic Wars had been resumed in 1803, American shipping had been the prey of both France and England, but the English, by virtue of their superior naval power, had been the more oppressive. In the United States, however, the Federalists and the Democrats had maintained their traditional lines of allegiance, with the Federalists favoring peace with England while the Democrats called for war. The issuing of Napoleon's Berlin Decrees, followed by the British Orders in Council, made the year 1807 a particularly gloomy one for American shippers, marked by increasing impressment of American seamen and other overt acts of agression against American vessels, with a prohibitive rise in the rates of marine insurance as the risks increased. In 1807 a group of Federalist merchants of Philadelphia unsuccessfully appealed to Congress to repeal the Non-Importation Act which, operative in November and December, 1806, was still on the statute books, though in suspension. In December the even more crippling Embargo Act had been passed.

Philadelphia had an ardent pro-war party opposed to her Federalist merchants. On July 2. 1807, a week before the Unitarians met to amend their Constitutional Rules, the Philadelphia Military Legion offered its services to the government as a result of public indignation over the *Chesapeake* affair. Within a year, troops were drilling and sham battles being waged in the streets as the war tempo increased, thanks in large measure to the unceasing propaganda effort being waged by Duane in the *Aurora*. Duane, for whom war with England was at least partly a private grudge fight, soon had an unwitting assistant in the person of Augustus John Foster, the British minister, who brought to the United States in 1810 a degree of obtuseness equalled only by that of his government.

The expression "rich Federalist shipping merchant" emerged from this period so thoroughly hyphenated as to be almost indivisible. The natural assumption, therefore, would be that the wealthy Unitarian merchants had by this time probably become Federalists, for economic reasons. Guy Bryan was an obvious exception, naming his son born on January 16, 1802, Thomas Jefferson Bryan,[72] but Vaughan was definitely a Federalist, and when Foster came to Philadelphia he put the unofficial British stamp of approval on him.[73] It is not known how many of the British-born members of the Philadelphia Unitarian Society had become American citizens by 1812, although five of them, at least, were naturalized by that time[74]. This is deduced from their membership in the Society of the Sons of St. George, which made United States citizenship a condition of membership. Whatever their official status, however, they had retained close ties of blood relationship and natural symathy with their homeland. Thus they were drawn by the strongest impulses, both economic and emotional, toward the Federalist cause and must have concurred in the action taken as late as 1812 by a Federalist convention in Philadelphia, stating "their firm and unqualified conviction that the United States are not impelled to the war by necessity, nor invited to it by expediency."[75] Nonetheless, the war came, and, with its coming, all British subjects in Philadelphia were required to register their names, occupations, and residences with the federal marshal. When mere opposition to the Non-Importation Act, based on economic necessity, had in 1807 labelled native Americans as pro-British and subjected them to abuse by the pro-war party, it is certain that Philadelphians of British birth must have borne some measure of public disfavor during the years of actual war. Still the Philadelphia Unitarians prospered and in that accomplishment was evidence not only of superior ability and daring but also of extraordinary tact and dis-

cretion. To whatever degree the founders of the society had originally sympathized with the principles of the French Revolution,
they had apparently amended that enthusiasm and were at this
time committed to the cause of England, both Old and New. It was
a curious situation, which found the society, predominantly English
by both birth and inheritance, in the midst of an American war
with England successfully conducting a campaign for funds in
America. In 1813, with the threat of invasion hanging over the
city, they opened a handsome new building for their religious purposes, and it was immediately filled by a sizeable body of respectable citizens, who lent both moral and financial support to the
enterprise.

NOTES

CHAPTER III

[1]There was no omnibus until December 7, 1831, when James Boxall began the operation of "Boxall's Accommodation" on Chestnut Street from the Merchant's Coffee House at Second Street to Schuylkill Seventh, making one round trip every hour and charging ten cents fare. Joseph Jackson, *Encylopaedia of Philadelphia* (Harrisburg, 1933), IV, 940–42.

[2]John F. Watson, *Annals of Philadelphia and Pennsylvania . . ., ed.* Willis P. Hazard (Philadelphia, 1881), I, 225.

[3]Ellis Paxson Oberholtzer, *Philadelphia, A History of the City and Its People* (Philadelphia, n.d.), I, 429. Cited hereafter as Oberholtzer, *City History*.

[4]*The Port Folio*, I (January 3, 1801), 4.

[5]Oberholtzer, *Literary History*, pp. 168, 176–79. Dennie required contributions to the *Port Folio* to be handed in no later than Wednesday. On Tuesdays contributors used to crowd the bookshop of the publisher, Asbury Dickens, until they decided to get together for social evenings at the homes of some of their number. This continued until Dennie's death in 1812. Jackson, IV, 1146.

[6]Oberholtzer, *Literary History*, p. 179.

[7]Oberholtzer, *City History*, I, 413.

[8]Priestley, *Memoirs*, I, 170.

[9]PROC, p. 56, entry dated March 16, 1807: "Since the date of the preceding meeting [August 24, 1800] the Society has not met for any purpose whatsoever."

[10]Frances Ann Kemble, *Records of Later Life* (New York, 1883), p. 403.

[11]Rutt, II, 483.

[12]Rutt, II, 506.

[13]Detlev W. Bronk, "Joseph Priestley and the Early History of the American Philosophical Society," *Proc. Amer. Phil. Soc.* LXXXVI (September 1942), 8.

[14]Priestley to Logan, January 25, 1804, in Smith *Chemistry in America* p. 127.

[15]Christie gave this account of his life in his Preface to his *Dissertations on the Unity of God . . .* (Philadelphia, 1808), pp. iii–xxxii.

[16]Eddowes, "Laying the first Corner-Stone," pp. 5–6.

[17]Priestley to Lindsey, n.d., "Received March 16, 1801 :" Rutt, II, 454.

[18]William Christie, *Select Psalms, ChristmasHymns, and other Devotional and Sentimental Pieces* (Philadelphia, 1821), p. 56.

[19]PROC, p. 57.

[20]PROC, p. 57.

[21]PROC, p. 58.

[22]All seven names are listed in CD, 1807 :
      William Bennett—multiple listing, identification impossible
      Josiah Evans, plaisterer [*sic*], 101 N. 6th St.
      Peter Harvy, coachmaker, near 58 S. 4th St.
      Alexander Napier, stonecutter, 399 High St.
      Thomas Trendel, teacher, 227 Market St.
      John Ward, shoemaker, 306 S. Front St.
      John Wright—multiple listing, identification impossible

[23]Eddowes, "Laying the first Corner-Stone," p. 5.

[24]PROC, p. 59. The following were listed in CD, 1807:
Peter Boult, merchant, 150 S. 6th St.
John Cluley, wire fender and cage maker, 34 S. 3rd St.
John Eddowes, china merchant, 27 N. 3rd St.
Ralph Eddowes, Jr., china merchant, 27 N. 3rd St.
Not listed were the following:
David Napier
Joseph Priestley Jr.—living in Northumberland but an occasional visitor to Philadelphia
Jonathan Walker

[25]COLLS, p. 10.

[26]Taylor, Memoir.

[27]PROC, p. 63.

[28]PROC, p. 63.

[29]Ralph Eddowes, unsigned manuscript draft, "On point of order," p. 5, CHURCH MSS.

[30]Both published in Philadelphia, 1807: Christie, *Dissertations*, p. xxix.

[31]This account is given by Christie, *Dissertations*, p. xxx.

[32]Eddowes, "Laying the first Corner-Stone," p. 6.

[33]Christie, *Dissertations*, p. xxix.

[34]Eddowes, "Laying the first Corner-Stone," p. 6.

[35]PROC, p. 114. Subsequently he delivered a package of twelve Unitarian publications to Vaughan for the church library, "with his good wishes for the success of the Establishment." Letter of May 5, 1818, Christie to Vaughan: CHURCH MSS.

[36]Eddowes, Owen, Taylor, Tucker, Vaughan, and Young, of the original, pre-1800 group; Bennett, Boult, Cluley, Ralph, Jr. and John Eddowes, sons of the founder, Evans, Harvy, Trendel, and Ward. Of those who had been present at the July meetings, not signing in August were Leishman, Alexander and David Napier, Walker, and Wright, as well as Christie. The name of Joseph Priestley, Jr. did not appear among the signatures on this date, but he signed again on May 13, 1808. He contributed $100 to the new church building before he left for England in 1812 (COLLS, p. 2). He died at Exeter, England, (DAB, XV, 226).

[37]*Merchants:* Ralph, Sr., Ralph, Jr., and John Eddowes, Boult, Taylor, Vaughan; *broker:* Tucker; *coachmaker:* Harvy; *plasterer:* Evans; *shoemaker:* Ward; *wire fender and cagemaker:* Cluley. CD, 1807. *Teacher:* Trendel. PROC, p. 58.

[38]*Constitution of the First Society of Unitarian Christians in the City of Philadelphia; Adopted, August 23, 1807* (Philadelphia, 1807), p. 19.

[39]Taylor married the widow of Nathaniel Thomas in 1811 (Taylor, Memoir). Vaughan never married.

[40]W. H. Furness, *Sermon on the Death of Mr. Ralph Eddowes. Preached March 31st, 1833* (Philadelphia, 1835), p. 12.

[41]Benjamin Vaughan to John Vaughan, September 23, 1874: Vaughan Papers.

[42]Washington bought six bottles of champagne from Vaughan in 1794 "as a sample," for $6. Quoted from "Washington's Household Account Book, 1793–1797," *Pa. Mag. of Hist. & Biog.*, XXX (April 1906), 181.

[43]*A History of the Insurance Company of North America* (Philadelphia, 1885), p. 133.

[44]This subject is developed at length in Roy F. Nichols, *Advance Agents of American Destiny* (Philadelphia, 1956).

[45]The manuscript collections of the American Philosophical Society contain many letters asking Vaughan for a great variety of favors and thanking him for aid given, as well as letters of introduction borne to him by visitors to the city. In the society's

Early Proceedings . . . (Philadelphia, 1884) are innumerable references to Vaughan.

⁴⁶The Unitarian pastor, William H. Furness, met there in 1824, at a breakfast which lasted five hours, John Quincy Adams, Albert Gallatin, and William Ellery Channing. W. H. Furness, *Recollections upon the Forty-Eighth Anniversary* . . . *January 19th, 1873* (n.p., n.d.), p. 7.

⁴⁷When Samuel Vaughan visited Philadelphia in 1784 he was on terms of close friendship with Washington, who, when Vaughan returned to England for the last time in 1787, wrote: "I shall be among those who will view your departure from this country with regret; at the same time I beg leave to add that I shall reflect with pleasure on the friendship with which you have honored me." Letter from Vaughan, November 12, 1787, in Fitzpatrick, XXIX, 313–14. For other letters from Washington to Vaughan see XXVII, 298–99, 430; XXVIII, 63–64, 326–27; XXIX, 6–7, 70; XXX, 237–41; XXXI, 354–46. Letters of Washington to the younger Vaughan are in XXIX, 468; Vol. 30, 243; Vol. 31, 453; and Worthington Chauncey Ford, ed., *The Writings of George Washington* (New York, 1891), XI, 144.

⁴⁸Entry for May 30, 1787, Washington's Diary: Ford, XI, 144.

⁴⁹Herbert B. Adams, *The Life and Writings of Jared Sparks* (Boston, 1893) I, 482–83.

⁵⁰Priestley to Lindsey, February 10, 1797: Rutt, II, 295.

⁵¹W. H. Furness in a letter to his sister-in-law, Mary Jenks, August 2, 1826: COLL. CORR. I.

⁵²Adams, *Jared Sparks*, I, 133.

⁵³Jefferson to Vaughan, November 5, 1801: MSS, APS; Scharf and Westcott, II, 1476.

⁵⁴Oberholtzer, *City History*, II, 970.

⁵⁵Quoted by J. S. Buckingham, *America, Historical, Statistic, and Descriptive* (London, n.d.), II, 67–69.

⁵⁶*An Historical Sketch of the Origin and Progress of the Society of the Sons of St. George* (Philadelphia, 1872), pp. 7–9, 62.

⁵⁷*Sketch of the Society*, pp. 12–13.

⁵⁹"Unitarianism in Philadelphia," *Christian Examiner*, March and April, 1828, p. 170.

⁶⁰Oberholtzer, *City History*, II, 102. The center of the fashionable quarter was then at Third and Spruce Streets.

⁶¹Talbot Hamlin, "Some Greek Revival Architects of Philadelphia," *Pa. Mag. of Hist. & Biog.*, LXV (April 1941), 124–25.

⁶²J. Andrews—PROC, p. 114; not in CD, 1811, 1813 (No CD, 1812)
Thomas Astley, merchant, cor. 3rd and Spruce Sts. (CD, 1808)
William Christie, translator, 180 N. 3rd St. (CD, 1811)
Samuel Darch—PROC, p. 114; not in CD, 1811, 1813
Thomas Harper, broker, 101 S. 2nd and 72 S. 5th St. (CD, 1811)
William E. Hulings, gentleman, 138 Pine St. (CD, 1807)
Thomas Jones—PROC, p. 114, no address given, identity uncertain
William Leishman, 383 Market St. (PROC, p. 81; not in CD, 1810, 1811)
John L. Palmer, merchant, 20 Swanson St. (CD, 1808)
Thomas Parker, s.e. cor. 9th and Severn Sts. (multiple listing in CD, 1808, but none under this address, given in PROC, p. 81)
William H. Smith, gilder and japanner, 165 S. 3rd St. (CD, 1811)
William Turner, storekeeper, 278 N. 2nd St. (CD, 1807)
James Cogan Warren, tanner and currier, 10 S. Broad St. (CD, 1811)
William Warren, trader, 385 S. 2nd St. (CD, 1811)

Robert Whittle, merchant, 15 S. 2nd St. (CD, 1809)

The CD listings given are for the year in which the individual became connected with the society, the year before or the year after.

[63]"Despatches from the United States Consulate in New Orleans, 1801–1803," *Amer. Hist. Review*, XXXII (July 1927), 801–24.

[64]"Despatches," *Amer. Hist. Review*, 804.

[65]MS note signed by Vaughan, July 13, 1807: CHURCH MSS.

[66]Palmer died April 15, 1809; Whittle on April 7, 1810. Ward "did not qualify." PROC, p. 81.

[67]Astley, Ralph and John Eddowes, Taylor, Turner, Vaughan, Warren, Young. CD, 1811.

[68]*A Century of the First Day or Sunday-School Society: A Sketch of the Beginning of Sunday Schools in Philadelphia* (Philadelphia, 1891), p. 6.

[69]Advertisement in *Gales's Independent Gazeteer*, September 16, 1796.

[70]Scharf and Westcott, I, 531.

[71]Scharf and Wesctott, I, 531; CD, 1813.

[72]REG I, 2.

[73]"One of the best men I was acquainted with at Philadelphia, and the most active in all charitable undertakings, was Mr. Vaughan, who was a native of England. . . ." Davis, *Jeffersonian America*, p. 253.

[74]Astley, Samuel Darch, Harvy, Taylor, Vaughan.

[75]Scharf and Westcott, I, 553.

IV

The Many-Sided Men

WHILE THE UNITARIAN SOCIETY WAS DEDICATING ITS FIRST CHURCH building on February 14, 1813, the British fleet was patrolling the Atlantic Coast. Philadelphia was as tightly bottled up as the greatest naval power in the world could contrive to make her. For several months during the winter it made little practical difference, actually, for nature had already sealed the Delaware River with ice, but when the thaw came in the spring fear of invasion came with it. The Federalist majority in the Select Council of the city did everything possible to avoid facing the local situation, but on May 6 a merchants' meeting decided that the city had to do something in its own defense and on May 13 the first volunteer American troops were marching down to Delaware to meet the threat before it could confront them on their own doorsteps. The Federalists continued to battle with their natural opponents, the Democrats, but the local political struggle in 1813 was a little less acrid than usual as both groups provided leaders for the common struggle against the enemy, which had invaded Maryland in April.

The records of the Unitarian Society for this period contain only three references to the war, but the members continued to have close ties with England. William Russell, one of the founders, gave up his residence in America and tried to return, in 1801, to an England which still rejected him. He had to take refuge in France, not being readmitted to his native land until 1814. Leishman, another of the founders, was enjoying a pleasure trip in England in 1812 when the war was declared, visiting William Vaughan, Belsham, and others, whom he was trying to interest in soliciting funds for the Philadelphia society's new building.[1] Boult, who had married Ralph Eddowes' daughter Sarah and had been a member of the society since 1807, returned to Liverpool around 1816.[2] Visitors came from England, too, beginning with Samuel Vaughan in the 1780's. English Unitarians sent gifts of tracts and books to the Philadelphia society and aided the work with cash contributions.[3]

When the governor of Pennsylvania issued his proclamation appointing August 18, 1814, as a day of fasting, humiliation, and prayer, the Unitarian Society recorded the following resolution at a meeting held for the purpose:

Resolved, That it does not appear to this Society that the objects specified by the said proclamation are such as to render the religious services therein recommended necessary or expedient.[4]

Similarly, when the president of the United States recommended in a proclamation that January 12, 1815, be observed as a day of public humiliation, fasting, and prayer, the society decided not to hold such services. Their reaction was very different in March, 1815, and they gladly complied with the presidential proclamation that on April 13 a day of thanksgiving be marked by appropriate services in the churches in "devout acknowledgment to Almighty God for his great goodness, manifested in restoring . . . the blessing of peace."[5]

With the opening of the new church building an entirely new spirit of optimism and self-confidence seemed to inspire the efforts of the group. The society advertised the opening in six daily newspapers for three days in advance and the Committee of Order, its governing body, announced that it would sit at the church on the next day for the letting of pews. On February 14 the ceremonies took place, with morning, afternoon, and evening services conducted in a crowded house,[6] and a collection for the building fund was taken up at each service. With a new building, a new charter of incorporation, and an official seal, the society in 1814 received as a gift from Vaughan its first official Register of Births, Baptisms,

Marriages, and Burials, and the secretary, Taylor, stood ready to record therein the births of children to members, pewholders, or other contributors.[7]

The new constitution, adopted on December 11, 1811, had specified that all applicants for admission to membership in the society had to be for twelve months previous to their application regular attendants at the meetings of the society for public worship. In 1814, when the new Register was opened, it was therefore possible that many of the families entered upon the records were not members of the society. Some of them may never have become members, but the majority were in due course formally admitted to membership and added their strength to the growing church. Altogether, in the period from 1813 to 1825, three families who registered the births of children apparently did not join the society; ten families had children baptized, several families having more than one child; four couples were married; and nineteen families had burials, some more than one, performed by the society, without actually having recorded membership in the society.

During the same period, however, these vital services were performed for a total of thirty-seven families who were either members at the time or eventually became members. Several of the new families were large ones, such as that of Guy Bryan, who in 1814 registered the births of eleven children, ranging in age from three to twenty-nine. Another large family group was that of John Joseph Marie Saulnier, whose wife and eight children, from the ages of twenty down to a newborn infant, were baptized on November 1, 1817, with a son born in February, 1819, baptized shortly after birth, as was another son born in December, 1820. The largest family of all, however ,was that of Thomas Harper, who registered eight children, aged from twenty-two to a new born infant, in 1814; five more in 1821, aged from five to another new infant; a fourteenth child in 1822; and the death of a fifteenth child, sixteen days old, in 1823. The sacraments were performed almost exclusively by Taylor, who between 1814 and 1824 baptized thirty-four persons and married ten, while Eddowes performed one marriage. Taylor conducted forty funerals during the same period, Eddowes one.

In 1810 the society had sought a burial-place for its deceased members and contributors, and had received permission to use the Free Friends' burial-ground. How many Unitarians were buried there or elsewhere before 1814 is not known, but in that year the society opened its own graveyard on land adjacent to the church and at the same time began recording funeral statistics along with other vital data in the newly acquired Register. Between 1814 and 1824, forty-four persons were buried in the churchyard, two in the Free Friends' cemetery. An elaborate scale of charges was set up. The gravedigger's fee was $3.50. The delivery of invitations to a funeral cost $2.00 for twenty-five written forms, $1.50 for oral delivery, if not over two squares from the church, fifty cents extra for each additional square. The bell would be tolled for a half-hour for $1.00, an additional $1.00 being charged for over a half-hour. The price of the hearse was fixed by its owner. No headstones were allowed in the burial-ground, only flat stones over the graves.

A pioneer champion of the protective tariff in the United States, John Melish, established a connection with the Unitarian Society during this period, his wife being buried in the churchyard with a service in the church by Taylor on February 2, 1817.[8] Born in Scotland in 1771, Melish first came to the United States in 1806 to set up a cotton-trading business in Georgia. In 1807 he returned to Scotland but came back to the United States in 1809 with his family. He travelled extensively in America and wrote many books on its geography, economics, and politics, his most notable work being *Travels through the United States of America in the Years 1806 & 1807, and 1809, 1810 & 1811*, which Jefferson read "with extreme satisfaction and information."[9] Melish settled in Philadelphia in 1811, where he engraved maps and continued to write and publish his own works until his death in 1822. He was very successful and at one time employed thirty persons.

An outstanding native Philadelphian, Dr. James Mease, became associated with the Unitarian Society in 1815 when his five children were registered in the church records.[10] Born of a wealthy shipping family, Mease attended the University of Pennsylvania, from which he received a B.A. degree in 1787 and an M.D. in 1792. Of the many books which he wrote, edited, or assisted in compiling, his historical and statistical *Picture of Philadelphia* was the most famous. He had other interests as well. An ardent horticulturalist who cultivated his own vineyard, he was active in 1802 with Vaughan in the organization of the Company for the Improvement of the Vine, of which he was elected a manager. Becoming a member of the Philadelphia Society for the Promotion of Agriculture in 1805, he served as an officer of that organization for many years, being successively its secretary, vice-president, and finally its president from 1844 until his death in 1846. Admitted to the American Philosophical Society in 1802, he was appointed a curator from 1824 to 1830 and a councillor from 1832 to 1836. He was one of the founders and a vice-president of the Athenaeum in 1814 and one of the medical assistants and a member of the Committee of Correspondence of the Humane Society for many years. In the War of 1812 he served as a hospital surgeon from September, 1814 to June, 1815.

Mease greatly admired Priestley, whom he described in the *Picture of Philadelphia* as "the amiable, the pious, the venerable Dr. Priestley."[11] However, there is no direct evidence that he was actually a member of the Unitarian Society. It was Mrs. Mease who paid the family's pew rent from 1826 to 1829,[12] and she was the only member of the family, according to extant records, whose funeral service was conducted by a pastor of the society. Mrs. Mease had been Sarah Butler, daughter of the rich Pierce Butler, member of the Constitutional Convention in 1787 and senator from South Carolina in the first Congress of the United States, and for many years a resident of Philadelphia, where he died in 1822. The Butler connection had its unhappy aftermath for Mease, in that his sons, John and Pierce, as a condition of inheriting tremendous wealth from their maternal grandfather, abandoned their father's name and took that of Butler. Dr. Furness, who conducted Mrs.

Mease's funeral service in 1831, "a delicate and difficult office," stated that "Dr. Mease . . . is treated as a mere cypher in the family."[13] His two sons, John and Pierce, rode with a servant in the first carriage in the funeral cortege while their father rode in the second carriage, an "impropriety" which "jarred" Furness. However, whatever Dr. Mease's position was in 1831, it is improbable that in 1815 Mrs. Mease would have been free to register the births of their five young children in the records of the Unitarian Society without at least having their father's consent.

Thomas Butler, brother of Mrs. Mease, did not attend his sister's funeral in 1831, nor had he had any intercourse with her for some time before her death because of his resentment at her sons' being allowed to take his father's name and so deprive him of the family property. In the early years of the newly reconstituted Unitarian Society, however, both the Meases and the Butlers apparently attended services, the names of Butler's three children being recorded in the Register in 1817.[14]

Butler injected a new note into the life of the society, that of southernism and all that that implied. Vaughan had had commercial ties with the South from the beginning. The Athenaeum's Record of Strangers from 1814 on is filled with the names of southerners whom he took to that organization's reading-room as his guests. Joseph Correa de Serra had written to him in 1815, while on a trip in the South, "What a great man you are in Charlestown!"[15] Colonel John Taylor in Columbia, South Carolina, in 1821, entertained a friend of Vaughan visiting Thomas Cooper "as a duty *incumbent* on the gentlemen of South Carolina toward Mr. Vaughan."[16] Senator William C. Preston stated: "We of the South are always your debtors, and I beg of you to give me, whenever you can, a chance of showing my sense of our obligations."[17] Another founder of the Unitarian Society, Gales, had become a leading citizen of Raleigh, North Carolina, at the end of the eighteenth century. Hulings had had an honored and prosperous career in New Orleans. Butler, however, noted in the society's Register as "of South Carolina,"[18] had been born into the American plantation tradition. His father organized and was the first president of the Southern Society in Philadelphia in 1818.[19] His father's property, which caused the estrangement of Butler and his sister, included hundreds of slaves, which were to be inherited by the younger Pierce Butler and were to be the cause of his eventual abandonment of the Unitarian Society.[20] Thomas Butler's presence in the congregation was the forerunner of that of many more southerners and southern sympathizers, who were to threaten the dissolution of the society in the two bitterly controversial decades preceding the Civil War.

Twenty-one persons are known to have joined the society between 1813 and 1825.[21] At least ten were merchants, three of whom were very affluent. James Wood had come from Manchester, England, with his wife in 1809, settling in Philadelphia where be became an importer.[22] That he was successful may be judged from the gift of $300 which he gave to the building fund of the new church in 1812.[23] He paid pew rent in March, 1813, and had three children baptized by Taylor in October of that year, but he did not sign the Constitutional Rules until May, 1815.[24]

Guy Bryan, associated with William Schlatter in 1805, in a business which conducted extensive trade with the West, lent tremendous strength to the society from the beginning of his association with it, his initial contribution of $200 to the new building being followed in due course by the purchase of four pews in the larger building subsequently erected on the same site.[25] Bryan's eleven children were registered in the books of the society in 1814 and he was a member of a committee appointed on April 9, 1820, but there is no record of when he became a member of the society.[26] He retired from business in 1817, but his sons, also active Unitarians, carried on, the firm name being changed from Bryan and Schlatter to Schlatter and Bryan. One of his daughters, Catharine, married John Ford, another merchant, who became a member of the society in 1822.

Thomas Fletcher, admitted to membership in 1823, was described as "a man of property and intelligence, with the undoubted rank of a gentleman."[27] He had been a goldsmith and jeweller in

Philadelphia for many years, from 1810 in partnership with Sidney Gardiner, who became a member of the Unitarian Society in 1825. Many members of the Fletcher family eventually came to Philadelphia from Massachusetts, including Charles and George, who joined their brother Thomas in the jewelry business and in the Unitarian Society in 1826 and 1827 respectively; their younger brother, Levi, who became an Episcopal clergyman and died as an Army chaplain in Mobile, Alabama, in 1839; and their mother, Hannah, who died of cholera in Philadelphia in 1832 and was buried in the Unitarian churchyard.[28] A nephew and namesake of Thomas Fletcher was a contributor to the society as early as 1825, distinguished from his uncle, who lived on Chestnut Street, by the notation "(Walnut Street)" after his name in the church's records. Thomas Fletcher (Walnut Street) left Philadelphia some time after 1829, and died in Burlington, Vermont, in 1855, but he left $1,000 to the Philadelphia society in his will.[29]

Thomas Fletcher (Chestnut Street) made frequent trips abroad to buy goods while his brothers and Gardiner travelled extensively in the United States, carrying their wares as far north as Boston and south to such points as Louisville.[30] Gardiner in 1823 journeyed to Mexico for the firm, riding on horseback from the Gulf Coast to Puebla, buying and selling. In spite of his physical misery during a sixteen-day attack of chills and fever, he became completely enraptured by what he saw. He wrote home to Fletcher: "You can have no ideas of the butis of natures works, untill you visit Mexico."[31] Though his knowledge of spelling was tentative, he was an able businessman, selling all his merchandise at a great profit. By 1827 the firm's Latin American outlets included Valparaiso, Chile, where they were trading such items as sealing wax, tobacco, steel, buttons, and swords.

One of the founders, Birch, had apparently at some point let his connection with the society relapse into an inactive state, because he was formally readmitted to membership on February 16, 1817, and signed the records on that day.[32] That he had always been one of the group from 1796 on, however, is suggested by the fact that he contributed $25 to the society in 1811.[33] His former business partner, Abraham Small, joined the society in 1818. Small was an Englishman, born in Taunton, Somerset, on April 11, 1765.[34] He had become Birch's partner in 1800 and their business "soon became large, for that period. They published many works of great merit, and received an extensive patronage."[35] The two men also participated jointly in the efforts made to develop Philadelphia's business and industry. As has already been noted, in 1802 they were two of the city's five representatives at the American Literary Fair. Small was one of the vice-presidents at a dinner given on November 17, 1808, by a group of manufacturers and mechanics of Philadelphia to celebrate the improvement of American industry and encourage its further development.[36] With Birch he was a manager of the Premium Society in 1813. Like so many others of the Unitarian Society, Small became a member of the Society of the Sons of St. George. Unlike most of his fellow Unitarians, he took an active part in politics, being a member of the Common Council of Philadelphia in 1820 and 1821, a variation from the Unitarian norm rendered more puzzling by his pastor's later comment that Small had "always been a timid man."[37] He was a convivial one, at least, for he and Birch, together with John Binns, Thomas Cooper, Dr. Edward Hudson, and Matthew Randall composed a group in 1820 known as The Club, which met for supper every Monday evening and discussed the affairs of the world. The meetings continued until Birch's death, in 1837, left Binns the lone survivor still resident in Philadelphia.[38]

Of the new occupations represented in the congregation, that of William Renshaw, famous for his Mansion House Hotel, enjoyed considerable publicity in the annals of the period.[39] The English-born Renshaw had leased the old Bingham house on Third Street above Spruce, with the original idea, in 1806, of establishing there The Exchange Coffee House as a center for marine business, the registering of vessels for sale, provision of space and facilities for auctioning, keeping of ships' letter-bags, etc. Earlier attempts at such a service had failed and Renshaw's did also, but he carried on as a hotelkeeper, naming his establishment the Mansion House Hotel. In 1812 he opened a new hotel on the southeast corner of Eleventh and Market Streets, built by Thomas Leiper and one of the first buildings in Philadelphia to be erected for use as a hotel. After two years, however, Renshaw found that he was too far away from the center of the city's life and moved back to Third and Spruce Streets. Because the building was now owned by the Washington Benevolent Society, he called his hotel the Washington Hall Hotel for a while, but eventually resumed his former name and it was as the Mansion House that the hotel became famous, not only in Philadelphia but all over the world, as one of the most elegant hostelries in America. Renshaw himself left Philadelphia in 1820 to take up the management of a hotel at the popular resort of Long Branch, where, it is noted, he had Joseph Bonaparte as a guest for at least a year. Renshaw became a member of the Unitarian Society on January 18, 1818, but three of his children had been baptized by Taylor and the birth of a fourth child registered on November 6, 1816, while a fifth child had been baptized on July 3, 1817, at the age of three months.[40] In the year before he left Philadelphia Renshaw suffered the loss of three of his children, who died between February and December and were buried in the Unitarian churchyard.[41]

One of the most active and able acquisitions of the society, and one whose connection was to be continued for two decades, was Samuel Vaughan Merrick.[42] Merrick was the son of John Vaughan's sister Rebecca and another English Unitarian, John Merrick, who had, from 1794 to 1797, been a tutor to the children of Benjamin Vaughan and had accompanied the family to America. He returned to England in 1798, married Rebecca Vaughan, and returned with her to Hallowell, Maine, where they spent the rest of their lives. Their son Samuel was born there on May 4, 1801. In 1816 Samuel came to Philadelphia and entered the counting-house of his uncle, John Vaughan. During the next four years Vaughan was so impressed by his young nephew's business acumen that in 1820, when Merrick was only nineteen years of age, Vaughan put him in charge of a fire-engine manufacturing plant which had just become his property when its owners, to whom he had lent money, were declared insolvent. Neither Vaughan nor Merrick understood mechanics, yet the venture prospered under their direction. Vaughan soon withdrew, however, and Merrick took John Agnew into partnership, the products of the firm of Merrick and Agnew quickly becoming famous for their superior workmanship. Merrick signed the records of the Unitarian Society in 1822 and on Christmas Day, 1823, was married by Taylor to Sarah Thomas, Taylor's stepdaughter, daughter of the late Nathaniel Thomas, one of the founders of the society.[43]

Merrick found that he needed additional knowledge of mechanics in order to run his business and he applied for admission to a mechanical institute in the city. Refused admission there, he decided to found his own organization for teaching and dissemination of information about the mechanical arts. Although Philadelphia was by this time well advanced, by American standards, in the development of manufacturing, its educational system was lagging behind its industrial progress. The Industrial Revolution was finally under way, with the change-over from hand labor to machines, but education in the new techniques had hardly begun. Merrick's decision to supply this need was at first ignored by the fifteen or twenty men he invited to meet with him to discuss it. He called a second meeting with the same lack of response, but finally interested in the project Professor William A. Keating of the University of Pennsylvania, who planned with him a gathering of about a dozen Philadelphians, mostly young men, who met at the Philosophical Hall on December 9, 1823. They agreed to form a society for the purposes Merrick had in mind and in due course an organizational meeting was held on February 2, 1824, in the County Court House at Sixth and Chestnut Streets. At this meeting the Franklin Institute was established, to give lectures in the mechanic arts and sciences, to provide for study a collection of models and minerals, to organize a library, and to encourage the development of the mechanic and scientific arts by the granting of premiums. A constitution was adopted, between 400 and 500 members enrolled, and a charter of incorporation was obtained on March 3, 1824. The officers appointed were James Ronaldson, president, who served until his death in 1841, Mathew Carey and Paul Beck, Jr. as vice-presidents, Thomas Fletcher, a member of the Unitarian Society, as treasurer, and Merrick as secretary. Merrick was also appointed a manager and served on the Committee of Finance and the Committee on Premiums and Exhibits. He became treasurer in 1828 and president in 1841, upon the death of Ronaldson, serving until 1854.

The Franklin Institute was always staunchly supported by Philadelphia Unitarians, the first membership list including twenty members of the society. The Vaughan family was especially devoted to its cause, with John a member from the beginning and William acting as an agent of the institute in England for many years, Petty, Benjamin's son, later performing this service.[44]

Undoubtedly the most illustrious new member of the society in the period from 1813 to 1824 was Thomas Sully, the artist, who was elected a member on April 9, 1815.[45] Sully was born at Horncastle, Lincolnshire, England, in 1783, and came to the United States in 1792 with his parents, three brothers, and five sisters. His parents were actors, who chose Charleston, South Carolina, as their new home because of the opening of a new theatre there by the elder Sully's brother-in-law. Sully early exhibited a talent for drawing and began studying art in 1798, first with his brother-in-law, a French expatriate named Belzons, and later with his elder brother, Lawrence. In 1805, two years after the death of Lawrence, Thomas Sully married his widow, who had three children, and in the following year moved with his family to New York, where he immediately experienced a measure of success, thanks to the patronage of the distinguished English actor, Thomas Abthorpe Cooper, who had met Sully in Richmond. In 1807 Sully visited Boston, where he made the acquaintance and profited by the instruction of the great master, Gilbert Stuart. Later in the same year he came to Philadelphia and liked the city so much that he decided to return and settle there, which he did in 1808, Philadelphia being his home for the rest of his life. In May, 1809, he became an American citizen, and it was in this character that he returned to England a month later to study for nine months with the assistance of the American, Benjamin West, and the Englishman, Sir Thomas Lawrence. Back in Philadelphia in April, 1810, he took up his painting at 56 South Eleventh Street, where he lived until 1812, when he moved his studio to the Hall of the American Philosophical Society. Here he painted for the next ten years, opening in 1817 a gallery for public exhibitions which became one of the show-places of the city. After living at several other addresses, in 1830 he finally settled at the house on Fifth Street below Chestnut, owned by Stephen Girard, where he lived until his death in 1872.

The increasing prosperity of Philadelphia, trickling down from the aristocracy through the solid bourgeoisie, made it a fertile field for a painter of portraits, and Sully enjoyed from the first the patronage of the leaders of Philadelphia's social, economic, intellectual, and political life.[46] The Biddles, the Hopkinsons, the Wetherills, John Sergeant, Benjamin Rush, Provost Andrews, Dr. Physick, Bishop White, Robert Walsh, Samuel Coates, Paul Beck, Jr., and many others sat for him before 1825. He painted political leaders, beginning with President James Madison in 1809, Mayor John Inskeep of Philadelphia in 1811, Governor Daniel D. Tompkins of New York in 1813 and again in 1818 when Tompkins was vice-president of the United States, former Governor Thomas McKean of Pennsylvania in 1819, Thomas Jefferson in 1822. Among the naval and military heroes he painted Stephen Decatur in 1814, Commander Jacob Jones in 1816 and 1817, the Marquis de Lafayette in 1824. He also painted his fellow Unitarians, Taylor in 1818, several portraits of Vaughan, Guy Bryan in 1825, and many others who were to become professed members of the society at a later date.

Sully became an active leader in the Unitarian Society's affairs, serving as a member of its governing body, the Committee of Order, from 1819 to 1822, and as a trustee from 1834 to 1837.

From the beginning of his residence in the city he also participated in many movements to promote the arts. He was a member of a group called the Pennsylvania Academicians, who had as their object the development of the newly established Academy of the Fine Arts, and served on a committee appointed to organize the management of the schools of the academy.[47] He was a director of the academy for sixteen years, resigning in 1831.[48] He joined many of his fellow Unitarians in the activities of the Franklin Institute, being a member of the Committee on Fine Arts and the Committee on Paints and Colors for the institute's first exhibition in October, 1824. He designed the institute's certificate of membership in 1830.[49] He also found many fellow Unitarians in the Society of the Sons of St. George, which he joined on January 23, 1818.

In 1820 Sully was one of the organizers of the Musical Fund Society of Philadelphia. The development of music had made a late start in Philadelphia, largely because of the Quaker opposition, but in the early years of the nineteenth century a small group of music lovers had begun to meet in their homes for evenings of musical enjoyment. By 1816 they were holding regular meetings in Sully's gallery at Fifth and Chestnut Streets, and finally in 1820 they organized the Musical Fund Society, their stated purpose at that time being to establish a fund for the relief and support of "decayed" musicians and their families. In 1831, however, this took second place after the primary purpose, which was "to reform the state of neglect into which the beautiful art of music had fallen."[50] At the first election of officers on February 29, 1820, Sully was named one of the Directors of Music. When the Board of Managers subsequently met on April 30, 1820, another Unitarian, William Y. Birch, was named one of the three trustees. The history of the Musical Fund Society written in 1858 indicated a continuing interest in its affairs on the part of the Philadelphia Unitarians, the list of members from 1820 to 1859 including four Unitarians among the managers, three among the directors, and forty among the general membership.

Under the Articles of Incorporation of 1813, the governing

board of the Unitarian Society continued to be called the Committee of Order but its members were now called trustees. The committee consisted of five members, elected in January of each year, who chose from among their own number a president, secretary, and treasurer. Ralph Eddowes, Vaughan, and William Turner continued to share the major burden of leadership on the committee during this period, Eddowes consistently chosen as president from 1813 to 1823, Vaughan as secretary from 1816 to 1824, and Turner as treasurer from 1813 to 1824, with a very few absences filled by pro tem officers. In March, 1820, Eddowes informed the congregation by letter that the removal of his family to their country home and the increasing infirmities of his own advancing years made it necessary for him to discontinue his public services and he asked to be relieved of his offices in the society within six months.[51] He was re-elected, however, until 1823. Astley continued until 1817 his service which had begun in 1808. Thomas Harper, elected in 1815, was re-elected in 1816, 1817, 1823, and 1824. William Y. Birch served from 1818 to 1824, Sully from 1819 to 1822, Jones in 1813, 1814, and 1818, Ford in 1823 and 1824, John Eddowes in 1813. Taylor was elected to the Committee of Order only in 1814 and 1815 when he also served as secretary, but he was, in addition, during this entire period rendering a service of paramount importance to the church in his assumption of sole responsibility for the administering of the sacraments and in the preaching which he shared with Eddowes and Vaughan.

The period from 1813 to 1824 was one of steady, though certainly not spectacular, growth for the Unitarian Society. The city's churches had increased from thirty in 1811 to forty-eight in 1825, yet there was still only one Unitarian church. In January, 1815, Taylor had recommended "a recurrence to the plan of teaching from house to house or conversing with individuals on religious subjects" in order to promote the increase of "practical religion,"[52] but this was not done. Evangelism was never a part of the Unitarian approach.

Philadelphia Unitarians were, however, conspicuous out of all proportion to their numbers in the secular activities of the period. The Pennsylvania Improvement Company had been formed at a meeting held on January 1, 1802, for the purpose of securing the development of inland communication and banking.[53] Guy Bryan had been a member of the organizing committee, which had petitioned the legislature to grant it a charter and an appropriation of $10,000. Unfortunately, the legislature had failed to do either. In the operations of the turnpike and navigation companies, however, several Unitarians took an active part, as directors in some instances, and, in the case of Thomas Harper, as a company officer, Harper serving as secretary and treasurer of the Schuylkill Navigation Company for several years.

When the Pennsylvania Society for the Promotion of Public Economy was instituted in 1817, "for ameliorating the condition of the poor and for removing or preventing the causes which produce mendicity,"[54] Vaughan was appointed a member of the Library Committee and served for many years. He was also one of the incorporators in February, 1819, of the Philadelphia Saving Fund Society, organized by a group of citizens "desirous of encouraging the poor in habits of economy and thrift."[55] Jacob Snider was the first president of the American Beneficial Society, incorporated in December of the same year. Guy Bryan was from 1813 to 1815 the president and a director of the American Fire Insurance Company, the first joint-stock fire insurance company in the United States, organized in 1810. Bryan was also one of the "ordinary directors" of the Second Bank of the United States when it was established in Philadelphia in 1816.

Unitarians continued to play an important role in the affairs of the cultural organizations of the city, as directors of the Pennsylvania Academy of the Fine Arts, stockholders of the Athenaeum, members and officers of the Academy of Natural Sciences, the Franklin Institute, the Musical Fund Society. A new charitable interest of Vaughan during this period was the Pennsylvania Infirmary for Diseases of the Eye and Ear, established in 1822, of which he was appointed a manager. Although practical politics was never a favorite field of operations for Philadelphia Unitarians, two of them served on the Common Council of the city at this time, Abraham Small from 1820 to 1822 and Thomas Harper in 1822.

Perhaps the most outstanding contribution to the life of Philadelphia by a Unitarian in this period, however, was that made by Vaughan through his connection with the American Philosophical Society. Dr. Caspar Wistar had for many years been providing in his home at the southwest corner of Fourth and Locust Streets every Saturday evening from November to April a series of informal gatherings of from fifteen to thirty persons chosen from among the intellectual elite of the city and visiting celebrities from all over the world. The Philadelphians were usually members of the American Philosophical Society. After Dr. Wistar's death in 1818, the men who had been regular guests at the Wistar parties decided to perpetuate the idea by means of a formal organization and in this effort Vaughan was a leading spirit. He wrote to Jefferson within a month of Wistar's death: "We shall try to keep up the Saturday evening meetings . . . and to endeavor to see strangers of merit passing through. We shall want the attractive magnet, but we shall derive pleasure from the attempt, and the recollection of the friend who established them, and gave them such interest."[56]

The Wistar Association was founded in the fall of 1818 by eight leaders of Philadelphia's life, all members of the American Philosophical Society: Zaccheus Collins, Reuben Haines, Thomas C. James, Peter S. Du Ponceau, Robert M. Patterson, Robert Walsh, and John Vaughan. By 1824 the number of members had grown to twenty-four, including such outstanding citizens as Robert Hare, Joseph Hopkinson, Nathaniel Chapman, Mathew Carey, Nicholas Biddle, Horace Binney, and John Sergeant. "The man, however, upon whom the association chiefly relied for its success was John Vaughan."[57] He served as dean of the association from 1818 until his death in 1841, assuming the labour of a general charge over the concerns of the Association, particularly of calling the annual meetings, making out the annual lists, distributing from week to week the cards of invitation, and attending with unremitting assiduity to various minor details. The Association is largely indebted to him for his attention to strangers, and for a fond and steady devotion to its interests and repute.[58]

In Vaughan's bachelor quarters in the building of the American Philosophical Society, where he lived from 1822 until his death, his celebrated breakfasts became the focal point of the Wistar Association's activities.

Though the Unitarian Society continued to be strongly mercantile in calling, during the period from 1813 to 1824 it welcomed, among others, the fire-engine manufacturer, Samuel Vaughan Merrick; the hotelkeeper, William Renshaw; the plantation owner, Thomas Butler; the printer and bookseller, Abraham Small; the physicians, James Mease and Isaac Heylin; the portrait painter, Thomas Sully. The tradition of public service which had been developed in England continued to characterize the Philadelphia society, with its members prominently engaged in a wide range of civic and philanthropic activities. With few college-trained men in the group, they fostered the principle of self-cultivation through their membership in societies of educational purposes and in the organization of the Franklin Institute. The group continued to be predominantly English, with Renshaw, Small, Sully and Wood, at least, among the new members, native Englishmen, but there was also a Gallic touch, if one correctly judges the origin of the Saulniers. Among the first arrivals in what was to be almost a mass migration of New Englanders were Merrick, born in Hallowell, Maine, and Thomas Fletcher of Massachusetts. A new solidarity began to develop with intergroup marriages being performed, such as that between Merrick and Sarah Thomas, James Taylor's stepdaughter. At least three other members who were active in the society during this period were married to daughters of members: Peter Boult, married to Sarah, daughter of Ralph Eddowes; Charles Shippen, married to Sarah's sister Martha; and John Ford, married to Catharine, daughter of Guy Bryan.

The Philadelphia society was apparently a peace-loving group from the beginning, with little or no interest in controversy. Its one stormy petrel, the Rev. William Christie, found that he had to go elsewhere to carry on his disorganizing efforts, but, having completely disorganized the dissident group which he took with him, he returned to the family fold and behaved with the required propriety from then on. The years from 1815 to 1825 were the period of the great Controversy which shook New England Unitarianism from top to bottom. but Channing and Morse fought it out with no help from the Philadelphia society as far as can be determined from extant records. The Philadelphia society had taken on the Quaker love of quiet. James Taylor in June, 1817, reported to Vaughan that during the services on Sunday morning, "the congregation was disturbed by the noise of a carriage passing and repassing on the pavement," and strongly recommended that a complaint should be made to the mayor of the city.[59]

The new church, holding three hundred persons, was well filled and was soon to be completely outgrown, although not all of those who attended services became members. Of those who did, as well as of many who did not, the family groups tended to be large, with the Bryans and Harpers probably outstanding. Filled as the church must have been with young families, however, the original leaders of the society were beginning to feel the passage of the years. In November, 1815, Vaughan then aged fifty-five, announced his intention of giving up the regular duties of the pulpit in January, 1816.[60] Significantly, it was to New England rather than Old England that the society looked for aid and guidance, writing immediately to the Rev. Drs. Freeman and Kirkland and Mr. William Ellery Channing, asking their help in obtaining a pastor. When in March, 1820, however, Ralph Eddowes, then sixty-nine, gave his notice of retiring from preaching responsibilities in six months from that date,[61] the society was still without an ordained leader. In 1823 James Taylor, aged fifty-six, resigned his office as lay preacher.[62] The society's problem seemed solved when the Rev. Samuel Barrett of Boston, after preaching seven Sundays for the society from July to September, 1823, was elected pastor on October 13, 1823, but Barrett unexpectedly declined the office.[63]

On February 17, 1824, the society approved the amending of its charter, inserting the word "Congregational" in its name, which thus became The First Congregational Society of Unitarian Christians. It stated, however, that "The term Congregational is used simply as expressive of the fact that this Society considers itself competent to manage its own concerns independently of the control of other religious societies."[64] The Commonwealth granted this amendment on March 19, 1824.Seven trustees were to be elected annually in April under the amended charter, only five of whom would be eligible for re-election in the succeeding year. The first governing board elected under the new system on April 19, 1824, consisted of Vaughan, Turner, Birch, Thomas Fletcher, Ford, Shippen, and Samuel H. Thomas.

The year 1824 was an exciting one in Philadelphia, made notable by the visit of Lafayette, comrade-in-arms of Washington, romantic hero of the American Revolution. His arrival in September was marked by the marching of troops and the ringing of bells. A sloop-of-war in the Delaware fired a salute as the General proceeded to a formal reception at the State House on Chestnut Street, where he passed under an arch built by Strickland, on which Sully had painted the arms of the city.

On August 15, 1824, while the city was in a froth of preparations for the reception of its distinguished foreign visitor, a young New England clergyman, William Henry Furness, preached for the first time to the Philadelphia Unitarian Society. Only twenty-two years of age, a graduate, the year before, from the Theological Department of Harvard, Furness had not yet received a charge of his own, but had been for three months assisting the Rev. Mr. Greenwood in Baltimore when he was invited to stop in Philadelphia on his way home and preach for the Philadelphia society. He did not particularly want to accept the invitation, for, as he later said, "I was homesick,"[65] but he did so, purely out of a sense of duty, he admitted later, and gratitude to the Philadelphia group for being so kind as to ask him. He preached for five Sundays, and then, to his amazement, a committee waited on him in September and offered him the pastorate of the church.

Furness' letter of acceptance, dated November 2, 1824, from his home in Medford, Massachusetts, is a classic of its kind.[66] Though its author was only twenty-two years old and had never had a permanent charge, the tone he took with the mature and substantial citizens of the Philadelphia society was haughty and condescending to a degree which would have been unforgivable had it not been so ingenuous. In the first place, he had waited two months before he gave his answer, and then he had done so with serious misgivings. "The salary which you offer me is, I doubt not, all that you can give. But as I do not possess the habits which would make the proposed salary sufficient, the doubt which I entertain concerning the success of my best efforts is increased by the fear that other cares & anxieties might demand my attention and distract my mind."

The worst drawback, however, as far as he was concerned, was Philadelphia itself, which had "cut off from all Christian communion" the members of the society and had arrayed old and powerful prejudice against them. Having thus made it very clear to the Philadelphia group that he did not consider their offer a particularly attractive one, Furness finally decided that it was no more than his duty to accept, "to prove the sincerity of my faith in the view of Christian truth to which we hold." The Philadelphia church was to be not only his first charge but his only one, his ministry continuing for fifty years of active pastorship and twenty-one years in emeritus status, until Furness passed quietly from this life on January 30, 1896, at the age of ninety-three. It was to be a pastorate of extraordinary richness and joy, a source of spiritual growth and strength not only to those who partook of the Unitarian faith but to all whose lives it touched in the greater community of the Philadelphia area.

NOTES

CHAPTER IV

[1]Leishman to Vaughan, October 20, 1812: CHURCH MSS.

[2]The birth of his daughter Lucy on July 20, 1816 was recorded in REG I, 6.

[3]Three contributions to the Building Fund from England were recorded in 1815 and 1817: CASH II; Charles Lean to Vaughan, June 27, 1816, and Taylor to Vaughan, November 1, 1817: CHURCH MSS.

[4]PROC, p. 154.

[5]PROC, p. 158A.

[6]Noted by Benjamin Rush in his "Commonplace Book, 1792-1813" under date of February, 1813, in Corner, p. 300.

[7]Presented to the society by Vaughan, March 13, 1814: PROC, p. 145. The only previous record of vital statistics was for two baptisms performed by Eddowes on April 2, 1797: PROC, p. 47.

[8]REG I,192. Melish gives an account of his life in his Introduction to his *Travels through the United States of America in the Years 1806 & 1807, and 1809, 1810 & 1811* (Philadelphia, 1815), See also DAB, XII, 486; Simpson, p. 690, and Marvin E. Wolfgang, "John Melish, An Early American Demographer," *Pa. Mag. of Hist. & Biog.*, LXXXII (January 1958), 65-81.

[9]John Melish, *A Geographical Description of the United States* (Philadelphia, 1816), p. 167.

[10]REG I, 4. See also DAB, XII, 486, and Simpson, pp. 689-90.

[11]James Mease, *The Picture of Philadelphia* (Philadelphia, 1811), p. 216.

[12]CASH II, 12, 13, 18, 33, 35, 37.

[13]Furness to Mary Jenks, February 28, 1831: COLL. CORR. I.

[14]REG I, 7.

[15]Correa de Serra to Vaughan, December 17, 1815: Misc MSS, APS.

[16]Cooper to Vaughan, June 20, 1821: Misc. MSS, APS.

[17]Preston to Vaughan, July 21,——:Misc. MSS, APS.

[18]REG I, 7.

[19]Scharf and Westcott, I, 593.

[20]*Infra*, p. 156 *et seq.*

[21]The dates given below indicate the CD from which they were taken, except as noted. They are in each case for the year in which the individual became connected with the society, the year before or the year after.

> John Bedford, patent ironbound shoestore, 296 High St. (1814)
> William Y. Birch, gentleman, 212 Walnut St. (1817) (Renewed connection)
> Thomas Fletcher, merchant, 325 Chestnut St. (1823)
> John Ford, merchant, 8 N. 7th St. (1823)
> Peter Harvy, coachmaker, 363 High St. (1814)
> Isaac Heylin, M.D. Palmyra Square (1824)
> Jacob Snider Law—not in CD, 1815; elected member April 9, 1815:PROC, p. 159A.
> George Lewis, merchant, 127 S. Front St. (1818)
> Samuel V. Merrick, fire engine maker, Pearson's Court back of St. James Church (1823)

Frederick K. Nidda, merchant, 28 N. 3rd St. (1814)

Samuel T. Porter, tin plate worker, n.w. cor. 13th & Filbert Sts. (1820)

William Renshaw, Washington Hall hotel, 120 S. 3rd St. (1818)

George Russell, saddler, 159 S. Johns St. (1820)

Charles Shippen, 27 S. 10th St. (1820, no occupation given)

Abraham Small, printer and bookseller, 112 Chestnut St. (1818)

James S. Smith, Jr. accountant, 165 S. 11th St. (1822)

Jacob Snider [Sr.], shoemaker, 5 N. 8th St. (1814)

Daniel Steinmetz, merchant, 22 Walnut and 291 Spruce St. (1814)

Thomas Sully, portrait painter, Philosophical Hall (1814)

Samuel H. Thomas, merchant, 107 and d.h. 246 Walnut St. (1823)
   Must have been a relative of Nathaniel Thomas, a founder. Address is
   the same as that of Taylor, who married Nathaniel's widow.

James Wood, merchant, cor. Front & Chestnut Sts. (1814)

[22]Scharf and Westcott, II, 1386.

[23]CASH II, 5, and a letter to Vaughan, March 3, 1813: CHURCH MSS.

[24]REG I, 1. His youngest son, James Frederic Bryan, born April 27, 1813, became a Roman Catholic in 1836 and eventually rose to the position of Archbishop of the Roman Catholic Diocese of Philadelphia. Scharf and Westcott, II, 1386–87.

[25]CD, 1805; COLLS, p. 1; UNNAMED, p. 23.

[26]REG I, 1–3; PROC, p. 171.

[27]Furness to Lucy Osgood, March 10, 1825:OSGOOD CORR.

[28]REG I, [202].

[29]Noted at meeting of the trustees of the church, April 1, 1856: TRUSTS III.

[30]A collection of Fletcher's papers at HSP contains 275 items, covering the years 1806–55.

[31]Sidney Gardiner to Thomas Fletcher, February 24, 1813: Fletcher Papers.

[32]PROC, pp. 114, 159B.

[33]COLLS, p. 2.

[34]Data on his tombstone. Edward W. Clark, *A Record of the Inscriptions on the Tablets and Grave-Stones in the Burial-Grounds of Christ Church, Philadelphia* (Philadelphia, 1864), p. 579. Small's wife Ann and five children were also buried at Christ Church between 1803 and 1825. Clark, pp. 579–80.

[35]Simpson, p. 91.

[36]Scharf and Westcott, I, 532.

[37]Furness to Mary Jenks, September 7, 1829: COLL. CORR. I.

[38]Binns, pp. 294–97.

[39]Scharf and Westcott, I, 525, 560; Oberholtzer, *City History*, II, 13, 51.

[40]PROC, p. 162B; REG I, 5–6.

[41]PROC, p. 193. Funeral services for all three were conducted by Taylor.

[42]DAB, XII, 557–58. Sheppard, *Reminiscences of the Vaughan Family*, gives a genealogy of the Merrick family (pp. 26–27) and a historical sketch of their activities (pp. 6–7.)

[43]PROC, p. 114; REG I, 96.

[44]George E. Pettingill, "Franklin, Priestley and the Samuel Vaughan, Jr. Manuscripts, 1775–1782," *Jour. of Franklin Instit.*, CCIIIL (March 1949), 195–204.

[45]PROC, p. 159A. The principal biographical source is Edward Biddle and Mantle Fielding, *The Life and Works of Thomas Sully (1783–1872)* (Philadelphia, 1921). See also DAB, XVIII, 202–5.

[46]A list of Sully's paintings, alphabetically arranged by subjects and numbering 2,631 items, is given in Biddle and Fielding, pp. 83–392.

[47]Biddle and Fielding, pp. 25–26.

[48]Biddle and Fielding, pp. 393–94. He was re-elected a director and elected president in 1842 but declined to accept election (pp. 394–95).

[49]Sydney L. Wright, *The Story of the Franklin Institute* (Philadelphia, 1938), pp. 24–25.

[50]Philip Goepp, ed., *Annals of Music in Philadelphia and History of the Musical Fund Society from its Organization in 1820 to the Year 1858* (Philadelphia, 1896), p. 62.

[51]PROC, pp. 170–71.

[52]PROC, p. 157A.

[53]Scharf and Westcott, I, 511.

[54]Scharf and Westcott, I, 589.

[55]Scharf and Westcott, I, 596.

[56]Quoted by Hampton L. Carson, *The Centenary of the Wistar Party* (Philadelphia, 1918), pp. 14–15.

[57]Carson, p. 16.

[58]Quoted from "Mr. Tyson's tribute," Carson, p. 16.

[59]Taylor to Vaughan, June 27, 1817: CHURCH MSS.

[60]PROC, p. 160A.

[61]PROC, pp. 170–71.

[62]RECS & MINS, p. 3.

[63]RECS & MINS, pp. 5–6, 32.

[64]RECS & MINS, p. 16.

[65]W. H. Furness, . . . *Discourse . . . January 12, 1875 . . . on the Occasion of the Fiftieth Anniversary of His Ordination* . . . (Philadelphia, 1875), p. 14.

[66]CHURCH MSS.

V

New Life From New England

WILLIAM HENRY FURNESS WAS BORN IN BOSTON ON APRIL 20, 1802, of solid New England stock.[1] His father being a bank clerk, young Furness' early years were passed in modest circumstances, distinguished, however, by the remarkable friendship he then formed with Ralph Waldo Emerson, when, aged five and four respectively, they shared a bench at Mrs. Whitwell's School. Their relationship continued with undiminished fervor down through the long years of their lives and ended only with Emerson's death, seventy-five years later. For Emerson, Furness was always "best of boys and best of men,"[2] with whom he had "the tie of school-fellow and playmate from the nursery onward . . . the true clan-ship and key that cannot be given to another."[3]

Electing the ministry as his vocation, Furness entered Harvard College, from which he graduated in 1820, and then went on to the Theological Department of that institution, receiving his degree there in 1823. His class later became famous in Harvard's history for its collection of theological giants, Furness being one of a group of five—the others, Ezra Stiles Gannett, Calvin Lincoln, Alexander Young, and Edward B. Hall, who was Furness' roommate—who, having gone through college and divinity school together, were to develop later into great leaders of the Unitarian Church.

Unitarianism in Boston by this time was enjoying the first flush of its Golden Morning. The Unitarian Controversy had rent the Congregational Church, pre-empting press and pulpit from 1815 to 1825, but by the end of that decade the Unitarians were in clear possession of the field in Boston, with only Old South remaining

114

WILLIAM H. FURNESS

Engraving on steel by John Sartain after the original portrait
by William H. Furness, Jr., 1861. Courtesy of the American
Unitarian Association.

in the Congregational camp. In the larger towns surrounding Boston they were only slightly less well off, claiming all but three churches, while in the Commonwealth of Massachusetts as a whole the Congregationalists had lost a full third of their strongholds. The Unitarian triumph was relatively localized. Of the 125 Unitarian churches in existence in the United States in 1825, 100 were in Massachusetts, most of these within twenty-five miles of Boston, with a score elsewhere in New England, and five located from New York south. But in the Boston area, the Unitarian faith enjoyed the leadership of every phase of community life. Law, medicine, theology, education, the fine arts, politics, commerce—all were ruled by Unitarians.

Young Furness lived through the furore of the Controversy and held his peace. As a student in Harvard's Theological Department, he listened dutifully to what Professor Andrews Norton had to say of sacred literature, heard Everett on the subject of the Septuagint, and took his Hebrew from Professor Sidney Willard. According to the Rev. Dr. Charles G. Ames, his Harvard biographer, however, "Whatever impressions were made on the student's mind by the courses of instruction, hardly a trace of them appears in his later authorship."[4] Of the Controversy itself, Furness remarked many years later that "It had snowed tracts, Trinitarian and Unitarian, over the land," and by the time he was ready to begin his life work the whole subject had simply become "rather wearisome."[5]

Furness delivered his first sermon in the fall of 1823 in Watertown, Massachusetts, and then preached for a few months in the Boston area, but did not receive a call to settle with any congregation. This situation he faced with undisturbed calm. "I felt not the slightest mortification, such a hearty dread had I of being settled in Boston, whose church-goers had in those days the reputation of being terribly critical, and rhetoric then and there was almost a religion. I felt myself utterly unequal to that position. All my daydreams had been of the country, of some village church."[6] In the spring of 1824 he had gone to Baltimore for three months and then had come the call from the Philadelphia society.

It was a cry from the wilderness, in terms of Boston Unitarianism, and Furness' initial hesitancy could not have been much abated by the sepulchral tone taken by his New England brethren at his ordination on January 12, 1825. Furness had had a hard time getting anyone to come to Philadelphia for the ceremony, for the journey from Massachusetts took two and a half days and the wintry winds were bitter. Those who finally came left their young friend in no doubt as to the magnitude of the sacrifice they were making on his account. Furness wrote to his future sister-in-law, Mary Jenks, on December 2, 1824:

I have not yet succeeded in getting a sufficient number of our Clergy to go on—I have had a great deal of fruitless trouble about it and have at last taken the advice of Mr. Henry Ware, who tells me I had better fix the day and send out the invitations and that then the ministers will have some conscience about the affair and feel the necessity of the case. It is a great shame that they should feel so little disposed to give me their *effectual* sympathy and aid. They give me *their blessings* and *good wishes* in abundance but as to a little sacrifice of personal comfort, they hang back. If I could possibly get along without them, I would try this very moment, but as an ordination is absolutely essential to all hope of success in Philad—If it were not I would be ordained here [in Massachusetts.][7]

They eventually did assemble, however, in the small, octagonal brick building at the corner of Tenth and Chestnut Streets: the venerable Dr. Aaron Bancroft, aged seventy, from Worcester, to deliver the Charge; the Rev. Henry Ware, Jr. and the Rev. Ezra Stiles Gannett, both from Boston, Ware to preach the Sermon and Gannett to extend the Right Hand of Fellowship to the new incumbent. The introductory prayers and Scripture reading were assigned to the Rev. William Ware, himself already manning an outpost of the Unitarian faith in New York City.

Dr. Bancroft tried to be cheerful. "Your brethren in the ministry, who will rejoice in your success, are distant from you; none will be here to encourage you by their aid and counsel, but you will not be forgotten."[8] The Philadelphia scene, however, he could view only with dismay.

Your situation is peculiar: you will have not only the usual trials of a minister's life, but many arising from your place in this city, surrounded by those who are warmly and conscientiously opposed to your faith, and separated from those who, with you, believe Unitarian Christianity to be the religion of the gospel. Your ministerial duties will be heavier, your language will be more liable to misrepresentation, and your conduct will be more strictly watched than those of most of your brethren.[9]

Mr. Henry Ware agreed that in the new situation to which his coreligionist had been called "there were circumstances of peculiar trial."[10] It was in the tone of one bidding Godspeed to a missionary dedicated to the conversion of deepest Africa that Dr. Bancroft enjoined, "Look up; the field is one of immense extent and promise."[11]

Channing had made his opinion of Philadelphia quite clear in a letter to Vaughan a decade earlier: "In your part of the country, religious opinions are hereditary, and unless I have been misinformed, the habit of sincere and fearless inquiry is hardly more common than in Constantinople."[12] With Boston, the center of American Unitarianism, more than two days' journey away, Philadelphia was a "frontier parish" in the opinion of his colleagues,[13] and to Furness "the place to be filled . . . looked lonely and formidable."[14] So it was, theologically speaking, Furness being the only minister of his denomination between New York and Baltimore.

Theological considerations aside, however, Philadelphia was actually not completely beyond the pale of civilization in 1825. It was true, that the War of 1812 had done deadly damage to the foreign trade which had once been the mainstay of the city's economy, and after the war this trade had been revived by way of the rival port of New York, which, among other attractions, offered a year-round accessibility impossible in Philadelphia, where the Delaware River was frozen solid for several weeks every winter. To New York also went more and more of the ships bearing new immigrants from Europe, and Philadelphia dropped to second place in population some time between the census of 1820 and that of 1830. Obvious and undeniable also was the additional fact that political primacy had passed on to the national capital at Washington.

On the credit side, nonetheless, there was much to be said for Furness' new home. New York could and did entice foreign shipping to her growing port facilities, but Philadelphia turned to the development of her inland communications and by 1825 she was enthusiastically constructing bridges, turnpikes, and canals. In 1824 an old dream had been renewed when a contract was let to construct a canal connecting the Delaware River with the Chesapeake. The Schuylkill Navigation Company, chartered in 1815 to work on her other river, had so well done its work in building dams, canals, and locks that in 1825 boats were able to navigate the Schuylkill from Fairmount in Philadelphia to Port Carbon in Schuylkill County, a distance of 110 miles. In the same period, work was also started upon projects to connect Philadelphia with New York by way of the Raritan River, and to open up the Lehigh Valley by a canal system. Meanwhile, the damming of the Schuylkill had provided water power which by 1819 had made possible the establishment of mill sites in outlying districts of the city such as Manayunk. At the same time, the vastness of the mineral resources lying to the north and west had begun to be realized, and the exploitation of Pennsylvania's coal and iron fields was beginning to change the whole fabric of the city's economic system.

Although it was true that in 1825 the Lenni Lenape Indians still roamed the streets of Philadelphia and William Swaim was not having much success in his attempt to convince his fellow Philadelphians of the benefits to be derived from a warm bath, the cultivation of the arts and sciences was flourishing. Philadelphia's resident artists were among the best in the country, including Thomas Sully, John Neagle, the Peales, Charles R. Leslie, and Thomas Birch. In sculpture she had William Rush and in architecture William Strickland, Thomas U. Walter, and John Haviland. The Musical Fund Society, organized in 1820, gave the city outstanding stature in the world of music, providing, in its hall opened in 1824, the first room devoted to musical purposes in the United States.

In spite of the fact that the gallery boys in the theatres often inundated the pit with showers of nutshells and apple peelings, and inebriated gentlemen in the boxes sometimes tumbled their companions out upon the stage, Philadelphia was a bright center of theatrical enterprise in 1825. All of the leading actors were to be seen upon her stage—John Dwyer, George Frederick Cooke, James William Wallach, Junius Brutus Booth, Edmund Kean, and many others. A new theatre was built on Chestnut Street in 1822, designed by William Strickland and adorned by pieces of sculpture done by William Rush. New York had still not outstripped Philadelphia even in the realm of theatrical management, although this fate was shortly to overtake her.

Philadelphia's pre-eminent position in the field of medicine had been established at the end of the eighteenth century by the School of Medicine of the University of Pennsylvania and this leadership she retained. New impetus was given to professional training by the establishment of the Philadelphia College of Pharmacy in 1821 and the Jefferson Medical College in 1825, while new additions were made to the already imposing list of the city's institutions for the care of the sick by the founding of the Pennsylvania Institution for the Deaf and Dumb in 1820 and the Pennsylvania Infirmary for Diseases of the Ear and Eye in 1822. In the natural sciences Philadelphia claimed such leaders as the entomologist Thomas Say, the geologist William Maclure, the botanist William Darlington, and the ornithologists George Ord and John James Audubon.

The first quarter of the century had, in fact, been particularly rich in new additions to the city's cultural and intellectual life, which already boasted of many "firsts," such as the oldest library in the United States, organized in 1731 by the Library Company of Philadelphia; the first society for the philosophical discussion of the arts and sciences, the American Philosophical Society, founded in 1743; the first university, the University of Pennsylvania, beginning with a Charity School in 1740 and assuming university status after its inclusion of medical courses in its curriculum in 1765; the first school for the teaching of the fine arts, the Pennsylvania Academy of the Fine Arts, founded in 1805. To these and many more were added the Academy of Natural Sciences in 1812, the Athenaeum in 1814, the Mercantile Library Association in 1821, and the Franklin Institute and the Historical Society of Pennsylvania in 1824. Under the leadership of such publishers as Mathew Carey and his sons, Henry and Edward, and his son-in-law, Isaac Lea, Philadelphia continued to be the literary center of the nation, a position from which she would not be dislodged by Furness' native city for yet another generation. The scene of the young New Englander's future labors was therefore not without certain attractions for his highly cultivated tastes. Nor was he alone for long. In August, 1825, he married Annis Pulling Jenks of Salem, Massachusetts, with whom he was to have a long and happy life.[15]

Furness suspected that the little group which came to see him in September, 1824, on behalf of the Philadelphia society was actually the greater part of the church body.[16] While this was not entirely true, it was symbolically true enough. Although at least forty-seven families had been admitted to membership from 1807 to 1825, only seventeen men signed the society's application for the amended charter in 1824.[17] Thomas Fletcher later described the society's situation at this time: "It was uphill work. Few seemed willing to join so *weak* a party, lest their temporal prosperity be affected. There were many attentive hearers, but at the end of ten years after the dedication of the first house of worship, there was no increase of members, and very little increase of means."[18] Apparently, though new members joined the group, the increase did not offset natural attrition by death, removal from the city, and other causes. The meetings of the society were not listed in the public press among the notices of church affairs, for, though the city was a center of American Protestantism, this meant extreme religious conservatism in all its forms. The Unitarians, according to Furness, were "about as obscure and despised as any company of Methodists or such like are in Boston."[19] Joining the society required a willingness to accept the burden of disfavor with which the denomination was regarded in the city and the membership was small. For the same reason it was highly selected, confirmed and steadfast in its devotion to the cause of religious liberalism.

Furness had been preaching in various churches from time to time for a little over a year before he settled in Philadelphia but none of his early sermons has been preserved.[20] It is possible, however, that they were more or less tentative and noncommittal, for Furness was an amiable young man, well adjusted to his world and happy with it as it was. On the other hand, it is at least suspicious that this extremely personable young clergyman, with all of the proper family and educational connections, received no offer of settlement in more than a year after his graduation. The accepted leader of Boston Unitarianism in 1825 was William Ellery Channing, who had at that time developed his theological convictions to the point of Arianism but no further. In 1816 he had told Vaughan quite frankly: "It is well known that I am far from agreeing on every particular with the leading men of your society. I certainly do not wish success to all your views."[21]

Furness, however, from the beginning seems to have been a convinced humanitarian, believing Jesus to have been entirely human, the son of God only as all men are sons of God. In this he was much closer to Priestley than he was to Channing and hence, presumably, close, as well, to the theological position of the Philadelphia society, with its predominantly English membership the direct inheritor of Priestley's theology. Furness himself stated: "This church in Philadelphia, composed almost exclusively of persons from the Old Country . . . was looked upon pretty much as a settlement of a small company of Mahometans, an exotic, having no root in the soil. Even the liberally disposed in New England were shy of it, as going altogether too far."[22]

What preconceived notions Furness' bride may have brought

to her new home in 1825 is not known, but, reporting to her sister in Salem her impressions of her first Sabbath in Philadelphia, she declared: "I could not have been more pleasantly disappointed than I was."[23]

When Vaughan had written to Channing in 1815, seeking his help in securing an ordained pastor for the Philadelphia society, Channing had replied that no ordinary minister would do for Philadelphia, where "the slumber of the mind can only be broken by some powerful excitement—and eloquence."[24] Furness supplied both. He had been richly endowed with every natural gift for success in his profession. Tall and handsome and of commanding presence, he was also friendly and approachable, full of good humour and quick to smile. His rich, mellow voice was superb, completely captivating all who heard him, and what he had to say went right to the hearts of his listeners, while at the same time they enjoyed the comforting assurance that their minds were being cultivated as well. In a word, Furness possessed in full measure that subtle, indefinable, but most precious of all qualities, "charm."

Thomas Fletcher said of Furness' coming: "Not more rapid and cheering is the revival of spring with its luxuriant verdure after a dreary winter, than was the change which succeeded this event. None but those who had so long waited for its advent can realize the happiness that was felt, when we saw our numbers increasing."[25] Fourteen new families joined the society in 1825, thirty-four in 1826, thirty-two in 1827, and eleven in the early months of 1828.[26]

Two outstanding new members were officially connected with the Franklin Institute, the teachers and scientists, James P. Espy and Walter R. Johnson. Espy was a native Pennsylvanian, born in 1785 of Huguenot stock.[27] His family had moved to Kentucky when he was an infant and there he grew up, entering Transylvania University in Lexington in 1803, from which he graduated in 1808. He taught in Ohio and Maryland before he arrived in Philadelphia, where he took up the teaching of the classics and mathematics and also became closely affiliated with the Franklin Institute, directing its School for Mathematics in 1824. In 1835 he began devoting himself to lecturing and studying meteorological problems, developing the theory of storms which won him the Magellanic Prize of the American Philosophical Society in 1836. He subsequently had a distinguished career as meteorologist for the War and Navy Departments, his first government appointment taking him to Washington in 1842.

Johnson was born in Leominster, Massachusetts, on June 21, 1794.[28] Graduating from Harvard University in 1819, he taught school in Massachusetts before coming to Philadelphia in 1821 as principal of Germantown Academy. He became the principal of the newly established Franklin Institute High School in 1826, continuing in that connection for ten years, and was also a professor of natural philosophy and mechanics in the institute. While serving in this capacity he prepared two textbooks and wrote innumerable articles on education for the *Journal* of the institute. Always an active promoter of public education, he lectured and wrote extensively on the subject of teacher training, advocated the public support of education, and was also active in many educational associations. He was the only teacher member of the Pennsylvania Society for the Promotion of Public Schools and was elected a member of the council of that body in 1829, thereafter playing a major part in the society's program. In 1836 he began the geological investigations which were to be his major interest for the rest of his life, concerning himself especially with the properties of coal and iron ore. When the new Pennsylvania Medical College was established in Philadelphia in 1839, functioning as a branch of Pennsylvania College at Gettysburg, Johnson was made its professor of chemistry and natural philosophy, which he remained until 1843, when the whole faculty resigned in a body. Meanwhile Johnson continued to produce many works on the properties of metals and engaged in research for the navy in the general field of thermotension. A member of the Academy of Natural Sciences in 1827, he served as an auditor, 1832–35; a curator, 1835–37; a member of the Publications Committee, 1836–37; and corresponding secretary

1841–48. He was a founding member of the Association of American Geologists, organized in April, 1840, became a member of the American Association for the Advancement of Science in September, 1847, and was elected the first secretary of the Association of American Geologists and Naturalists and a member of its Standing Committee in 1848–49. He moved to Washington in 1848, dying there in 1852. His biographer at the Franklin Institute summed up his career: "Probably he was not a great man, but typical of those who were busy developing American science during the early nineteenth century and contributing to the nation's industrial development."[29] Furness considered his going to Washington a great loss to the Unitarian Society.[30]

The printing and bookselling business, so well represented in the beginning of the society's history, first by Birch and later by Abraham Small, provided several new members: Lawrence Johnson, James, Jr. and John Kay, John Mortimer, Robert H. Small, and James Webster. Of these, at least Johnson and James Kay, Jr. are known to have been born in England.

Johnson's marriage to Sarah M. Murray on May 3, 1825, was the first performed by Furness in Philadelphia.[31] Johnson was then the proprietor of a stereotype foundry at 17 Cyprus Alley. In his business he was actually the partner of Jedidiah Howe, although the two men operated at different addresses, and this partnership continued until Howe's death in 1834. Johnson had been born in Kingston-upon-Hull, England, January 23, 1801, and had been baptized in the Church of England in March of the same year. At the age of twelve he had begun to learn the printing business. Leaving England for America in 1818 with his parents, he had gone first to Albany, New York, but had then resumed the printing trade in New York City. In 1823 he removed to Philadelphia, where he became a United States citizen on June 19, 1828. Until 1825 Philadelphia publishers had sent to New York the few books they entrusted to the stereotype process, but gradually they began to give this work to Johnson and Howe. In 1833 Johnson added type-founding to his business and with George F. Smith bought from Richard Ronaldson the Philadelphia Type Foundry established in 1796. With the introduction of the new process of electrotyping, Johnson surpassed all his rivals and became an outstanding figure in Philadelphia, at his death in 1860 leaving an estate valued at $800,000. After a succession of changes in personnel and name, the firm was incorporated with the American Type Founders' Company in 1892.

Johnson was active in many phases of Philadelphia's life. He became a member of the Franklin Institute in 1825, a life member in 1835. He was a trustee of the Union Academy of Philadelphia when it was chartered in 1851. He was elected a member of the Philadelphia Society for the Establishment and Support of Charity Schools in 1852, a member of the Historical Society of Pennsylvania in 1854. He was president of the Commonwealth Bank of Philadelphia and held directorships in several insurance companies, transportation companies, and coal companies. Always a patron of social reforms for the protection of workers, one of his last acts, with the other leading founders of Philadelphia, was to secure by petition to Congress a modification of the copyright law to protect the letter-cutters, engravers, and originators of designs. When Johnson died, a special meeting of gentlemen was held in the office of J. B. Lippincott and Company in his memory, with laudatory speeches and resolutions delivered by many of the outstanding men of the city.

Although Johnson had been born and baptised in the Church of England, he began paying pew rent in the Philadelphia Unitarian Society in 1827 and remained a devoted member of the society.[32] His first wife died in 1834 and in 1837 he was married to Mary Winder by Mayor John Swift of Philadelphia. The second Mrs. Johnson was a staunch member of the First Presbyterian Church of the Rev. Albert Barnes, a point discussed at some length in the family genealogical study though the same work does not refer in any way to the fact that Johnson himself was an equally devout member of the Philadelphia Unitarian Society.[33]

A contemporary of Johnson, James Kay, Jr.,[34] born in England in 1802, was barred from Oxford University because of the liberal religious views of his father, who shortly thereafter moved with his family to the United States. The elder Kay later became a well known Unitarian clergyman in Northumberland, Pennsylvania, and subsequently in Harrisburg. James Kay, Jr., with his brother John, was a printer and publisher for many years in Philadelphia, bringing to his work outstanding intellectual gifts and innate good taste, cultivated by his classical education to an unusually high level of performance. Although his firm specialized in law and educational works, he was also accomplished in the arts and had many friends in the artistic circles of the city. When he died at his home in Philadelphia on April 22, 1856, he was mourned especially by "the friends of social reform, of which, for the last fifteen years, he had been a prominent, judicious, and devoted advocate."[35]

Rembrandt Peale, the portrait painter, paid pew rent to the society in December, 1825.[36] His son Henry had been buried by Furness in September and his daughter Eleanor married by the Unitarian pastor in October to Thomas Jacobs, who either then or shortly thereafter became a pewholder.[37] There is no later record however, of any further connection of Peale himself with the society.

Representation from another branch of the arts, engraving, began in this period, the first newcomer from this field being Gideon Fairman.[38] Born in Newtown, Connecticut, on June 26, 1774, Fairman was sent to Isaac and George Hutton in Albany, New York, to learn silver-plating engraving. He set up his own business in Albany in 1796 and achieved considerable prominence as an engraver of vignettes. Moving to Philadelphia in 1810, the following year he joined George Murray, a newly arrived Scotch engraver, and John Draper, a native Pennsylvania craftsman, to form the bank-note engraving firm of Murray, Draper, Fairman and Company. Bank-note engraving was at that time a relatively new art. The paper money used during the colonial period and in the early years of the Republic had been exceedingly poor in quality, printed from wooden blocks on an inferior grade of paper, and had lent itself easily to counterfeiting, with the resultant evil of loss of public confidence as well as loss of revenue. In the last years of the eighteenth century, however, great technical improvements began to be made, many of them the work of Fairman. According to one estimate he was, as well, "considered to have the greatest talent and taste of any of the vignette engravers in the country, and few equals in Europe,"[39]; and he seems to have been the attraction which shortly drew to Philadelphia a whole group of engravers who became associated with him in business. Charles Toppan,[40] born in Newburyport, Massachusetts, in 1796, travelled to Philadelphia in 1814 with Fairman's younger brother, David, and entered the firm of Murray, Draper, Fairman and Company. Two years later Toppan's teacher in Newburyport, Jacob Perkins, well known inventor of several revolutionary new processes in bank-note engraving, also took a position with the firm, as did Asa Spencer of Connecticut, inventor of the geometric lathe for engraving.

The stereotype steel plate devised by this group was considered proof against counterfeiters and the firm was urged to enter it in the prize competition being conducted by the Bank of England in 1819 for a means of preventing bank note forgeries, a crime from which the bank was suffering heavily at this time. Fairman, Toppan, Perkins, and Spencer went to England and submitted their method of "engine-turning," which, though it failed to win first prize, was greatly praised and led to their association with Charles Heath, the English engraver, in a new firm, Perkins, Fairman and Heath. The new business prospered and Perkins stayed on in London until his death in 1849, but the others returned to the United States after a few years. In 1822 Fairman established the firm of Fairman, Draper and Company, which later became Fairman, Draper, Underwood and Company. Fairman died on March 18, 1827. Spencer was associated with the firm, through its various changes in name, from 1825 until at least 1847, at which time he was senior partner in what was then called Spencer, Hufty and Danforth. Toppan returned to the United States in 1825 but lived in New York for a while before settling again in Philadelphia, where he worked with several other engravers of bank notes until in 1858 the firm of Toppan, Carpenter and Company, which he then headed, merged with several other leading engraving firms to form the American Bank Note Company. Toppan was elected the first president of the new firm, which office he held until 1860, when he declined re-election and resigned.

It was apparently the pastor's personality which drew Fairman to the Philadelphia Unitarian Society. Furness said of him that "a little while after I came here, he became interested in our Church and altho' he has been indifferent to Church going, he became a constant attendant. . . . Indeed I believe he loved me with warm affection and it was impossible not to reciprocate the feeling."[41] Fairman, who was generally referred to as "Colonel," having achieved that rank during the War of 1812, was, according to Furness, "one of the handsomest men I ever saw. His figure was perfect. His disposition particularly amiable. Washington Irving once said that if he were compelled to live with one man all his life and he were permitted to choose that man, it should be Colonel Fairman."[42] In March, 1827, Fairman unfortunately suffered a paralytic stroke for which his physician treated him by drawing from him a basin full of blood and cupping him on the heart.[43] He died the next day. After his death his family continued to be active in the church. His widow Furness considered "one of my most devoted and valued friends."[44] Both of his children eventually married members of the congregation, Caroline in 1830 becoming the wife of Evans Rogers, one of the wealthiest men in the society, George in 1834 marrying Ellen, daughter of Sidney Gardiner.[45]

Toppan began contributing to the church in May, 1826, and was very active down through the years, being elected a trustee in October, 1844, although he declined election.[46] At the same time he took a prominent part in the cultural life of the city, with membership in many societies, serving as a director of the American Art Union Association, the Pennsylvania Academy of the Fine Arts, and the Franklin Institute. Widely travelled, he died in Florence, Italy, in October, 1874.

Two of Toppan's business associates were also identified with the Unitarian Society. S. H. Carpenter, a member of the firm of Toppan, Carpenter and Company, organized in 1845, shared a pew with Toppan in 1828, and was associated with the church as late as 1842.[47] Henry E. Saulnier, an engraver with the same firm from 1846 to 1860, had been baptized in 1817 at the age of six by James Taylor and was married by Furness in 1838.[48]

Spencer's recorded connection with the Unitarian Society began in June, 1826, when he made a contribution to the church.[49] He began paying pew rent in July, 1827, but the only other reference to him in the church's records are tragic ones, seven of his children, most of them infants, being buried in the church burying-ground between 1828 and 1844.[50]

One of Fairman's most famous pupils in the art of engraving was Cephas G. Childs, who began paying pew rent in the Unitarian Society as early as 1828.[51] Childs was born in Bucks County, Pennsylvania, in 1793. In 1812 he was apprenticed to Fairman but the following year enlisted in the Washington Grays, serving with that unit for the rest of the War of 1812. Entering the engraving business for himself in 1818, he appeared in the *City Directories*, from 1818 until 1845 as a historical and landscape engraver, and was considered quite a good engraver of portraits in stipple and landscapes and vignettes in line. He persuaded Henry Inman, the portrait painter, to join him in 1830 in the lithographic firm of Childs and Inman, which became Childs and Lehman in 1833 upon the withdrawal of Inman and the addition of George Lehman. Childs gave up engraving in 1845 to devote himself to journalism, in which he had been engaged from 1832 when he became an editor of the *Commercial Herald* of Philadelphia. After that paper merged with the *North American* in 1840, he became the commercial editor of the latter journal, which he purchased, with Walter Colton, in 1842, subsequently selling his interest in 1845, though he retained his editorial post until 1847. He established the *Commercial List and Philadelphia Price Current*, of which he was proprietor and editor from 1832 to 1852. From 1830 to 1845 he was a director of the Pennsylvania Academy of the Fine Arts, from 1839 to 1851 secretary of the Board of Directors of the Philadelphia Board of Trade, of which he was a charter member, and from 1855 to 1864 president of the New Creek Coal Company, except for a brief interval in 1858–59.

In November, 1828, Childs shared his pew with another engraver, William E. Tucker, a native of Philadelphia, born in 1801, who had been a pupil of Francis Kearney in Philadelphia and had also studied in England.[52] Tucker was considered an excellent craftsman in line and stipple portraits and landscapes but devoted the latter part of his life almost exclusively to bank-note engraving. The list of his signed works includes pieces published by Childs and another Unitarian, James Kay, Jr.

The largest group of newcomers, however, was that of the merchants, who continued to join the society in growing numbers, at least twenty-eight of them becoming affiliated between 1825 and 1828. The overwhelming majority of them lived within a few blocks' radius of High Street and the Delaware River, with their shops attached to their dwellings, and they dealt in everything from the lace fringe and military articles sold by Henry Duhring to the wholesale and retail groceries of Henry Lentz, the china of John C. Stanbridge, and the hosiery and gloves of Joseph Todhunter.

Two new sets of partners were included, New England merchants all—Benjamin R. Cheever and George Fales, Baldwin Gardiner and Lewis Veron.[53] Also from New England, Charles and George Fletcher, brothers of Thomas Fletcher, joined him as jewellers and silversmiths at 130 Chestnut Street and as members of the Unitarian Society during this period. Sidney Gardiner, his partner since 1810, became a fellow Unitarian in 1825. The relationship of the two Gardiners, Baldwin and Sidney, to each other is not known, but Baldwin Gardiner was Mrs. Thomas Fletcher's brother.[54] Lewis Veron was also closely bound into the family picture, one of Thomas Fletcher's children being named Lewis Veron Fletcher and another Melina Veron Fletcher.[55] Veron was living with Thomas Fletcher in 1828.

Still another New England merchant who joined the society in this period was Charles Leland, a wholesale dealer in Leghorn hats at this time.[56] Leland was to become famous through his son, Charles Godfrey, who in 1857 began publishing his celebrated humourous ballads in dialect under the pseudonym of "Hans Breitmann." The future author, with his brother Henry, was baptized by Furness in 1828.[57] He retained the family pew until he entered Princeton College, although his father had returned to the Anglican faith a year or two before.

Thomas H. Jacobs, a merchant at 19 Dock Street, was married to Eleanor, daughter of Rembrandt Peale, by Furness in 1825 and took a pew in the church.[58] In 1829 he gave up his pew and moved to Washington but he subsequently returned, his five children being baptized by Furness in 1837.[59]

Dexter Stone, a merchant at 9 South Ninth Street, began contributing to the society in 1825.[60] His firm, the commission house of Grant and Stone, in 1837 became the Philadelphia agent of the great English bankers, Baring Brothers and Company, and was considered one of their most important connections in the United States.[61]

Of all the new merchant members of the Unitarian Society, however, the most important from the historian's point of view was Joseph Sill.[62] Born in Carlisle, Cumberland County, England, in 1801, of a family in modest circumstances, he left school at the age of twelve. When he was eighteen he came to the United States and settled in Philadelphia, where he worked as a clerk for Spackman and Little, until his marriage on October 16, 1825, to Jane Todhunter, daughter of another English merchant and member of the Unitarian Society, Joseph Todhunter.[63] After their marriage the Sills opened a gentlemen's furnishing store on Chestnut Street opposite the State House, where they lived from 1825 to 1850. They took a pew in the church in 1828 and Joseph became a trustee in 1831, continuing in that capacity until his death in 1854. He was, in addition, one of Furness' closest personal friends, seeing him daily. When Sill decided to begin a diary in 1831 he initiated a day-by-day account of the affairs of the society which is invaluable, not only as a revelation of the inner workings of the society, possible only from one who was both an officer of the church and a friend of the pastor, but also as a warm and intimate picture of one immigrant Englishman and how he fared with Philadelphia society from 1831 to 1854.

Sill was almost a perfect example of what David Riesman calls an "inner-directed" man. He had been a poor boy in England who had come to the United States to better himself, and this goal he kept steadily in mind. Life was real and very earnest for him, a terribly serious business that could not be taken lightly. There was a great deal of "self" in him—he was filled with self-esteem but was also self-critical, highly self-conscious, and forever driven by a self-improving urge. Yet he was also a fond parent to his seven children and he was acutely sensitive to the social ills and maladjustments of his day. He not only went to church every Wednesday night and twice on Sunday but recorded in his diary every day the text of the sermons, his own reaction to them, and minute observations on the attitudes and behavior of other members of the congregation. Many of these he unfortunately found wanting. Together with his often ponderous solemnity and intense moral earnestness, however, he had a great capacity for enjoyment and took full advantage of all the cultural and recreational opportunities which the city had to offer. These ran the gamut from lectures at the University of Pennsylvania to tightrope walking and exhibitions at the Chestnut Street Theatre, dramatic performances by the Kembles and strolls in Laurel Hill Cemetery, Philharmonic concerts and visits to the menagerie on the open lot at Thirteenth and Spruce Streets. Living on Chestnut Street directly across from the State House, he had a first row seat for the elections for many years, though his acid comments expressed disgust with the followers of all political parties. He was interested in art, buying many pictures even when he could ill afford to do so and painting a bit himself. He wrote stories which he contributed to the local periodicals. He took up sports as seriously as he did everything else, always with an eye to self-improvement, playing cricket like the good Englishman he never ceased to be even when he had become an equally good American, riding horseback, hiking, playing quoits. He joined organizations and usually became an officer in them, for he was a man who thrived on responsibilities accepted and discharged. His major interest in this area was the Society of the Sons of St. George, of which he became a life member on April 23, 1829, a steward in 1832 and 1833, secretary from 1834 to 1841, vice-president from 1842 to 1847, and president from 1848 until his death in 1854. The diary contains it all, in ten manuscript volumes.

There continued to be a strong English tone to the society with the coming of such new members as Lawrence Johnson, the Kays, Sill, and the Todhunters, but with the beginning of Furness' pastorate the influence of New England gradually came to predominate over that of Old England. Furness himself never gave up his New England ties. He had made it a condition of his acceptance of the Philadelphia post that he be given six weeks' leave every year, with a substitute supplied at the expense of the society, in order that he might return "to the Eastward" to his paternal home. [64] Even in 1834 he wrote of "that yearning of the heart with which I turn to that place, once my home—the house of my father. . . . If I were to give up for an indefinite time the idea of visiting New England with my family, it would cost me a pang only less than that produced by the separation of the grave." [65]

His father, to whom he was especially devoted, never became reconciled to his living in Philadelphia, and his wife was still "not very much attached" to the city in 1842. [66] Furness himself in 1847, when his daughter became engaged to Dr. Leonard Abbott, found it "a comfort . . . that he is a Boston man," for "I should love to leave *all* my children in New England when I die." [67] This hope was frustrated, for his daughter broke her engagement to Dr. Abbott and later married a Philadelphian, Dr. Caspar Wister. Only one son, William Henry, Jr., actually went to New England to live, settling in Cambridge, Massachusetts, around 1863, where he died in 1867.[68] However, the only son to go to college, Horace Howard, by-passed Philadelphia's University of Pennsylvania in favor of Boston's Harvard.[69] In a speech given at the Academy of Music in Philadelphia on November 10, 1859, the senior Furness referred to himself as "a New Englander, and so an American of the Americans, as we New Englanders, with our well known modesty, account ourselves." Conviction underscored the intended humour.

Although Philadelphia's foreign trade had never recovered from the effects of the War of 1812, it had been replaced by strong mercantile ties with the ports of New England. In 1827 trade with the ports east of New York was valued at $7,750,000—nearly half of which was with Boston. Among the other New England ports involved were Providence, Hartford, Nantucket, New Bedford, Portsmouth, Portland, Salem, Newburyport, Hingham, and Stonington. Migration followed in the wake of trade, and such New England merchants as Benjamin Cheever and Thomas Rotch,[70] from New Bedford, John W. Patten from Roxbury,[71] the Fletchers, the Gardiners, Charles Leland, and George Fales came to live in Philadelphia, joining the Unitarian Society there. Charles Godfrey Leland noted in his *Memoirs:* "My parents, on coming to Philadelphia, had at first attended the Episcopal Church, but finding that most of their New England friends held to the Rev. W. H. (now Dr.) Furness, an Unitarian, they took a pew in his chapel."[72]

There was much visiting back and forth, and apparently Philadelphia's climate, much maligned by natives, held certain attractions for New Englanders, as Furness remarked in 1831, "It is getting to be common for Boston people to come here to pass the Spring to avoid the East winds."[73] In addition to family and business connections, close cultural ties were maintained by the "labours of love," as Furness called them, performed for him by such New England friends as Emerson, Channing, Gannett, and a host of others, who preached for him from time to time. Furness stated in 1871: "When I first became the pastor of this church . . . scarcely six weeks passed that some one of my brethren in the ministry from Boston or its vicinity—the headquarters of the Unitarian denomination—did not stand in this pulpit, and thus keep up a living connection with the main body."[74]

Ties with the South also were strengthened by the trading carried on by such merchants as Fletcher and Gardiner, and by the presence in the congregation of such men as William E. Hulings and Thomas Mellon,[75] retired "gentlemen," both of whom had made fortunes in New Orleans.

More and more wealthy men were joining the society, some of them under rather unusual circumstances. Thomas Hulme was a member in 1825. A particularly impressive Communion Service had been conducted in December of that year, Furness wrote to his mother-in-law, and

had touched the heart of a young lady who comes regularly to our Church and who belongs to a rich family the majority of whom with the father at the head not only have no religious faith but I fear scoff at all religion. Mr. Hulme the father will not come at all. He found that a regard to appearance must impel him to let his family attend some Church, so he took a pew in ours because he says in his coarse way there is less nonsense there than in the other places of public worship.[76]

Sidney Gardiner took a pew in 1825, became a faithful attendant and was "warmly interested in the Church," bringing his four children to Furness to be baptized in 1826. Furness was so highly gratified that he told his sister-in-law all about it in a letter, even though he questioned the propriety of his expressing his elation thus openly. "Mr. Gardiner is a man that you would call fashionable. . . . Before I came here, he never went to Church scarcely at all. . . . He is my greatest—my best pledge of success."[77] Oddly enough, though, he went on to say of Mr. Gardiner: "I don't intend to say that he is now what you would call a religious man—tho' he is unexceptionable in his manners and habits—but there is evidently a sense of Religion increasing upon him."

Furness took tremendous professional pride in the growth of the society, writing to Mary Jenks in November, 1825:

I have never seen the Church so full. Is it a wrong feeling, my dear Mary, with which I look down upon the pews when they are full? I assure you I can't have a more delightful sensation than that which fills my heart when I rise to prayer and the people rise all around me . . . I would not exchange the gratification with which I perceive the increase of my society for the richest station on earth. I hope I do my duty to these people.[78]

In January, 1826, he wrote: "My society increases beyond my expectations. . . . Hardly a week passes that some one does not take a pew or a seat."[79]

Though he had come to Philadelphia with misgivings, Furness quickly found much to admire in his new home and began to resent the pity which his New England relatives felt for him in his exile. He rebuked his mother-in-law in May, 1826: "While we are surrounded by such devoted friends as we have here, don't let it be dreamed that I am a martyr. The idea is ridiculous."[80] Nor were his consolations only spiritual. He was a very practical young man. "Indeed this is a favored city. I believe there is more comfort and convenience here than anywhere else in the U. States . . . especially the dwellings of the rich Quakers look so simple and yet so large and comfortable and costly withal that it is impossible not to feel that there is a great amount of happiness enjoyed here."[81] He was particularly impressed by the quantity and variety of food available in Philadelphia. "Our market is glutted with cantelopes, water melons, peaches and every sort of eatable vegetable," he wrote to Mary Jenks in August, 1826. "Indeed there is no finer sight in Philad[a] than the market. You may walk a mile and a half amidst heaps of every kind of produce. . . . For less than half a dollar *we* can supply ourselves with a dinner wh. besides meat shall be composed of almost every kind of vegetable and fruit."[82]

The Furnesses were at this time living in a house on the north side of Chestnut Street, between Thirteenth and Broad, in a part of the city "which is built up and *improved*, as the Yankees say. The part which lies between Broad Street and the Schuylkill is like the country. As we live near Broad you perceive we are almost in the country."[83] Although they liked this house, chiefly because it "looks so *genteel*," they finally found it too "far off from every-body" and moved to Eleventh Street near Chestnut, where "the whole square opposite the house is open and filled with full grown trees of every kind, willows, elms, etc."[84]

The growing prestige of the society was reflected in the appointment of Furness in 1827 as one of the thirty-six Directors of Public Schools named by the Select and Common Councils of Philadelphia. He took these duties very seriously, although in 1830 he admitted: "The system of public schools is a doubtful one in my mind. The more I think of it, the less certain I feel."[85] The new members who entered the society at this time carried on the tradition of public service established by the founders. Thomas Mogridge had been one of the group of gentlemen who formed in 1821 the Accountants' Society of Pennsylvania to alleviate the shortage of accountants and young men who wished clerkships, and he was elected a member of the Committee on Charity of that organization in 1822. Jonas Green was one of the attending physicians and surgeons for Philadelphia serving the Philadelphia Dispensary in 1828, and Joseph Todhunter was a member of the Board of Education in the same year. Several of the new members continued the tradition of Unitarian support of the Society of the Sons of St. George, the Franklin Institute, and the Academy of Natural Sciences. On the national level, the importance of the Philadelphia Society was recognized by the nomination of James Taylor as a vice-president of the American Unitarian Association, organized coincidentally, in 1825, the same year in which Furness was ordained pastor of the Philadelphia society.[86]

The growing affluence of the congregation and a conscious seeking for social recognition, as well as a need for more space, were revealed at the special meeting of the society held on December 1, 1827, when it was stated that

it must be obvious to every one that the erection of a new and elegant Building upon a more eligible site than the present and sufficiently capacious to contain twice the number of persons would add to the respectability of the society and doubtless induce many to join it who entertain similar religious views and sentiments with ourselves but cannot be accommodated to their satisfaction in the present Church.[87]

Finding no site better than the one then occupied, however, the society decided to dismantle the Octagon Church and build again on the same ground, to which was added the adjoining lot to the north on Tenth Street, the design for the new structure, Doric in style, being provided by William Strickland without charge. He was later paid $500 for the actual plans. Desiring to have their edifice "classed among the ornaments of our City," to "attract the notice of Strangers as well as Citizens,"[88] the society succeeded in achieving its purpose, the new church, which was occupied by the society until 1885, being included in most books describing the city as among the outstanding church edifices of Philadelphia. The foundation of the new building was laid with appropriate religious ceremonies on March 24, 1828. It was officially opened and dedicated "to the grand cause of human goodness" on November 5, 1828, and Furness declared that on that day, "almost for the first time in Philadelphia, I felt as if I were really in a church."[89]

Furness reminded the people of the purpose of the society: "You have not reared this structure merely to gratify your taste or to display your wealth. . . . Your views have been, I trust, altogether more enlarged. . . . [I]t is your aim to help forward the advancement of the world in all that is excellent and happy."[90] Recognizing the fact that the Unitarians "are everywhere regarded with a feeling of distrust and prejudice . . . a denomination of Christians every where spoken against," he urged the members to enlighten the community as to the real meaning of Unitarianism, "and opposition of every sort will die away."[91]

SECOND CHURCH EDIFICE, Tenth and Locust Streets, Philadelphia, 1828
Designed by William Strickland. Built by the Unitarian Society
on the site of the Octagon Church. Engraving by Cephas G. Childs
after the drawing by H. Reinagle. Courtesy of the
Historical Society of Pennsylvania.

NOTES

CHAPTER V

[1]There is no full-length biography of Furness. Sketches of his life are in DAB, VII, 80, and ACAB, II, 565–66. A denominational account is given in Samuel A. Eliot, ed., *Heralds of a Liberal Faith* (Boston, 1910), III, 133–38. Munsell's (pub.) *American Ancestry* (Albany, 1889), IV, 206, contains a genealogy of the Furness family under the name of William Eliot Furness. The various obituary pieces which appeared at the time of the pastor's death are also helpful, the best of these being those of the Rev. Charles G. Ames for the *Harvard Graduates' Magazine*, June 3, 1896; Joseph G. Rosengarten for the *Proceedings of the American Philosophical Society, Memorial Volume I* (Philadelphia, 1900), 9–17; and the Rev. John W. Chadwick in the *Christian Register*, February 6, 1896, pp. 83–84.

[2]H[orace] H[oward] Furness, ed., *Records of a Lifelong Friendship, 1807–1882. Ralph Waldo Emerson and William Henry Furness* (Boston, 1910), p. 167.

[3]H. H. Furness, *Records of a Lifelong Friendship*, p. vi.

[4]Ames, p. 2.

[5]W. H. Furness, *Fiftieth Anniversary*, p. 17.

[6]W. H. Furness, *Fiftieth Anniversary*, p. 14.

[7]COLL. CORR. I.

[8]Henry Ware, Jr., *A Sermon delivered at the Ordination of the Rev. William Henry Furness . . . January 12, 1825 . . .* (Philadelphia, 1825), p. 43.

[9]Ware, *Ordination Sermon*, p. 41.

[10]Ware, *Ordination Sermon*, p. 28.

[11]Ware, *Ordination Sermon*, p. 44.

[12]Channing to Vaughan, August 12, 1816: Misc. MSS, APS.

[13]Edward Everett Hale, "Reminiscences of the Unitarian Pulpit, III, William Henry Furness," *Christian Register*, LXXVIII (March 2, 1899), 240.

[14]W. H. Furness, *Fiftieth Anniversary*, p. 15.

[15]Mrs. Furness died June 11, 1885, aged 83. REG II, 155.

[16]W. H. Furness, *Fiftieth Anniversary*, p. 14.

[17]Birch, Ralph Eddowes, Thomas Fletcher, Ford, Harper, Merrick, Nidda, Shippen, Small, Snider, Sully, Taylor, Thomas, Turner, Vaughan, Warren, Wood, RECS & MINS, p. 27.

[18]*Proceedings of a Meeting of the Members and Pew-Holders of the . . . Society . . . 28th September, 1846* (Philadelphia, 1846), p. 2, in W. H. Furness, *Sermons, Addresses, Articles*.

[19]Furness to Mary Jenks, September 20, 1825: COLL. CORR. I.

[20]Furness stated in his *Forty-Eighth Anniversary* sermon: "I have lately been destroying my old, or rather I should say my young sermons; and as, in preparing them for the flames, I have caught sight now and then of their quality, I have only admired the more the patience of those early friends of mine [who bore with me]."

[21]Channing to Vaughan, August 12, 1816: Misc. MSS, APS. There were, however, several theologically more advanced Unitarians in New England, notable among them Freeman at King's Chapel, Boston, who had been in close touch with English Unitarianism for many years. Wilbur, II, 392–95.

[22]W. H. Furness, *Forty-Eighth Anniversary*, p. 19.

²³Mrs. Furness to Mary Jenks, September 6, 1825: COLL. CORR. I.

²⁴Channing to Vaughan, August, 12 1816: Misc. MSS, APS.

²⁵*Proceedings . . . 28th September, 1846*, p. 2.

²⁶By the terms of the second article of the amended charter of March 13, 1824, after that date membership was based on pew occupancy, payment of pew rent, and contributions within a stated framework of time and money (REGS & MINS, 24). No journal listing pewholders, as such, from 1824 to 1828 has been found. Thus membership for any individual during this period must be deduced from entries in CASH II, with supplemental information in REG I, which recorded vital statistics but without comment as to membership. Cash Account I cannot be located, hence the dates hereinafter noted for the beginning of individual connections with the church may not be the earliest such dates.

²⁷Teacher, 150 Mulberry St.: CD, 1825. The account of his life comes chiefly from DAB, VI, 185–86.

²⁸This account of Johnson's life comes from George E. Pettingill, "Walter Rogers Johnson," *Jour. of Franklin Instit.*, CCL (August 1950), 93–113. Pettingill's main purpose was to present for the first time a bibliography of Johnson's writings, which he listed on pages 102–13, a total of 124 items, including books, pamphlets, and articles in periodicals and newspapers, although he stated that the list of newspaper articles was not exhaustive.

²⁹Pettingill, "Johnson," p. 102.

³⁰Furness to Mary Jenks, September 9, 1848: COLL. CORR. II.

³¹REG I, 96; Furness to Mary Jenks, September 14, 1831: COLL. CORR. I. The account of Johnson's life is taken from Robert Winder Johnson, Sr. and Lawrence Johnson Morris, *The Johnson Family and Allied Families of Lincolnshire, England. Being the Ancestry and Posterity of Lawrence Johnson of Philadelphia, Pennsylvania* (Philadelphia, 1934), pp. 55–69.

³²CASH II, 20. It is known that he paid $200 for a pew as late as 1847. UNNAMED, p. 29. There is no record of his funeral, but the records were especially faulty in 1860.

³³The propensity on the part of non-Unitarian descendants of Unitarians to omit the mention of Unitarianism in family chronicles has been a part of the English tradition as well as the American. One English biographer of Joseph Priestley even accomplished the notable feat of eliminating all mention of Unitarianism from his work, according to Raymond V. Holt, *The Unitarian Contribution to Social Progress in England* (London, 1938), pp. 14–15.

³⁴Simpson, pp. 621–22.

³⁵Simpson, p. 621.

³⁶CASH II, 2.

³⁷REG I, 96, 196.

³⁸Accounts of Fairman's life are in ACAB, II, 403–4; David McNeeley Stauffer, *American Engravers upon Copper and Steel* (New York, 1907), I, 81–82; George C. Groce and David H. Wallace, *The New-York Historical Society's Dictionary of Artists in America (1564–1860)* (New Haven, 1957), p. 219.

³⁹Robert Noxon Toppan, *A Hundred Years of Bank Note Engraving in the United States* (New York, 1896), p. 7.

⁴⁰This account comes from *Memoir of Charles Toppan* (Old Newbury, Mass., 1880); Stauffer, I, 273–74; Groce and Wallace, p. 633; and Toppan, pp. 3–4, 8–13.

⁴¹Furness to Mrs. Jenks, March 25, 1827: COLL. CORR. I. Fairman's first recorded contribution was made February 27, 1826: CASH II, 3.

⁴²Furness to Mrs. Jenks, March 25, 1827: COLL. CORR. I.

⁴³Furness to Mrs. Jenks, March 25, 1827: COLL. CORR. I.

[44]Furness to Mary Jenks, July 3, 1834: COLL. CORR. II.

[45]REG I, 98, 101.

[46]TRUSTS III.

[47]He signed the anti-slavery Protest in that year.

[48]REG I, 6, 104.

[49]CASH II, 14. Accounts of Spencer's life appear in Stauffer, I, 258, and Groce and Wallace, p. 595.

[50]CASH II, 18; REG I, 198, 200, 201, 202, 205, 212; UNNAMED, pp. 209–10.

[51]CASH II, 23. This account of Childs' life comes from DAB, IV, 69–70; Mantle Fielding, *Dictonary of American Painters, Sculptors, and Engravers* (Philadelphia, n.d.), p. 64; Stauffer, I, 47–48; and Groce and Wallace, pp. 124–25.

[52]UNNAMED, p. 302. This account of Tucker comes from Groce and Wallace, pp. 638–39, and Stauffer, I, 277.

[53]Cheever was treasurer of the New England Society of Philadelphia in 1823 (CD, 1823). Fales was described as a New England Whig in Anon. *Wealth and Biography of the Wealthy Citizens of Philadelphia* (Philadelphia, 1845), p. 10.

[54]Baldwin Gardiner to Thomas Fletcher, January 10, 1829: Fletcher Papers.

[55]Lewis Veron Fletcher to Thomas Fletcher, September 20, 1831: Fletcher Papers; REG I, 195.

[56]Paid pew rent September 23, 1825: CASH II, 1; CD, 1825.

[57]REG I, 10. Charles Godfrey Leland's *Memoirs* (New York, 1893) contain many references to the family's connections with the Philadelphia Unitarian Society.

[58]REG I, 96; UNNAMED, p. 62.

[59]REG I, 16.

[60]CASH II, 2.

[61]Ralph W. Hidy, *The House of Baring in American Trade and Finance* (Cambridge, Mass., 1949), pp. 230, 247, 250, 286, 348.

[62]This account of Sill's life comes chiefly from his ten-volume "Diary:" MSS, HSP, the facts of his early life specifically from II, 260–64; IV, 43, 436. He is also included in Simpson, pp. 888–89.

[63]REG I, 96. Todhunter was a native of Highhollows, Cumberland County, England. *Memorial Exhibition of Portraits by Thomas Sully*, p. 106.

[64]Furness to the society, November 2, 1824: CHURCH MSS.

[65]Furness to Mary Jenks, September 2, 1824: COLL. CORR. II.

[66]Mrs. Furness to Mary Jenks, September 2, 1842: COLL. CORR. II.

[67]Furness to Mary Jenks, November 29, 1847: COLL. CORR. II.

[68]ACAB, II, 566; Groce and Wallace, p. 246.

[69]DAB, VII, 78.

[70]A native of New Bedford, Mass., Rotch married Susan Ridgway, daughter of the wealthy Philadelphia merchant (Furness to Lucy Osgood, June 10, 1829: OSGOOD CORR.). He began paying pew rent June 24, 1827 (CASH II, 35). The listing of his name in CD, 1827, contains only the notation "inquire at 181 Chestnut Street."

[71]Noted by Furness, who married him and baptized his children, in letter to Lucy Osgood, May, 16 1837: OSGOOD CORR.

[72]Leland, p. 49.

[73]Furness to Mary Jenks, April 4, 1831: COLL. CORR. I.

[74]W. H. Furness, *Robert Collyer and His Church, A Discourse delivered . . . November 12, 1871* (Philadelphia, n.d.), p. 5.

[75]He paid in full, $300, for a pew September 6, 1828: CASH II, 27. Listed in CD, 1828, "Gentleman, 79 Pine St." In Anon., *Wealth and Biography*, p. 16, he was declared to be worth $100,000, having made his money in New Orleans.

[76]Furness to Mrs. Jenks, December 2, 1825: COLL. CORR. I.

[77]Furness to Mary Jenks, November 6, 1826: COLL. CORR. I.

[78]Furness to Mary Jenks, November 21, 1825: COLL. CORR. I.

[79]Furness to Mary Jenks, January 31, 1826: COLL. CORR. I.

[80]Postscript in Mrs. Furness' letter to her mother, June 16, 1826: COLL. CORR. I.

[81]Furness to Mrs. Jenks, April 2, 1827: COLL. CORR. I.

[82]Furness to Mary Jenks, August 8, 1826: COLL. CORR. I.

[83]Furness to Mary Jenks, October 9, 1826: COLL. CORR. I.

[84]Furness to Mrs. Jenks, March 25, 1827: COLL. CORR. I.

[85]Furness to Mary Jenks, June 8, 1830: COLL. CORR. I.

[86]George Willis Cooke, *Unitarianism in America* (Boston, 1902), p. 134.

[87]RECS & MINS, p. 51.

[88]RECS & MINS, p. 53.

[89]W. H. Furness, *A Discourse preached . . . November 5, 1828* (Philadelphia, 1828), p. 5; Furness to Mary Jenks, November 9, 1828: COLL.CORR. I.

[90]Furness, *Discourse preached . . . November 5, 1828, p.* 6.

[91]Furness, *Discourse preached . . . November 5, 1828*, pp. 6–7.

VI

The Respectable Reformers

THE YEARS FROM 1828 TO 1839 MARKED A DEFINITE EPOCH IN THE
life of the Philadelphia Unitarian Society. The rapid increase in
membership which followed the establishment of Furness as pastor
was signalized by the building of the new church edifice, more than
twice the size of its predecessor, but a qualitative change in the
society's thinking took place as well. No longer was the society's
membership predominantly English, its leaders refugees from
foreign oppression, desiring only peace in which to rehabilitate
themselves. The new spirit animating the society was American,
self-assured, dynamic, and determined to make a practical success
of the enterprise. The strong infusion from New England, where
Unitarianism had won an overwhelming victory, inevitably colored
events in Philadelphia, for, having tasted the pleasures of community prestige, the new members had no intention of accepting
anything less in their new location. Soberly and quietly, but nonetheless determinedly, they built up a substantial following and
looked forward to ever increasing "respectability" in terms of
community acceptance. The steady development of their plans was
interrupted dramatically in 1839, when their pastor, breaking all
the unwritten laws of the society, openly challenged the status quo
on the forbidden subject of abolitionism.

By coincidence this period approximately covered a phase of
national growth which has been variously described as "The Age
of Jackson" and "The Age of the Common Man." It was a dynamic
period, characterized on the national level by unparalleled develop-

ment, demographically, economically, and politically. The rate of population increase, both naturally and by immigration, exceeded all previous records, generating a propulsive force which took the frontier westward until the nation stretched from the Atlantic to the Pacific. At the same time there was an increasing concentration of population at centers of trade and commerce, and cities began to emerge where only wilderness or small towns had been a few years before. The Industrial Revolution was in full stride, concentrating workers in factories but sending the products of their labor to ever expanding markets and raising the general standard of comfort and convenience everywhere. The nation was filled with enthusiasm, bursting with optimism, convinced that all good things were waiting just beyond the horizon and that all it took was a bit of "get up and go" to make all dreams come true. Certain basic convictions were recognizable as components of the American Dream—a belief in the existence of a positive moral order in the universe, with absolute standards of right and wrong, and the former inevitably triumphant over the latter; faith in the inevitability of progress, with society capable of infinite improvement until it reached perfection; the conviction that the United States was favored beyond all other nations and was divinely ordained to lead the rest of the world in the way in which it should go.

The Unitarians could not have been described as "common men" for by theology alone they were marked as quite uncommon in the Philadelphia community, nor were they, with possibly a few exceptions, Jacksonian in politics or social aspirations. They did, however, share the American Dream. Progress was the aim of all and action the order of the day. For the Unitarians, generally, universal perfection was to be obtained through humanitarian reform. They had cast off the Calvinistic tenet which held that all men were by nature sinners, eventually, if not immediately, to be punished by an angry God. Unitarians believed that all men were essentially good, created by a loving Father in His own image and therefore partaking of a measure of Divine goodness themselves. It was obvious that physical, economic, social, or political circumstances often made it impossible for men to realize their potentialities, but it was equally obvious that it was every man's duty to change such circumstances so that all men could live as their Heavenly Father had intended.

For the Unitarians themselves this was more often than not an academic problem, for as a group they were upper middle class, usually, though not always, bountifully endowed with the world's goods. They looked on their less fortunate fellows, however, with compassion and a well-bred concern for their problems, which they implemented by action through a great number of well-organized efforts. They attacked with concentration and thoroughness the problems of prisons, institutions for the insane, the deaf, the dumb, the blind, the issues of women's rights, peace, temperance, slavery. Always their aim was a moral and religious one. As all men were equal in the sight of God, so should they be given an opportunity to achieve equality on this earth. The levelling was to be upward, however. The ideal to be achieved was ultimate, individual perfection and there was to be no surrender to mass mediocrity.

Although the romanticism of the age recognized the supremacy of feelings over thought processes and the Unitarians were true romanticists in this sense, they kept emotionalism under control. "Enthusiasm" was definitely frowned upon. They wished no sudden conversions, such as the moral reformers of the Burnt-Over Area of New York were exploiting with such noisy success. Everything was to grow gradually, but quietly, better and better, simply because it was God's intention from the beginning that that was the way it was to be. All that men had to do was to obey their own best impulses and all would be well. Actually, Unitarianism's humanitarian reform movement was simply a part of a world-wide movement for human betterment at this time, which had been and would continue for many decades to be manifested in political and social upheavals all over the world. The local scene in Philadelphia was a microcosm in the macrocosm of world reform.

The Philadelphia society was in 1828 at last beginning to be everything that a Unitarian society seemed inevitably to be. The great majority of its people were well-to-do members of the middle class, who had met the world on its own terms and wrested an economic victory from it. They were concerned about the welfare of their immortal souls, as most nineteenth-century Americans were, but they did not make theology a preoccupation or an avocation. They required of their pastor only the regular reassurance that God was indeed in His Heaven and all was right with His world. As intelligent men they daily saw proof that there was much room for improvement in society, and as kind and decent individuals they did whatever they could to alleviate distress and misery where they saw it. They were in no way militant in the face of adversity, however. They gave no encouragement to fanatical reformers.

As Furness looked down upon his congregation at the end of 1828 he could well be gratified by the solid phalanx of wealth and dignity with which he was surrounded. The new edifice would cost approximately $28,000 and it was decided to finance its construction and maintenance by a new expedient in the society's history, the sale of pews. With space for eight hundred people, it was proposed to value the 186 pews on the ground floor and the thirty pews in the gallery at a total of $33,600, prices for individual pews ranging from $400 to $50, according to size and location. An annual levy of 10 per cent was to be made on the value of each pew to support the operations of the society. The sale of pews was accordingly opened on November 11, 1828, with seventy pews let or sold at that time, and the record of these transactions affords the first and only reasonably complete record there is of the membership of the society at any given time during this period. The seating arrangement by assigned locations also presents a graphic picture of the relative prominence of the various families in physical location, at least, which apparently corresponded rather closely to the more intangible elements of leadership as well.

As the pastor faced his congregation he was flanked on his right by John Vaughan, Thomas W. Morgan,[1] William W. Potter,[2] Thomas Rotch, Joseph Sanderson,[3] the Fairmans, and Thomas

Haven.[4] On his left were Ralph Eddowes, Jr., Charles Leland, James Hill,[5] Joseph Todhunter, Judge Joseph Barnes,[6] John Wyeth,[7] and Thomas J. Natt.[8] Directly in front of him on the right were the Bryans and the Fords,[9] followed by such outstanding members as William Y. Birch, Isaac Elliott,[10] Abraham Small, and Thomas Fletcher. In front of Furness to his left were Thomas Butler, James Taylor, Thomas Mellon, Lewis Veron, Samuel Vaughan Merrick, Isaac Heylin,[11] Thomas Harper,[12] Joseph Sill, and Henry Duhring.[13] All these, substantial citizens all, and many more, formed the congregation which soon filled the new church. By Christmastime, 1829, there were so many well-to-do members in the congregation that when an anonymous gift of two fifty-dollar bills was delivered to Furness by messenger, the pastor could not be certain who the donor was, any one of a dozen of his flock being possibilities.[14]

The newcomers joined for various reasons. Hard-headed men of the world like Barnes, presiding judge of the United States District Court from 1826 to 1835, were drawn by the intellectuality of its theology. Barnes told Furness that he had decided in favor of the Unitarian Society because "he was tired of going home every Sunday and unpreaching the sermon to his children. At the presbyterian churches he was compelled to tell his children in so many words that the things said in the pulpit were not true."[15] Many, seeking consolation in the bereavement which was a tragically recurrent phase of daily life, found solace in the compassionate preaching of Furness. From the depths of his own sorrow in the death of his first child in infancy the Unitarian pastor found the words to comfort others and to reconcile them to their losses. Many had need of sympathy: George Fletcher and his wife, whose three small children died of scarlet fever within four days; the Spencers, who lost six children in eight years; the Elliotts, who lost five; and many others. Many, however, came joyfully, simply to share in the thrilling experience of being a part of Furness' congregation. He loved life as it was but he knew that it could be even more wonderful, and this sense of expectancy, this challenge to take part in the glories that could be, brought more and more people to hear him. He confessed in 1829 that "The excitement is sometimes too great for me."[16]

Between 1828 and 1839 there was a steady development in the society along the lines already marked out. The merchants formed the largest occupational group among the new members, at least forty who joined during this period making their living in trade and commerce. This reflected the situation in the society as a whole, in which almost seventy-five per cent of the active leadership was in the hands of merchants. During the period from 1828 to 1839, calculating on the basis of seven trustees being elected each year, a total of eighty-four terms were served by twenty-six trustees. Of the eighty-four terms, fifty-six were served by fourteen active merchants, six terms by two retired merchants. Vaughan served for the entire period, Sill from 1831 on, Sill's father-in-law, Joseph Todhunter, from 1828 to 1833, Morgan from 1829 to 1833, and thirteen others for less than five years each. Of the ten non-merchant trustees, Elliott, the conveyancer, served longest, from 1830 to 1836, and the artist Sully the next longest term, from 1834 to 1837.

The pastor's seventeen-year-old brother James came to Philadelphia at his urging in 1839, to live with him and to work for Dexter Stone.[17] The job with Stone did not materialize but, thanks to the efforts of Vaughan and others, another position was obtained for James in a store where, working from seven in the morning until late at night, he earned enough to clothe himself. In 1835 he returned to Boston but was back in Philadelphia again in September, 1837, when he took a pew in his brother's church. In that year he was listed in the *City Directory* as an accountant. By 1839 he was an auctioneer at 22 North Second Street.

Furness was especially happy over the arrival of the two Havens, Charles Chauncey and Thomas, who moved to Philadelphia "from the Eastward" in 1829, "lovely additions . . . to our flock."[18] Thomas Haven brought with him eleven children. Both families were to be intimately connected with the Furnesses by marriage. Thomas, then widowed, married Ann M. Furness in 1841, and one of Charles's daughters married Horace Jenks, brother of Mrs. Furness.[19] Thomas became a trustee of the society in 1832, Charles in 1835.

George Merrill, a commission merchant in Boston, was a friend of Ralph Waldo Emerson, who wrote to his brother William in February, 1830, that Merrill "to my great regret is leaving the Second Church and the First Town to settle in Philadelphia."[20] When Emerson arrived in Philadelphia the following month to spend some time, Merrill was there to greet him with Furness and Vaughan and to help him find a place in which to live. Merrill served the Unitarian Society with great devotion for over a decade and was finally elected a trustee in April, 1843. In October of the same year, however, he returned to New England to live, his departure being recorded by the society with a vote of thanks for his services to the church, its sunday school, and the Vaughan Charitable Association, which had been established after the death of Vaughan in 1841.[21]

Another notable addition was Frederick Cabot, who was connected with the society as early as 1833, when he had a child baptized by Furness.[22] The Cabots left Philadelphia in 1837, at which time Furness described their departure as "a heavy loss."[23] They left two infant children buried in the churchyard.[24]

Benjamin A. Farnham was a merchant in business at 8 South Front Street in 1837 when his marriage to Lydia R. Harper, daughter of Thomas Harper, one of the pillars of the society, marked his first recorded connection with the church.[25] He became "a devoted and valued member"[26] and was in April, 1847, elected a trustee.

Evans and William E. Rogers were brothers, hardware merchants at 52 High Street in the firm of Rogers and Brothers, when they bought a pew in the Unitarian Society in December, 1828.[27] When Evans Rogers married Caroline, the daughter of Colonel Fairman, on March 4, 1830, Furness said of him that he was "very rich, has a splendid house, splendidly furnishd—is very liberal and very solid in his character . . . has got his money not by speculation but by 17 years devoted to his business as a hardware merchant."[28]

The fee of fifty dollars given to Furness for the marriage ceremony was unprecedented in its generosity, five or ten dollars being
the average he received. Not until 1837, for the wedding of Judge
Barnes's daughter, did he again receive as much, and only three
other weddings before 1864 provided that fee.[29] By 1845 Evans
Rogers was rated as one of the city's seven millionaires in a curious
volume by an anonymous "Member of the Philadelphia Bar,"
Wealth and Biography of the Wealthy Citizens of Philadelphia.[30]

In 1829 the china merchants James and Sampson Tams bought
a pew in the Unitarian Church.[31] The Tams family was English but
had lived in Philadelphia as early as 1823.[32] Both James and Sampson were listed in 1830 as only associate members of the Society of
the Sons of St. George, indicating that they were at that time not
American citizens, but Sampson became a regular member, and
presumably was then a citizen, in 1832. The family firm, Tams and
Brothers, including a third brother, William, acquired great wealth
in the importing of chinaware, Sampson being listed in the anonymous 1845 volume as the possessor of $200,000.[33]

Though the merchants still had their shops and stores in the
business district within a few blocks of the Delaware River and a
few blocks above and below High Street, more than half of them
now lived in houses apart from their businesses, further west in
the city. Jesse Godley, who bought a pew in 1832, had a store at
53 High Street but lived at the corner of Eleventh and Arch
Streets.[34] Thomas Haven's shop was at 91 South Front Street, his
home at the corner of Thirteenth and Walnut Streets.[35] Joshua
Tevis conducted his business at 14 Church Alley but lived on
Walnut Street near Broad.[36] In April, 1832, the Furnesses moved
to a new house, never before occupied, on "the right side (the
South side)" of Spruce Street, the third door from Broad Street.[37]
Here they had the Merrills as neighbors and Furness marvelled at
the physical stamina of Merrill, who had to travel seventeen blocks
each day to his business at 11 South Wharves.[38]

Though the merchants were the most numerous group among
the new members, other occupations were represented. From the

law, in addition to Judge Barnes, came John Cadwallader, who shared a pew with the Meases, having married Dr. Mease's daughter,[39] and Charles S. Cope, attorney and counseller and deputy clerk of the Orphans Court.[40] William R. Dinmore, treasurer of the Chestnut Street Theatre, took a pew in April, 1837.[41] Charles and Elisha Townsend were originally clock and watchmakers and Charles remained in that occupation, but Elisha made a curious decision in 1831 to give up watchmaking and devote himself to dentistry.[42] Furness' comment that one married pair of Townsends, first name not stated, addressed each other as "thee," indicates a Quaker origin.[43] Jacob Farnsworth, the owner of a carpet warehouse, bought a pew in the church and his wife, late of Boston, was considered by Furness "one of the best women in my society" in 1831, but the family moved to New York in 1835.[44] The Masons, James Servetus and Eliza Priestley, apparently a brother and sister, brought an obviously confirmed family tradition of Unitarianism to the society. James, a successful blacking manufacturer, was married by Furness in 1834, and continued "a member of this Church, and a liberal supporter of it, for over half a century," until his death in 1888.[45]

Edward Dodge, a brother-in-law of Enoch W. Clark and a partner in the banking business of E. W. Clark & Company, established in January, 1837, bought a pew on June 26, 1839.[46] The pursuit of unearned increment became a favorite pastime during this period of national expansion and in 1832 claimed Charles Leland, who in that year sold his hat business to Charles S. Boker, father of the future dramatist, George Henry Boker, and thereafter engaged in real estate speculation.[47] In 1837 he bought a large property at Third and Market Streets, the site of Congress Hall, and another large purchase was the old Arch Street Prison, then vacant, which he tore down and on the site built a block of private homes. Another real estate broker, Alexander McCay, had five children baptized by Furness between 1830 and 1836.[48]

The family of Jacob Thomas is known to have been connected with the society at least as early as 1830.[49] Multiple listing of innumerable Thomases in the *City Directories* makes it impossible positively to identify the Unitarians of that name, but Jacob, who died in 1854 at the age of eighty-six, left three generations of his family then active in the church.[50] He was a trustee from 1836 to 1844. Charles J. and Joseph M. were his sons. His daughter Eliza married another Unitarian, Isaac Elliott.[51]

Another family connection of outstanding importance to the society, that of the Bradfords, was also made at this time. Samuel Bradford had been born in Boston in 1803.[52] Ralph Waldo Emerson, born in the same year, and William Henry Furness, a year older, were his earliest friends and the three began school together, forming a close friendship which endured until Emerson's death in 1882 and Bradford's in 1885. Bradford did not accompany his two friends to Harvard but entered a counting-house in Boston when he was fifteen years old and remained there for eight years. After an unsuccessful business venture in Portsmouth, New Hampshire, he moved on to New York in 1827, and finally to Philadelphia in 1830, where he lived for the rest of his life.

Bradford had been born into the Unitarian tradition. He and his two friends, Furness and Emerson, had been in the same catechism class as small boys, under the tutelage of the Rev. William Emerson, the poet's father, at First Church, Boston, where Bradford's father was one of the oldest members. Undoubtedly, when Bradford arrived in Philadelphia he joined Furness at the Philadelphia Unitarian Church, although the first record of his connection is the burial of his sister Lucy in the churchyard on March 17, 1837. It is certain that the Bradfords became one of the most active of the society's families.

On March 31, 1830, two weeks after his arrival in Philadelphia, Bradford took a position in the office of the newly organized Little Schuylkill Navigation, Railroad and Canal Company, and on January 13, 1833, he was elected treasurer and secretary. He and his sister rented a small house on Spruce Street near Broad, to which he brought his bride, Elizabeth Ann Wood, whom he married on March 23, 1835. In 1838 the treasurer and secretary of the Philadelphia and Reading Railroad Company wished to retire and on January 8 of that year Bradford was elected to succeed him, retaining his position with the Little Schuylkill at the same time, since little had thus far been done by the Philadelphia and Reading. In May, 1843, however, the latter company became so active that Bradford resigned from the Little Schuylkill and devoted all his energies thenceforward to the Philadelphia and Reading Company.

Philadelphia continued to be a great publishing center and three additional publishing and bookselling families of importance established a connection with the Unitarian Society. Henry C. Carey, son of Mathew Carey and from 1824 to 1836 the head of the family firm, took a pew in the Unitarian Church from 1833 to 1836.[53] He had been baptized a Roman Catholic as an infant and had been married in the Catholic church. Eventually he was to hold a pew in St. Mary's Episcopal Church in Burlington, N.J., where he was buried. From 1833 to 1836, however, his religious affiliation was Unitarian and throughout his life he continued a close association with the leaders of Philadelphia Unitarianism. This took place naturally through their mutual interest in the many public activities, organizations, and associations of Philadelphia. When Carey established at his home on Walnut Street the weekly meetings known as "Carey's Vespers," Furness and William D. Kelley, who joined the Unitarian Society about 1846, were conspicuous among the regular guests.[54] William A. Blanchard, who became a member of the Carey firm in 1833 after more than twenty years' employment with the house, also joined the Unitarian Society during this period, as did the Desilvers, Charles, Robert P., and Thomas, Jr.[55] The Beresford family of printers was still another addition from the world of books.[56]

When the artist, Hugh Bridport, was married by Furness to Rachel, daughter of Joseph Todhunter, on May 26, 1830, it is probable that he also became affiliated at that time with the Unitarian Society, of which the Todhunters were active members, although the first record of Bridport's pew ownership was made in 1859. Bridport was born in London in 1794 and had already exhibited three miniatures at the Royal Academy when he followed his brother George to America, around 1816, and settled with him in Philadelphia where they established a drawing academy. Described as a portrait and lanscape painter, a miniaturist, an engraver, a lithographer, and an architect, Bridport exhibited many times at the Pennsylvania Academy of the Fine Arts between 1817 and 1843 and at the Artists Fund Society in 1844 and 1845.

To the tradition of engraving established by the Unitarians Fairman, Toppan, Spencer, Carpenter, Saulnier, and Childs was added the contribution of John Sartain, whose first connection with the Philadelphia Unitarian Society was made shortly after his arrival in Philadelphia in 1830.[57] Sartain was an Englishman, born in London in 1808. At the age of fourteen he chose the career of engraving and was apprenticed to John Swaine. Here his work attracted the attention of William Young Ottley, who introduced him to the art world of London and whose sponsorship made possible his first important work, the engraving of eighteen new plates and the finishing of fourteen incomplete ones for Ottley's historical sketch of early Florentine painters. In January, 1830, Sartain married Swaine's daughter and six months later, appropriately enough on July 4, he and his wife left London for America. They landed in Philadelphia, intending to go on to New York, but on the ship Sartain had met a prominent merchant named Ralston, who gave him a letter of introduction to John Vaughan. The latter, exercising his customary hospitality, not only gave the young Englishman a hearty welcome but suggested that he show some of his prints at the exhibition then in progress at the Franklin Institute, which he did, with signal success. After a brief trip to New York, he was urged to return to Philadelphia by Sully, who offered the persuasive argument of a commission to engrave the portrait he had just painted of Bishop White. The painter John Neagle, who had married Sully's stepdaughter Mary, also gave him a commission and Henry C. Carey ordered from him an engraving of Sully's "Miss Jackson." Thus importuned, Sartain decided to settle in Philadelphia.

Having executed plates for the *Gentleman's Magazine*, the *Casket*, and *Godey's Lady's Magazine*, in 1841 he became associated with *Graham's Magazine*, for which he contracted to execute a plate for every issue, a pioneer work in that it established the tradition of pictorial illustrating in American magazines. Sartain's tremendous success with this venture led him into an unfortunate one with *Campbell's Semi-Monthly Magazine*, of which he became the proprietor in 1843, and also an unprofitable connection with the *Eclectic Magazine*. In 1847 he was the proprietor and editor of the quarto *American Gallery of Art*. The following year he purchased with William Sloanaker the *Union Magazine* of New York and began the publication of *Sartain's Union Magazine of Literature and Art*. This was an overwhelming artistic success, claiming as contributors the best of the current writers, including such men as Longfellow, Lowell, Simms, and Poe. Unfortunately, it was a financial failure, and Sartain worked for seven and a half years after its demise in 1852 to pay off its debts. He confined himself chiefly to general engraving after this fiasco, executing the staggering total of 1,500 plates during his long and busy lifetime.

Sartain's career was a distinguished one, recognized by many honors both at home and abroad. Having introduced mezzotint engraving into the United States, he was the first person to make a profitable career of this work. To Philadelphia's life he contributed outstanding leadership in the world of art, serving as a member of the Artists Fund Society for many years and as its president in 1844; affiliated with the Pennsylvania Academy of the Fine Arts in the same year and continuing his service to that organization for twenty-three years in various capacities, as member, director, and secretary, designing the rooms and galleries of its new building in 1872. He was for fourteen years vice-president of the Philadelphia School of Design for Women, of which his daughter Emily became principal in 1886. In 1875 he was chief of the bureau of art for the Centennial Exhibition, a post which brought him additional international honors.

Sartain's official connection with the Unitarian Society began in 1830, when he had his first child, Kenneth Samuel, born October 8, 1830, baptized by Furness on November 18.[58] From the beginning of his American life, however, he was closely associated with the leaders of the society, notably Vaughan and Sully, and he became an active leader himself, serving as a trustee for many years.

In 1832 a brilliant bird of paradise startled the dovecote of Philadelphia and came to rest for a time in the unlikely shelter of the First Unitarian Church. Responsible for this addition to Furness' flock was Pierce Butler, son of Dr. James Mease, who had been baptized by Taylor as a small boy and had continued his membership in the society. At the age of twenty-two he was rich, handsome, and of unimpeachable social connections. He was, apparently, also proud, arrogant, and accustomed to having his own way. When the enchanting English actress, Fanny Kemble, came to Philadelphia in 1832 in the course of her American tour with her father, Charles Kemble, Butler fell in love with her and, after pursuing her up and down the East Coast for two seasons as she proceeded from city to city on tour, he finally persuaded her to marry him in June, 1834.[59] It was a tragic mistake for both of them. A more dissimilar pair it would be difficult to imagine—Fanny, brilliant, sensitive, imaginative, the darling of two continents, accustomed to excitement and the adulation of a glittering and sophisticated world; Butler, rigid, narrow-minded, unimaginative, conventional, and, above all, dull. All that they had in common were pride and stubbornness.

The life into which Butler introduced his bride was almost Quakerlike in its simplicity. "My life, and all its occupations, are of a sober, neutral tint," she wrote to a friend in London in October, 1834.[60] The Butler Place on Old York Road near Germantown where the young couple established themselves, little better than a farmhouse at that time, was an intellectual desert as far as Mrs. Butler was concerned. Six miles away from the center of culture in Philadelphia, she found herself reduced to "a little housekeeping . . . a little music . . . feeding and cleaning a large cageful of canary-birds . . . strolling around the garden, watching my bee-hives." [61] Even the birth of her first child, Sarah, in May, 1835, failed to compensate her for the world she had given up. Her husband, having won her, obviously felt that he had done all that was necessary. Summing up her existence, she declared in 1837:

I live alone . . . much alone bodily, more alone mentally; I have no intimates, no society, no intellectual intercourse whatever; and I give myself up, as I never did in my life before, to mere musing, reverie, and speculation—I cannot dignify the process by the title of thought or contemplation. [62]

At the same time she belatedly found intolerable the institution of slavery, from which, she had known from the beginning, her husband drew his ample fortune. As early as June, 1835, she had written

a long and vehement treatise against negro slavery, which I wanted to publish with my Journal, but was obliged to refrain from doing so, lest our fellow-citizens should tear our house down, and make a bonfire of our furniture—a favorite mode of remonstrance in these parts with those who advocate the rights of the unhappy blacks. [63]

A visit with her husband to the Butler rice and cotton plantations on the coast of Georgia in 1838 had apparently made her realize for the first time, however, how intimately involved in the evils of slavery her husband was and she was both horrified and disgusted by his callousness to the suffering for which he was responsible. She kept an account of her visit but in deference to her husband's wishes did not publish it at this time. It was published in 1863 as the *Journal of a Residence on a Georgian Plantation in 1838–39*, chiefly to convert British public opinion to the northern cause.

In 1835 Mrs. Butler had provoked a public furore with another *Journal*, embodying her reactions to American life as seen during her tour with her father before her marriage. Her husband had foreseen the acute embarrassment which would result for all concerned if the work were published and had demanded that she not release it, but the manuscript had been promised to Carey, Lea &

Blanchard and Mrs. Butler insisted upon honoring that commitment. Her attempt to placate her husband by permitting him to "edit" the proofs had only led to further arguments, as she defended her sprightly writing from his determination to reduce it to his own uninspired standards. The *Journal* as it finally appeared contained enough of the author's uninhibited comments to cause an uproar in Philadelphia society. She had deleted proper names from the narrative as a concession to her husband's sense of propriety but the blank spaces only intrigued her readers the more and the identification of the deletions became a favorite game among Philadelphians for many years. The general popular opinion was, however, that the work was too frank in its criticisms, and many thought that its refreshingly vivid language was vulgar for a lady.

Mrs. Butler's conduct, from the beginning, was considered highly unconventional in Philadelphia, yet it appears to have been simply that of a spirited young woman accustomed to a free and natural expression of the joy of living. One of her "sins" was her delight in horseback riding without an escort, which her husband regarded as an intolerable eccentricity of behavior. It did, in fact, provoke a comment from the staid Joseph Sill, who was sufficiently moved by his encounter with Mrs. Butler on horseback to note in his diary that "She look'd uncommonly well in her riding dress." [64]

She had another fervent admirer in the pastor of her husband's church. Though she had been a member of the Church of England and had been married in Christ Church in Philadelphia, Mrs. Butler began attending services at the Unitarian Church with her husband after their marriage. Furness called on her at once and "was greatly struck with her modesty and naturalness and her brilliant power of conversation." [65] How far removed her new life was from her old was indicated by Furness' further comment, "It would be impossible to suppose from her manners that she had ever appeared on the stage." Her incompatibility with her husband having become obvious within the first few months of their marriage, Mrs. Butler seems to have turned to the consolation of religion, attending Unitarian services regularly and reading diligently the works of such Unitarian divines as Channing to while away the lonely hours at the farm. She wrote to her friend, Harriet St. Leger, in London in October, 1835:

You ask if I am going through a course of Channing—not precisely, but a course of Unitarianism, for I attend a Unitarian Church. I did so at first by accident (is there such a thing?), being taken thither by the people to whom I now belong, who are of that mode of thinking and have seats in a church of that denomination, and where I hear admirable instruction and exhortation, and eloquent, excellent preaching, that does my soul good. . . . I am acquainted with several clergymen of that profession, who are among the most enlightened and cultivated men I have met with in this country. Of course, these circumstances have had some effect upon my mind, but they have rather helped to develop, than positively cause, the result you have observed.[66]

When Channing came to Philadelphia, which he did rather frequently, preaching at the Unitarian Church and giving public lectures, his visits to the Butler farm were high points in the dreary existence of its mistress. She stated many years later: "After my first introduction to Dr. Channing, I never was within reach of him without enjoying the honor of his intercourse and the privilege of hearing him preach."[67]

Many Philadelphians escaped from the heat of the city during the summer months by boarding in the country and the Furnesses stayed near the Butlers in July and August of 1836. Mrs. Butler clung desperately to their society and Furness became "an excellent and highly valued friend,"[68] while he admitted in a letter to Bronson Alcott in September of that year: "She has taught me a great deal,—I mean in comparison with what I knew before."[69] The friendship continued down through the years. Mrs. Butler made a noteworthy conquest of the very young Horace Howard Furness, born in November, 1833, "mothering" his love of Shakespeare, according to his grandson, and undoubtedly was a later source of inspiration to him in his choice of Shakespearean scholarship as his life's work.[70] The Butlers and the Meases had long been valued members of the Unitarian Society and the elder Furness accepted what must have been a painful role during the unhappy years preceding the final breaking up of Pierce and Fanny Butler's marriage. When the two principals no longer communicated with each other except through a third party, Furness acted in that capacity together with the legal counsels involved, his correspondence with the husband and wife being entered in the testimony offered in the suit for divorce brought by Butler in 1848.[71]

The whole fabric and texture of an ultraconservative Philadelphian's attitude toward the marriage relationship is revealed in the statements issued separately by Butler and his wife in connection with the divorce action. Butler felt that his demands were minimal and completely reasonable: "If you can consent to submit your will to mine, we may be reconciled and may be happy," he told his wife in December, 1842. "I firmly believe that husband and wife cannot live happily together upon any other terms."[72] Mrs. Butler's impassioned plea for equal rights as a partner in marriage, eloquently expressed in her *Narrative* in reply to his suit, he dismissed with contempt. "Nothing is required to show the error of this principle of equal rights in marriage. . . . No one, who is not morally or intellectually astray, can fail to feel and see the heartlessness and falsity of the pretension."[73] Public opinion in general by no means upheld Butler's attitude. Furness found his demands harsh and told him so,[74] while even the otherwise conservative Sill recorded in his diary the hope that Butler would be unable to prove his charges against his wife.[75] Butler sued on the grounds of desertion but his wife's defense was that he had forced her to leave him by his harsh and inhuman conduct. She exercised almost inhuman self-restraint in not referring to the Schott divorce action in 1844. James Schott, Jr. had permitted his wife to secure an uncontested divorce, but had subsequently challenged Butler to a duel as "the other man" and set forth the whole story in a printed statement dated July 29, 1844.

Judgment was eventually entered by default against Mrs. Butler, she having given up her fight in return for certain financial arrangements made in favor of her two children. She never married again but, returning to the life she loved, achieved much fame, material security, and happiness, living until the age of eighty-three. Butler, on the other hand, continued a bitter, irascible course. In 1859 he had to sell his slaves to pay his debts, and his pro-southern activities during the Civil War led to his imprisonment in the federal prison on Governor's Island for five weeks in the summer of 1861. He died on Butler's Island in Georgia in August, 1867, at the age of fifty-seven.

While the westward migration was the dramatic phase of American growth during this period, Philadelphia's increase in numbers was also notable and filled with portent. In 1820 the city's population, with that of the adjoining suburbs, had numbered 137,097. By 1830 it was 188,961; by 1840 it was 258,037. The Unitarian Society in this period grew from 18 resident families in 1825 to 120 families in 1830[76] and to 150 voting members in 1833:[77] The members continued to produce large families, the Thomas Havens having eleven children, the Barneses and Kirks nine each, the Pattens eight, the Duhrings and Sills seven, the Sullys, Elliotts, and Jacob Snider, Jrs. six, the Robert H. Beresfords, Bradfords, George Fletchers, Lelands, and William Henry Furnesses each five. So large did the society grow, in fact, that in December, 1835, an attempt was made to establish a second Unitarian group in a room over the Northern Liberties Reading-Room. but this came to nought.[78]

Though America had not yet become a melting-pot in the sense it was to be so described at the end of the century, it was beginning to feel the effects of the "new" immigration of Irishmen at this time. Since these immigrants were almost exclusively Roman Catholic, the Unitarian Society was obviously not officially affected by their coming. An exception seems to have been the family of Samuel and Sarah Christy, who had five children baptized by Furness in November, 1825, an occurrence so unusual, apparently, that Furness noted after their names in the Register the word "Irish."[79] The new immigration did, however, have an effect upon the members of the Unitarian Society in other ways. Many of the

Irish became domestic servants, of whose indifferent training and general slothfulness the Furnesses complained bitterly. Mrs. Furness became so desperate that she tried to persuade her husband to give up their house and take rooms in a boarding-house but this they never did. A humourous sidelight on the contrast between the unlettered Irish immigration and the comparatively cultivated German influx a decade later was provided in Furness' description of their German servant girl in 1849, "who spoke no English but read Schiller, Goethe, etc., wrote an exquisite German hand . . . but utterly stupid in household matters."[80]

Furness applied the universal American panacea as well as he could, teaching those who were teachable to read and write, and he assisted financially by remitting his fees in those few instances when he was called upon for professional services for which the applicants were unable to pay. The poverty of many of the immigrant Irish challenged the humanitarianism of the Unitarians and met a generous response. The Furnesses themselves visited forty-five poor families during one winter, "most of them Catholicks and Irish."[81]

The society continued to receive new members from England, among whom were Bridport, William and Frederick W. Harrold,[82] William Kirk,[83] Sartain, and the Tams brothers. The English influence was so strong, in one instance, that Furness accepted a fee in English pounds sterling when he married Richard Y. Pease to Mary E. Dawes on June 10, 1835.[84] The major part of the growing membership, however, came from New England, among which newcomers Barnes, Bradford, Cabot, the Havens, and Merrill were outstanding.

Among the native Philadelphians beginning to join the church the most sizeable group was that of the Quakers, of the party called Hicksite. Elias Hicks, a native of Long Island, had been preaching extensively throughout the Quaker meetings all over America for fifty years before his doctrinal soundness was questioned by the Pine Street Monthly Meeting in Philadelphia in 1819. He received a stronger rebuke from the ten Elders of Philadelphia in 1822, and in 1827 the Yearly Meeting split the Society of Friends into two parts in the Great Separation which the Quaker historian Rufus M. Jones called "the greatest tragedy of Quaker history."[85] Though the dissident group was given the name of Hicksite, the presence of Hicks himself was merely coincidental, as the causes for the schism lay deeper, in the world-wide movement described by Jones as a "profound transformation which occurred in the nineteenth century, and which carried a large proportion of the membership of the Society of Friends, both in England and America, over from a mystical basis to what for want of a better term may be called an evangelical basis."[86] Most of Philadelphia Quakerdom called itself Orthodox but actually it followed the new course, closely akin to the current evangelism of other Protestant sects. The rural areas overwhelmingly took the Hicksite position, conserving the principle of the Inner Light which they felt to be the essential element of Quakerism. Of Hicks himself, Jones said that, though "he is often thought of as a leader of 'Unitarianism' . . . [t]hat judgment is not warranted by the facts."[87] However, Jones conceded that "it is possible to think of his position as pointing toward Unitarianism." Lucretia Mott, on the other hand, a Hicksite herself, insisted that Hicks "was, nevertheless, unitarian in sentiments, whether they [other Quakers] know it or not."[88]

Whatever the theological merits of the case, the fact remains, as recorded by Furness, that there were many Quakers in the Unitarian congregation by 1830, their number being sufficiently large that their disapproval of music in the church services had to be reckoned with. He wrote to Mary Jenks on December 27, 1830, that at the evening service the night before there had been "an anthem finely sung. But there are too many Quakers in our society to like such a display."[89] On January 3, 1831, he reported to Miss Jenks: "The publisher of a Quaker paper belongs to my Church and he wishes to make it as much of a Unitarian paper as he can. He has 2000 Quaker subscribers and I am going to assist him with communications, as much as I can. . . ."[90] After the Separation, Orthodox Quakers held possession of most of the city's meeting-houses and the Philadelphia Hicksites had few places in which to worship. They were welcomed gladly by the Unitarian Society.

Vaughan's tradition of outstanding hospitality was carried on by Furness, whose home became a center for both local and visiting celebrities, domestic and foreign. Mrs. Furness' first morning "at home" in Philadelphia, when she received twenty-two callers, was an augury of things to come. In 1830 she wrote to her mother and sister that the house was "so thronged with company that at times I have hardly had time to think."[91] Philadelphia's strategic location on the road between New York and Washington made it a convenient stopping-off place at which to break the long and wearisome journey, a fact which Furness faced realistically when he accepted the charge in Philadelphia, making it one of the conditions of his acceptance that he be given sufficient means to enable him to act as host to travelling Unitarians. In 1834 he was honored by a six weeks' visit from Harriet Martineau, the famous English Unitarian then touring the United States, who came armed "with many letters to the first people here and our humble dwelling has been all but thronged."[92] Furness had met Miss Martineau when he preached one Sunday in New York and had invited her to make his house her home when she visited Philadelphia. She accepted literally, bringing a companion, Miss Jeffrey, with her. Poor Mrs. Furness, who had to cope with the housekeeping problem thus created, wistfully maintained that even if the visit had "given three times the inconvenience it did," it would have been worthwhile.[93] Among those who called to see Miss Martineau were such disparate personalities as Mrs. Fanny Kemble Butler and Bishop White. The Furnesses were soon case-hardened hosts, who took in their stride such surprises as the unexpected arrival of Josiah Quincy, the new president of Harvard, whom Furness found in his study one morning, playing with the infant Furness son. Emerson was a frequent visitor at the house and preacher at the church, although his advanced thinking was not to the liking of most members of the society.

Another of Furness' New England friends who made a strong though shortlived impression on Philadelphia at this time was Amos Bronson Alcott. [94] Alcott first met Furness when he visited Philadelphia in May, 1828, and it was Furness who introduced him to the Swedenborgian minister, Dr. Maskell W. Carll, who taught a school for young ladies, and Dorothea Dix of Boston, then much interested in infant schools, who, in turn, gave him a letter of introduction to Mathew Carey. These connections eventually led Alcott to return to Philadelphia in 1830 at the invitation of the Quaker merchant, Reuben Haines, and open a school for children with William Russell, a Scottish educator, first in Germantown and later in the city itself. Although born an Episcopalian and intended for holy orders by his mother, Alcott had grown away from the Episcopal Church by 1827 and was taking much pleasure in the preaching of such Unitarians as Henry Ware, Jr., John G. Palfrey, William Ellery Channing, and Ezra Stiles Gannett. On May 23, 1830, he married the sister of a Unitarian clergyman, Samuel J. May, and with her came to Philadelphia in December, together with Russell. The newcomers were received by an influential circle, including Roberts Vaux, Robert Walsh, Dr. James Rush, Dr. George McClellan, and the Unitarians, Furness, Taylor, and Vaughan. After attending a Wistar Party, Alcott came to the following conclusion about Philadelphia in 1831:

Compared with Boston, there seems to exist here all the plainness and simplicity of manners for which the city is distinguished. The subjects most cultivated, and on which conversation generally turns, seem to be the physical sciences; while those most discussed in Boston are the metaphysical and ethical. The influence of the Friends upon conversation, manners, and thought is apparent; subjects connected with utility, comfort, and practical morals seem most congenial to their minds. [95]

The death of Haines in 1833 led to the abandonment of the Germantown school and Alcott moved into the city in April, establishing there a school with fifteen pupils. His students included, in addition to William Henry Furness, Jr., Leland's young son, Charles Godfrey, who later said of his teacher:

Mr. Alcott was the most eccentric man who ever took it on himself to train and form the youthful mind. . . . His forte was "moral influence" and "sympathetic intellectual communion" by talking. . . . All of the new theories, speculations, or fads which were beginning to be ventilated among the Unitarian liberal clergy found ready welcome in his dreamy brain, and he retailed them all to his pupils, among whom I was certainly the only one who took them in and seriously thought them over. Yet I cannot say that I *really* liked the man himself. He was not to me exactly sympathetic—human.[96]

Alcott, with Russell, tried very hard to promote public interest in education in Philadelphia, a project which claimed another New Englander, Walter R. Johnson, a Philadelphian by adoption and a member of the Unitarian Society. Under the urging of these men the Philadelphia Association of Teachers was formed in 1831, to give lectures and issue a monthly magazine, the *Journal of Instruction*, which lasted only from January to March 15, 1832, its editors including Alcott and Johnson. Alcott returned to New England for a visit in the summer of 1833 and never came back to Philadelphia. He had provoked mixed reactions among the Philadelphians for whom he had labored, but in Furness he had had a friend. Emerson wrote to Furness in October, 1837: "I shall always love you for loving Alcott. He is a great man."[97]

Though much interested in Unitarianism and married to the sister of a Unitarian clergyman, Alcott himself never joined a Unitarian society, his religious mysticism taking him into the ranks of the Transcendentalists, of which group he was an outstanding member. Another schoolmaster came to Philadelphia in 1831, however, who was a Unitarian minister and who became an active member of the Unitarian Society. The Rev. Martin Luther Hurlbut, born in Southampton, Massachusetts, had long been resident in Charleston, South Carolina. When he opened a school in Philadelphia in 1831, Furness declared, "I regard him as quite an acquisition to our Society."[98] Charles Godfrey Leland, having been subjected to Alcott, was placed in Hurlbut's school in 1838 and found him an "ungenial, formal, rather harsh man."[99] Furness found him even worse when the struggle over abolitionism took place in the society.

The Unitarian Society grew larger and stronger and as it did its members became more and more conspicuous in the city's activities. In the American Philosophical Society Vaughan was still treasurer and librarian, resident in the hall of the society. He welcomed to membership during this period from the Unitarian fellowship his nephew, Samuel Vaughan Merrick, and Carey in 1833 and Espy in 1835. In 1835 Merrick joined him in the Wistar Association. Vaughan was a member of the Executive Council of the Historical Society of Pennsylvania from 1829 to 1841 and a vicepresident of the Athenaeum from 1836 to 1841. At the Franklin Institute, Thomas Fletcher was vice-president, Toppan and Merrick were managers, and Espy and Walter R. Johnson were serving on committees. Vaughan, Sully, and Childs were directors of the Pennsylvania Academy of the Fine Arts and Sartain was a controller of the Artists' Fund Society. Thirty-one Unitarians were members of the Musical Fund Society between 1828 and 1839, two served as officers at the Academy of Natural Sciences, three as council members of the Pennsylvania Horticultural Society. When the Board of Trade was organized in October, 1833, Evans Rogers was elected to the first Board of Managers. Vaughan was performing a varied consular service as vice-consul for Sweden and Norway from 1829 to 1839, for Brazil from 1830 to 1839, for Portugal from 1828 to 1830 and from 1837 to 1839, and acting as consular agent for Austria in 1839. Seven Unitarians were directors of banks, five served on the boards of insurance companies, eight were involved in the affairs of turnpike, railroad, navigation, and coal companies as officers, managers, or directors. Sampson Tams became a director of the Philadelphia Steam Tow Boat Company, which was chartered in 1832 to break up the ice in the Delaware River in the wintertime.

The Unitarians began to take a greater interest in practical politics, with Merrick and Elliott serving on the Common Council in 1833 and Elliott on the Select Council in 1837. Merrick and

Elliott were Whigs. An unsuccessful candidate for the Select Council on the Democratic ticket in 1839 was Evans Rogers. In October of the same year he served on a committee to arrange for the reception of President Van Buren upon his visit to Philadelphia.[100] Willis H. Blayney, son of one of the founders of the society, Dr. Arthur H. Blaney, and a member himself, was one of the High Constables of Philadelphia during this period.

When the city began to think seriously of the possibilities of gas illumination for Philadelphia, Merrick was appointed by councils in 1834 to go abroad and study the European experience with gas lighting. The first inflammable gas for lighting purposes had been demonstrated successfully in Philadelphia in 1796 and the question of its further use had been a matter of controversy ever since. Merrick had been an early advocate of gas for street lighting and it was in order to further this cause that he ran for and was elected to the Common Council in 1833. As a result of his favorable report upon his European observations, the construction of the Philadelphia Gas Works was authorized on March 1, 1835, with Merrick given charge as chief engineer of building the plant and distributing gas to the city. The Gas Works was completed in February, 1836, and the following year Merrick resigned to return to private business.

The well-established prosperity of Philadelphia Unitarians was attested by the fact that during the Panic of 1837 there was only one failure among the members of the society, that of John W. Patten, a leather merchant, and this, according to Furness, was "honorable."[101] Patten recovered quickly, moreover, and in 1845 was listed among the wealthy men of Philadelphia. At least one Unitarian, Sill, was made painfully aware of Philadelphia's social snobbery when he realized that, though he was intimately associated with many prominent men in his various "benevolent activities" and was occasionally invited to breakfast with them, he was never invited to their evening parties. He confided to his diary, "The only reason I can assign to it is, that I am engaged in a Retail business—that I am a shopkeeper!"[102] He was deeply hurt but told himself that such feelings were unworthy and determined to rise superior to them. The social prestige of at least some of the Unitarians, on the other hand, was indicated by the fact that when the exclusive Philadelphia Club was organized in 1834, among the members that year were John Butler and Thomas Rotch, Timothy M. Bryan becoming a member two years later.

In addition to being men of property and prestige and active participants in the affairs of the city, the Philadelphia Unitarians were involved in many philanthropic causes. Furness in 1839, commenting on the fact that Philadelphia was justly noted for the number and efficiency of its benevolent institutions, undoubtedly was entirely innocent of the cynicism which the disillusioned generation of today would impute when he declared that "it is a great step made in the progress of the world, and a striking proof of the power of Christianity, that active benevolence has become so fashionable, and so sure a way to respectability and personal success."[103] Charity was simply a part of the code of *noblesse oblige* of this era.

The Society of the Sons of St. George was concerned with the special problems of English immigrants. Between 1829 and 1839, Merrick, Sill, Joshua Tevis, James and Sampson Tams, and Joseph M. Sanderson joined the society, of which Joseph Todhunter was secretary from 1827 to 1833, followed in that office by Sill from 1834 to 1841, while William Todhunter served as treasurer in 1835 and 1836, Birch was a steward from 1822 to 1829 and again from 1831 to 1833, Sill serving in the same capacity in 1832 and 1833.

Rapid economic change during the 1830's created serious problems of human maladjustment and consequent misery as it attempted to keep pace with the growing industrialization of the country. Poverty was widespread and relief still largely a matter of private charity. In this the Philadelphia Unitarians did their share, the problem being almost a preoccupation with such a man as Sill, whose diary is filled with his pondering on the subject. He was inclined to agree with the majority opinion that insolvency was the result of indolence or vice or both, and yet, during the bitter winter of 1836, he began to suspect that perhaps the unfortunate did not always deserve their fate, and whether they did or not he believed that they should be helped. Mrs. Furness, always involved in works of charity, had one particular protege, Mrs. McClure, who had been abandoned with four small children. Though she must have been sorely tried by this poor creature, whose habitual intoxication thwarted all Mrs. Furness' attempts at rehabilitation, yet Mrs. Furness continued to believe her "a victim of our heartless social arrangements."[104] When the interdenominational Union Benevolent Association was formed, in an attempt to gain a complete picture of the needs of all the city's poor, Mrs. Espy served as secretary of the association, and Mrs. Furness and Mrs. Fairman were very active in its affairs.[105] An attempt was made to raise the educational level of the lower classes by the establishment of the Apprentices Library, of which James Kay, Jr. was a manager in 1830.[106]

The outstanding beneficence of the Philadelphia Unitarians during this period, however, was the Pennsylvania Institution for the Instruction of the Blind, which received a charter from the Commonwealth of Pennsylvania on January 27, 1834. Vaughan was considered the founder of this institution,[107] while it owed its financial independence to Birch, who made it the residuary legatee of his will in 1837, his legacy amounting to over $180,000. Sill stated that Birch left this money to the institution chiefly because of his fondness for Vaughan, who had founded it.[108] When the institution was first organized, Bishop White was named president, but Birch was one of the vice-presidents, Vaughan the treasurer and a member of the Admissions Committee, and Jacob Snider, Jr. the recording secretary. When the first annual meeting was held on March 3, 1834, Sill acted as secretary, Birch, and Snider were re-elected vice-president and recording secretary, respectively, and Elliott was elected treasurer to replace Vaughan, who had resigned that office. Vaughan continued as a manager. An especially important accomplishment during the year had been Snider's devising of a method of printing for the blind, raising entire letters on the page rather than the Braille symbols. Snider's publication of the Gospel of St. Mark was the first book for the blind ever printed in this form and drew to the Philadelphia institution the attention of the whole civilized world.

Vaughan had been instrumental in bringing to the institution as its first principal, the brilliant Julius R. Friedlander, a Silesian Jew, who was already teaching the blind in a small school of his own in Philadelphia. Although he lived only until 1839, before his tragically early death at the age of thirty-six Friedlander had become famous for his work with the blind and had established the Pennsylvania institution on a firm, working basis which assured its future success. Though Friedlander was not a member of the Unitarian Society, he was warmly regarded by its membership and Furness preached a memorial discourse on the occasion of his death. Unitarians continued to take an active interest in the welfare of the institution and to give it generous financial support. Birch was honored by the institution when he died by the erection of a memorial plaque in the school and a monument over his grave, which was in a lot owned by the institution in Laurel Hill Cemetery. Friedlander was buried with similar honors within the same enclosure. Vaughan was elected president of the institution in 1837 and continued in that office until his death.

A preoccupation with cemeteries was characteristic of this age. Sill, together with his contemporaries, liked nothing better than a stroll in Laurel Hill Cemetery, which was incorporated in 1836 and began to receive great numbers of deceased Unitarians. *A Guide to Laurel Hill*, published in 1851, declared: "The salutary effects of ornate and well-preserved cemeteries on the moral taste and general sentiments of all classes, is a most valuable result, and seems to have been appreciated in all ages, by all civilized nations."[109] It supplied a public want, ministered to the public taste, and elevated human thoughts to "those spiritual associations which should ever be connected with death."[110] Unhappily, the Unitarians, like all other Philadelphians, lived intimately with death in this period, as they had earlier. Many of the families in the society suffered crushing multiple tragedies as part of the normal course of events, the especially high mortality rate for the newly born and their mothers and for young children casting a pall of constant apprehension over family life when it was not actually immersed in grief. The cholera epidemic which struck Philadelphia in 1832 was regarded by many as an instance of Divine punishment, a view supported by the Commonwealth when August 9, 1832, was declared a day of fasting, humiliation, and prayer. Sill rejected the notion of Divine wrath and appeasement as a repulsive one, accepting widespread chronic illness and premature death as a natural part of existence which had to be endured. He and Furness recorded among their own families and those of their friends an unending procession of chills, fevers, "fits," headaches, and other assorted ills, for which the medical treatment available often seemed worse than the disease. Mrs. Ford, suffering from "an inflammation of the stomach," was cupped half a dozen times with eighteen cups at a time, leeched, and blistered, after which she unaccountably seemed better.[111] Gould, another member of the congregation, got into the hands of a practitioner whom Furness described as a "quack," who relied on the use of steam in treating his patient for apoplexy, inflammation of the brain, and pleurisy, keeping poor Gould drenched in perspiration and plying him with cayenne pepper at the same time.[112] William Henry Furness, Jr., not yet three, had five ounces of blood taken from his arm as a cure for a cough.[113] Death won many easy victories against such adversaries, and even the sunny-tempered Furness admitted that the losses in his congregation "have had an effect on my mind which they ought not to have had. They have depressed me with a sense of the utter insecurity and vanity of human things. I feel oftener and more overwhelmingly than I should that we are all walking in a vain show."[114] That this was no passing mood is indicated by his writing more than a year later: "How I wonder every day I live at the intense interest which we allow ourselves to take in a scene of things so transitory. I put on a cheerful countenance and try to make those about me happy. But indeed . . . I feel nothing more deeply than the nothingness of this world."[115]

Life did have its lighter side, however. For Unitarians like Sill there was the world of the theatre, of which Philadelphia had a goodly share, and the somewhat less dignified exhibitions of equestrians, trained bears, balloon ascensions, and the like. There were concerts and the opera and both active and spectator sports. There were the pleasures of self-improvement, lectures, study, and the exhibitions of the fine and practical arts. There was, above all, the joy of leisurely social intercourse, freely indulged in by all, by the women who kept to their houses or visited other ladies at their homes, and by the men who went to business. Visiting began early in the day, long breakfast sessions to which friends were invited being a regular feature of the social system, carried to the heights of perfection by Vaughan but practiced on a lesser scale by ordinary househollders as well. After breakfast came the casual callers. Mrs. Furness received twenty-two such calls one day at home, while Sill's diary is filled with résumés of long chats he had with his male friends at his place of business, Furness in particular seeming to have made it a regular practice to drop in at the Sill store almost every morning. Large parties were given at home in the evening and Sill, for one, thoroughly enjoyed on such occasions the pleasures of dancing, but the pastor frowned on such frivolity. The first time he saw a waltz danced the performers were a nine-year old boy and his younger sister, but Furness commented that "it is the first time I ever witnessed an exhibition of *that* dance & I never desire to see older persons undertake it."[116] His taste led him to the soberer joys of such gatherings as the Wistar Parties and Carey's Vespers, where intellectual conversations on a high level were the featured entertainment. An evening party at the home of Nicholas Biddle, thronged with ladies of high fashion, impressed him only with "the barbarism of the age," making him feel "as if I were amongst Indians."[117] Many thought he should not even be present at such gatherings. He wrote to Mary Jenks on January 3, 1831: "I have just had the reproach cast upon me of having been twice at parties where dancing was going on!"[118]

The most fascinating of all public diversions, however, continued to be politics. It was a never ending performance, as election followed election throughout the year, replete with comedy, tragedy, pathos, and bathos. Sill had a front seat for this show, living on Chestnut Street across from the State House, where all elections were held until 1850, and his reaction was, "A pox on both your houses." He thought the partisans of both parties coarse and vulgar but consented to serve on a Vigilante Committee at the polls in spite of his distaste because he felt it was his duty as a responsible citizen.[119] Jefferson and John Adams had made a melodramatically coincidental departure from this life on the fiftieth anniversary of the declaration of American independence and a pleasant glow of public approbation was now accorded both by most people. Furness in August, 1826, admitted such a change of heart. "In youth with our parents we hear only one side in politics. I confess the name of Jefferson has been associated in my mind with what is bad and wrong—but since I have read, I cannot help according both to him and to Mr. Adams my cordial respect."[120] All Americans joined together in 1832 in celebrating the one hundredth anniversary of the birth of Washington, who had now become the symbol of national patriotism.

The bitter struggle of Hamilton-versus-Jefferson lived on, however, personified by Henry Clay and Andrew Jackson. Philadelphia gave its heart to Jackson in 1824 and in 1828, but when the bank expired, so, apparently, did the city's love for Old Hickory. In 1832 the city's vote was against Jackson, though he retained his hold on the industrial areas of Kensington and Southwark. Those Unitarians who recorded their political preferences were definitely anti-Jackson. When a town meeting of Philadelphia Whigs convened on July 7, 1828, to record their support of Clay's American System, the advertisers of the gathering included the Unitarians William Y. Birch, Cephas G. Childs, Thomas Harper, John Jennings, Benjamin Tevis, and Samuel H. Thomas. Among other actions taken, this group

Resolved, That, in our opinion, neither the education, the habits, nor occupations of General Jackson have been of a kind to qualify him for the duties of the first civil magistrate of our country; and that, whatever his military merits may be, his unfitness for the office of President of the United States is manifested by the whole course of his public life.[121]

Furness struggled manfully to overcome his inherited prejudice against Jefferson but he was incapable of self-restraint as far as "that man," Jackson, was concerned. In April, 1829, he wrote, that "As to General Jackson, it is a poor creature—the perfect slave and tool of his party and a dull tool, too,"[122] but by July, 1832, the tool had proved to have a sharp cutting edge and Furness exploded:

At present the Veto which the old Mummy at Washington has put on the Bank bill has quite taken the place of the cholera. I don't know whether it is right or wrong but the provoking thing is to have a man destroying such institutions who is not competent to form an opinion on the subject and knows no more about the . . . Bank, etc. than I do.[123]

Sill was an ardent supporter of Clay on purely emotional grounds, for, as an importer of goods from England, he wanted free trade and confessed that the arguments of the protectionists were "beyond my comprehension."[124] At this time Henry C. Carey agreed with him, in spite of his father's convictions to the contrary. It was not until 1844 that the younger Carey was suddenly converted to protectionism and within a few years he found within the Unitarian Society one of his ablest and most tireless workers in the protectionist cause, William D. Kelley. A member of the house of Adams returned to the Philadelphia Unitarian Church for a brief visit in 1832, when John Quincy Adams, appointed a member of the committee to study the bank situation in Philadelphia, attended services on March 25 and April 10.[125]

Though the Philadelphia Unitarian Society had by no means won universal community approbation by 1839, there was no denying that its position had been greatly improved. Responsible for this improvement beyond any other single factor was the personality of its pastor. His approach was simplicity itself.

175

If a person is prejudiced the plainest statements of which language is capable are of no use. The clearest words will be misinterpreted. It is best to hold one's peace. Let us only take care to show our religion in our lives, in our general demeanour, in the sweetness of our tempers, in patience and forbearance. Such an exhibition will soften the hearts of others and gradually they will acquire such respect for you that what you may say will be listened to with attention and with more favorable disposition.[126]

Before Furness' irresistible charm the opposition simply melted away. Emerson wrote to him in 1838: "How can you keep so good a nature from a boy to man. . . . Every word that comes or ever came to me from you or of you is good . . . and every year is adding the riches of high accomplishments to your image."[127]

Furness flatly opposed sectarianism and disavowed any desire to make proselytes, declaring that he regarded the existing differences of religious opinions "not only as natural and inevitable, but as positively useful."[128] When the Roman Catholics were finally accorded the full privileges of citizenship in Great Britain in 1829, he preached a sermon praising that action which was well received by the Catholic clergy of Philadelphia.[129] The following year he preached a sermon on the Jews by special request, the many Jews who attended this service expressing themselves well pleased by his efforts. "You can't think how cordially I am met and greeted by the children of Israel," he wrote to Mary Jenks in January, 1830.[130] One of his special friends was Miss Rebecca Gratz.

Furness encountered prejudice in his own home. One of his servants was taken from his house by her mother, "who appears to be a very good woman [but] is unwilling that she should stay with us on acct. of our religious sentiments. I told her I was sorry she had scruples without any foundation but so long as she had then it was her duty to obey them."[131] His own mother-in-law, a strict Calvinist, objected to his religious opinions, but his disarming reaction was: "If she dreads the thought of Unitarianism and thinks it is sealing her ruin only to come and live with us, why is it not just as fair to take the opposite view and hope that she may do us good and herself too by coming here."[132]

In 1836 Furness published *Remarks on the Four Gospels*, the first of a series of twenty-two books which during his lifetime he was to devote to the exploration of the nature of Jesus and the explanation of the nature of the Gospels. Apparently, when confronted with this declaration of faith in cold print, certain members of the congregation suddenly realized for the first time whither their pastor had been leading them, for even Sill, one of the most devoted of his parishioners, was moved to write of the new work in his diary, "These new ideas did not seem to find favour with the Church." He had hoped "they would either have been discarded from his mind or kept close within his own bosom; but it has proved otherwise, and he has, I believe, publish'd the Book upon his own responsibility, without much, if any, consultation either with the Trustees, or members of the Congregation. I think it unfortunate that he has thus proceeded."[133] However, such was Furness' hold upon Sill's affections that, admitting that "I cannot impute any improper motives to him," Sill decided that he would "endeavour to keep my mind open to conviction on the subject."[134]

Furness' theological position was fully stated, in its essentials, in this first book, and it remained practically the same throughout his long life. "Believing Jesus Christ to have been a man, a man indeed of miraculous gifts," he felt that "in him we have a new and original specimen of human nature."[135] "Jesus Christ was such a man as has never existed before nor since . . . Do I derogate from God in so conceiving him? Oh, no! How is the Creator revealed in so Divine a Man, the Father glorified in so God-like a Son!"[136] For him, Jesus was a great teacher and prophet, though only "a humble peasant of Judea,"[137] who brought men the Truth which has been taught through all the ages, the wisdom of eternity.

The life of Jesus of Nazareth, his words, acts and sufferings, being real, being facts, are a part of the grand and all-instructive system to Creation— they constitute a page, nay, a chapter, and at once, the profoundest and the clearest chapter in the vast volume of God. Nowhere do I see spiritual and eternal things so clearly revealed, so touchingly expressed, as in his life.[138]

177

In sermon after sermon, as well as in book after book, the same ideas were expressed. Often the words were identical, prompting even so devoted a friend as Sill to pepper his diary with the comment, "This has been preached before!" or, even more emphatically, "This has been preached before!!" Furness admitted that he had great difficulty in writing sermons, often reaching Saturday without an idea for the next day, and he used "the dear old subject" again and again. He remarked to the Rev. John W. Chadwick in 1870: "I suppose you write many sermons: I write only one, but I keep on writing it over."[139]

Furness did have one more string to his bow, however, and he loosed it in 1839. On July 13 of that year he wrote to his sister-in-law, Mary Jenks: "What do you think? Sunday before 4th July I preached *out* about Slavery. . . . It was a great effort for me to undertake. Pierce Butler sitting before me, the holder of hundreds of slaves & the majority of the congregation of an opposite way of thinking."[140] He had tried desperately to avoid the issue. For fourteen years he had been gradually winning not only the love of his congregation but the respect and friendship of the Philadelphia community, and he knew that everything he had worked for was jeopardized by his espousal of the antislavery cause. But he was "impelled by a sense of duty that I could in no wise resist."[141] Stronger than his distaste for controversy and his desire for approval was the current of reform in which he found himself caught up at last, a world-wide movement which caused great multitudes to work for many causes, for women's rights, the reform of prisons, the amelioration of the lot of the deaf, the blind, the morally crippled, the insane. For Furness the irresistible call for help came from the enslaved Negroes and in their service he spent the next thirty years. He had measured the cost but on July 13, 1839, he was finally ready to pay the price his conscience demanded. "It is a great relief to have preached this sermon—not that I want to be an advocate of abolition, but I wanted to have my own opinions fully known, & I believe they are now."[142]

NOTES

[1]Merchant, d.h. 45 S. 8th St.: CD, 1825. He began paying pew rent September 14, 1827: CASH II, 19.

[2]Proprietor of the vegetable catholicon, 13 S. 9th St.: CD, 1829. He began paying pew rent May 12, 1828: CASH II, 35.

[3]Keeper of the Merchants' Coffee House, S. 2nd St., cor. of Bank Alley: CD, 1829. He rented half a pew on November 1, 1828: UNNAMED, p. 35. He was married by Furness on February 24, 1829, to Elizabeth, daughter of Joseph Todhunter: REG I, 98.

[4]Merchant, 91 S. Front St., d.h. cor. Walnut and 13th Sts.: CD, 1831.

[5]Boot and shoemaker, 15 S. 11th St.: CD, 1825. He began paying pew rent September 11, 1827: CASH II, 19, but had been married by Taylor on September 12, 1822: REG I, 96.

[6]President Judge, District Court of City and County of Philadelphia, 11 Sansom St.: CD, 1829. He was commissioned October 24, 1826, and served until April 21, 1835: John Hill Martin, *Bench and Bar of Philadelphia* (Philadelphia, 1883), p. 78. Furness in a letter to Mary Jenks in April, 1829: COLL. CORR. I, stated that Barnes "recently joined us."

[7]Gentleman, 77 Wood St.: CD, 1829. He was married by Furness to Mrs. Lydia Allen on May 2, 1826: REG I, 97, and took half a pew on November 11, 1828: UNNAMED, p. 301

[8]Looking glasses and print store, 134 High St.: CD, 1825. He began paying pew rent July 11, 1826: CASH II, 14.

[9]Merchant, 8 N. 7th St.: CD, 1823. He was elected a member March 31, 1822: PROC, p. 181. That Ford was married to Catharine Bryan, daughter of Guy Bryan, is deduced from a reference to Mrs. Ford's mother's death in a letter from Furness to Mary Jenks, August 15, 1826: COLL. CORR. I. Guy Bryan bought him Pew 96 in November, 1828: UNNAMED, p. 23.

[10]Conveyancer, 82 Chestnut St.: CD, 1828. He began paying pew rent October 1, 1827: CASH II, 21.

[11]M.D., Palmyra Square: CD, 1824. Mentioned as a member November 9, 1824: RECS & MINS, p. 33. There is no record of his election.

[12]Merchant, 459 High St.: CD, 1814. Signed records December 20, 1812: PROC, p. 114.

[13]Lace fringe and military store, 53 N. 3rd St., d. City Hotel: CD, 1828. He began paying pew rent December 16, 1827: CASH II, 22.

[14]Furness to Mary Jenks, January 1, 1830: COLL. CORR. I.

[15]Furness to Mary Jenks, April, 1829: COLL. CORR. I.

[16]Furness to Mary Jenks, October 30, 1829: COLL. CORR. I.

[17]Furness to Mary Jenks, April 2, May 12, September 7, October 12, and December 3, 1829: COLL. CORR. I.

[18]Furness to Mary Jenks, October 30, 1829: COLL. CORR. I.

[19]REG I, 105; Furness to Lucy Osgood, June 28, 1847: OSGOOD CORR.

[20]Ralph L. Rusk, ed., *The Letters of Ralph Waldo Emerson* (New York, 1939), I, 293.

[21]RECS & MINS, p. 129.

[22]REG I, 14.

[23]Furness to Mary Jenks, June 8, 1837: COLL. CORR. II.

[24]UNNAMED, pp. 251–52; REG I, [204].

[25]CD, 1837; REG I, 103.

[26]REG II, 161.

[27]CD, 1828; CASH II, 27.

[28]REG I, 98; Furness to Mary Jenks, March 5, 1830: COLL. CORR. I.

[29]Kerr-Hurlbut, 1838 (REG I, 104); Barton-Roch, 1843 (REG I, 107); Clark-Sill, 1855 (REG I, 113).

[30]Anon., *Wealth and Biography*, p. 18.

[31]CASH II, 27.

[32]Tams and Co., china merchants, 192 High St.: CD, 1823.

[33]Anon., *Wealth and Biography*, p. 20.

[34]UNNAMED, p. 28; CD, 1833.

[35]CD, 1831.

[36]CD, 1837.

[37]Furness to Mary Jenks, May 3, 1832: COLL. CORR. I.

[38]Furness to Mary Jenks, June 26, 1832: COLL. CORR. II.

[39]Attorney at law, 88 S. 4th St.: CD, 1831; UNNAMED, p. 27.

[40]Attorney and counsellor and deputy clerk of the Orphans Court, h. 22 N. 7th St.: CD, 1839. He bought a pew April 6, 1839: UNNAMED, p. 28.

[41]Treasurer, Chestnut St. Theatre, 191 S. 9th St.: CD, 1837; UNNAMED, p. 28.

[42]CD, 1831, 1833; Furness to Mary Jenks, October 26, 1831: COLL. CORR. I.

[43]Furness to Mary Jenks, December 6, 1830: COLL. CORR. I.

[44]134 Chestnut St., d. h.first door above U.S. Mint, 7th St.: CD, 1831; Furness to Mary Jenks, January 3, 1831: COLL. CORR. I.

[45]95 Callowhill St.: CD, 1835–36; REG I, 102.

[46]Banker, 25 S. 3rd St., h. 76 S. 4th St.: CD, 1839; Scharf and Westcott, III, 2100: UNNAMED, p. 28.

[47]Leland, p. 67.

[48]186 S. 5th St.: CD, 1831; REG I, 11, 13, 14, 16.

[49]REG I, 199.

[50]W. H. Furness, *Discourse delivered October 22, 1854, occasioned by the Decease of Jacob Thomas and Eli Griffith* (Philadelphia, n.d.)

[51]Included in description of Eliza and her brother James, painted by Sully in 1811. Biddle and Fielding, p. 296.

[52]This account is from Samuel Bradford, *Some Incidents in the Life of Samuel Bradford, Senior, by his Son. Also, the Autobiography or a Brief Narrative of the Life of Samuel Bradford, Junior, to January 1, 1879* (Philadelphia, 1880).

[53]This account comes from William Elder, *A Memoir of Henry C. Carey* (Philadelphia, 1880); Arnold W. Green, *Henry Carey, Nineteenth Century Sociologist* (Philadelphia, 1951); and DAB, III, 487–89; UNNAMED, pp. 33–34.

[54]Charles H. Cramp, "Carey's 'Vespers,' " MS dated November 11, 1908, in the Edward C. Gardiner Collection, HSP.

[55]UNNAMED, p. 28.

[56]Robert H. Beresford, printer, 23 Blackberry Alley (CD, 1833) was married by Furness in 1829 (REG I, 98) and had five children baptized by him in 1833 (REG I, 14). Robert G., also a printer, was present at a meeting April 15, 1839 (RECS & MINS, p. 109), William on April 16, 1838 (RECS & MINS, p. 106).

[57]The sources for this account were his own *Reminiscences of a Very Old Man, 1808–*

1897 (New York, 1899); DAB, XVI, 371–72; Fielding, p. 317; Groce and Wallace, p. 558; and Stauffer, I, 234–36.

[58]REG I, 12.

[59]This account comes from Frances Ann Kemble, *Records of a Girlhood* (New York, 1883); Frances Anne Butler, *Journal* (Philadelphia, 1835), 2 vols.; F[rances] A[nn] Kemble, *Journal of a Residence on a Georgian Plantation in 1838–39* (New York, 1863); Frances Ann Kemble, *Records of Later Life* (New York, 1883); two documents covering the Butler divorce: *Pierce Butler vs. Frances Anne Butler, Libel for Divorce with Answers and Exhibits, in Court of Common Pleas, Philadelphia* (n.p., n.d.) and *Mr. Butler's Statement, originally prepared in aid of his professional counsel* (n.p. n.d.); *A Statement of James Schott, Jr.* (n.p., 1844); and Margaret Armstrong's biography, *Fanny Kemble, A Passionate Victorian* (New York, 1938).

[60]Mrs. Butler to Mrs. Jameson, October 26, 1834: *Records of Later Life*, p. 2.

[61]Mrs. Butler to Harriet St. Leger, June 27, 1835: *Records of Later Life, p.* 22.

[62]Mrs. Butler to Harriet St. Leger, November 14, 1837: *Records of Later Life*, p. 71.

[63]Mrs. Butler to Harriet St. Leger, June 27, 1835: *Records of Later Life*, p. 22.

[64]Sill, VI, 212.

[65]Furness to Mary Jenks, October 22, 1834: COLL. CORR. II.

[66]Letter dated October 31, 1835: *Records of Later Life*, p. 24.

[67]Footnote to letter written to Harriet St. Leger, March 1, 1836: *Records of Later Life*, p. 28.

[68]Mrs. Butler to Harriet St. Leger, August 29, 1836: *Records of Later Life*, pp. 39–40.

[69]F[ranklin] B. Sanborn and William T. Harris, *A. Bronson Alcott* (Boston, 1893), I, 244.

[70]Horace Howard Furness Jayne, in his Introduction to his edition of *The Letters of Horace Howard Furness* (Boston, 1922), I, xx–xxii. The elder Furness had done the same for Mrs. Butler. In his letter to Alcott on September 17, 1835 (*supra*, footnote 69) he wrote: "I have tried to urge Mrs. Butler to attempt a work on Shakespeare—that is her mission."

[71]*Pierce Butler vs. Frances Anne Butler*, pp. 8–13, and exhibits 2–10, pp. 35–42.

[72]*Mr. Butler's Statement*, p. 69.

[73]*Mr. Butler's Statement*, pp. 75–76.

[74]Furness to Butler, December 16, 1844: *Mr. Butler's Statement*, pp. 137–38.

[75]Sill, VIII, 358.

[76]Furness to Mary Jenks, December 27, 1830: COLL. CORR. I.

[77]Sill, I, 333.

[78]W. H. Furness, *An Address delivered in the Room over the Northern Liberties Reading-Room, . . . December 13, 1835* (Philadelphia, 1836); Mrs. Furness to Mary Jenks, August, 1837: COLL. CORR. II.

[79]REG I, 13.

[80]Furness to Mary Jenks, December 26, 1849: COLL. CORR. II.

[81]Mrs. Furness to Mary Jenks, December 20, 1842: COLL. CORR. II.

[82]William Harrold began paying pew rent for himself and his son, Frederick W., January 1, 1826: CASH II, 2. When William Harrold signed the Athenaeum's Record of Strangers on November 6, 1814, he gave his home address as "England."

[83]Little is known about this family beyond Furness' note in REG I, 13, when he baptized the infant son of William and Elizabeth Kirk on October 28, 1831, that the father was an Englishman. Eight of the Kirk children were baptized by Furness between 1831 and 1851, and the birth of a ninth recorded in 1835: REG I, 13, 15, 17–21.

[84]REG I, 102.

[85]Rufus M. Jones, *The Later Periods of Quakerism* (London, 1921), I, 435.

[86]Jones, I, xiii.

[87]Jones, I, 443.

[88]Anna Davis Hallowell, ed,. *James and Lucretia Mott. Life and Letters* (Boston, 1884), p. 209.

[89]Furness to Mary Jenks, December 27, 1830: COLL. CORR. I.

[90]Furness to Mary Jenks, January 3, 1831: COLL. CORR. I.

[91]Letter dated May 12, 1830: COLL. CORR. I.

[92]Furness to Mary Jenks, November 26, 1834: COLL. CORR. I. In her two-volume account of her tour, *Retrospect of Western Travel* (New York, 1838), Miss Martineau declared (I, 39) that the Furnesses were "my American brother and sister." Furness felt that she presented them "as large as life and a great *deal larger.*" Furness to Lucy Osgood, January 28, 1838: OSGOOD CORR.

[93]Mrs. Furness to Mary Jenks, December 27, 1834: COLL. CORR. I.

[94]This account is based on Sanborn and Harris; and Dorothy McCuskey, *Bronson Alcott, Teacher* (New York, 1940).

[95]Sanborn and Harris, I, 157.

[96]Leland, pp. 46–47.

[97]Sanborn and Harris, I, 242.

[98]Furness to Mary Jenks, September 13, 1831: COLL. CORR. I. He had been in Philadelphia earlier, a son being buried in the church burial-ground August 17, 1825: REG I, 196. He paid pew rent August 16, 1826: CASH II, 14, and his wife was baptized by Furness on September 29, 1826: REG I, 9.

[99]Leland, p. 73.

[100]Philadelphia *Public Ledger*, October 2, 1839.

[101]Furness to Lucy Osgood, May 16, 1837: OSGOOD CORR.

[102]Sill, II, 278–79.

[103]W. H. Furness, *A Discourse occasioned by the Death of Julius R. Friedlander, Delivered . . . March 24, 1839 . . .* (Philadelphia, 1839), p. 5.

[104]Furness to Mary Jenks, November 17, 1848: COLL. CORR. II.

[105]Furness to Mary Jenks, January 27, 1831, and January 30, 1832: COLL. CORR. I.

[106]CD, 1830; Scharf and Westcott, II, 1208.

[107]Richard Henry Lee, undated letter to Vaughan (Misc. MSS, APS) referring to the institution, stated: "I have never witnessed so touching and so admirable a charity. It is perfectly astonishing—I rejoice to find that you are its founder, for so Mr. Friedlander tells me."

[108]Sill, II, 89.

[109]*A Guide to Laurel Hill Cemetery Near Philadelphia* (Philadelphia, 1851), p. 20.

[110]*Guide to Laurel Hill Cemetery*, p. 19.

[111]Furness to Mary Jenks, March 9, 1832: COLL. CORR. I.

[112]Furness to Mary Jenks, January 27, 1831: COLL. CORR. I.

[113]Furness to Mary Jenks, January 27, 1831: COLL. CORR. I.

[114]Furness to Mary Jenks, July 3, 1834: COLL. CORR. II.

[115]Furness to Mary Jenks, September 9, 1835: COLL. CORR. II.

[116]Furness to Mary Jenks, September 20, 1825: COLL. CORR. I.

[117]Furness to Mary Jenks, March 3, 1836: COLL. CORR. I.

[118]Furness to Mary Jenks, January 3, 1831: COLL. CORR. I.

[119]Sill, II, 228.

[120]Furness to Mary Jenks, August 2, 1826: COLL. CORR. I.

[121]*Report of the Proceedings of the Town Meeting in the City of Philadelphia, July 7th, 1828* (n.p., n.d.), p. 7.

[122]Furness to Mary Jenks, April 2, 1829: COLL. CORR. I.

[123]Furness to Mrs. Furness, July 13, 1832: COLL. CORR. II.

[124]Sill, I, 6.

[125]Sill, I, 99.

[126]Furness to Mary Jenks, May 23, 1831: COLL. CORR. I.

[127]H. H. Furness, *Records of a Lifelong Friendship*, pp.6–7.

[128]W. H. Furness, *Address delivered in the Room over the Northern Liberties Reading-Room*, p. 3.

[129]W. H. Furness, *A Discourse preached . . . May 24, 1829, Occasioned by the Recent Emancipation of the Roman Catholics throughtout the British Empire* (Philadelphia, 1829); Furness to Lucy Osgood, June 10, 1829: OSGOOD CORR.

[130]Furness to Mary Jenks, January 27, 1830: COLL. CORR. I.

[131]Furness to Mary Jenks, October 20. 1829: COLL. CORR. I.

[132]Furness to Mary Jenks, June 22, 1830: COLL. CORR. I.

[133]Sill, II, 6.

[134]Sill, II, 17.

[135]W. H. Furness, *Remarks on the Four Gospels* (Philadelphia, 1836), pp. 60, 113.

[136]Furness, *Remarks on the Four Gospels*, p. 164.

[137]Furness, *Remarks on the Four Gospels*, p. 143.

[138]Furness, *Remarks on the Four Gospels*, p. 144.

[139]Obituary of Furness in *The Christian Register*, February 6, 1896, p. 84.

[140]COLL. CORR. II.

[141]W. H. Furness, *A Discourse delivered January 5, 1851* (n.p., n.d.), p. 4.

[142]Furness to Mary Jenks, July 13, 1839: COLL. CORR. II.

VII

Antislavery Pulpit

PHILADELPHIA WAS BITTERLY HOSTILE TO ABOLITIONISM WHEN Furness began his antislavery preaching. It had not always been so. The first formal protest against slavery in the United States had been made in a memorial drawn up by a group of Germantown Quakers under the leadership of Pastorius in 1688, and in 1780 Pennsylvania was the first state in the Union to adopt an anti-slavery law. Thereafter no child was born into slavery in Pennsylvania and all those then enslaved were freed after they reached the age of twenty-eight. Of the twenty-four antislavery conventions held in the United States from 1794 to 1828, twenty were held in Philadelphia.

"The Pennsylvania Society for promoting the Abolition of Slavery, for the relief of free Negroes, unlawfully held in Bondage, and for improving the Condition of the African Race," founded in Philadelphia in 1775, was the first antislavery society in the United States. It was the best of the state societies, quiet and unspectacular in its methods but tremendously successful in its results. Not only did it secure protective legislation for Negroes; it made certain that the laws worked, checking violations and assisting Negroes in law suits in defense of their legal rights. That which it had accomplished for Pennsylvania it tried to bring about on a national level by petitioning the federal government and distributing antislavery propaganda. Meanwhile it helped Negroes in its own state to find employment and assisted them financially when they were in need. Non-violent but quietly persistent, the society was highly respected and among its members were to be found influential leaders in both local and state affairs. At least two Philadelphia Unitarians belonged to the society, Joseph Todhunter, noted in the *City Directory* of 1829 as a member of its Electing Committee, and Sill a member from 1832 on.

Unfortunately, although Philadelphia bore the name of the City of Brotherly Love, a certain segment of its citizens had always been astonishingly prone to unfraternal violence. They usually found what they considered a worthy cause for their outbursts of rowdyism. During the War for Independence the Quakers had been attacked for their lack of martial fervor, the Tories for their failure to abandon old loyalties in favor of the revolutionary cause. When President Washington objected to the undiplomatic antics of Citizen Genêt, pro-French Philadelphia mobs threatened violence to their erstwhile military hero, while during the period of the XYZ Treaty negotiations President Adams declared:

The multitude in Philadelphia . . . was almost as ripe to pull me out of my house as they had been to dethrone Washington in the time of Genêt. Even the night of the fast-day, the streets were crowded with multitudinous assemblies of the people, especially that before my door, and kept in order only . . . by a military patrol, ordered, I believe, by the Governor of Pennsylvania.[1]

No great international issues were needed, however, to start riots. In 1819, for instance, a balloon which could not ascend at Vauxhall Gardens as advertised caused a mob of 35,000 enthusiasts to lay waste the entire establishment and rob the proprietors of $800. An excuse could always be found. When all other forms of excitement failed, there were always fires to start in order to rush to their extinguishing, a stimulating exercise which could be counted upon to degenerate later into a brawl, and there was always an election in progress somewhere at which heads could be broken or even shooting indulged in.

By 1820 the Negroes had begun to be singled out as the particular victims of mob violence. Up to that point, under the protection of the Pennsylvania Abolition Society and with a generally favorable public opinion, they had made considerable economic progress. They practiced trades, conducted small businesses, and held practically a monopoly in some occupations, most notably in the catering business. In 1814 they owned an estimated $250,000 of city property and five years later their assets were thought to be worth more than $1,000,000. Word of the relatively happy situation of Philadelphia's Negroes inevitably travelled South to their less fortunate brethren and the Quaker City became the goal of fugitives from southern slavery. As the first large city north of the Mason and Dixon Line on the main route of travel between North and South, Philadelphia naturally served as an important station on the Underground Railroad, which functioned with ever increasing efficiency. Unfortunately, however, once they got to Philadelphia, too many of the fugitives stayed there, penniless, untrained, completely unassimilable, swarming together in slums of their own creation. Poverty, idleness, and congestion inevitably produced degeneration and crime, and their general misery was made a charge against the Negroes who were its principal victims.

Fanny Wright's lectures on race equality in 1829 provoked riots in Philadelphia as they had done elsewhere, but by this time no definite excuse was any longer needed to start an outbreak of violence against Negroes. They were attacked in the streets for no reason at all, their property defaced, their homes destroyed. The kidnapping of Negro children for sale in the South had become so serious a threat that in 1827 city councils had felt called upon to adopt punitive legislation for the protection of Negro families. Meanwhile, though it was the mobs who defied the law and broke heads and blasted the lives and hopes of their fellow citizens, many of the "respectable" gave consent by their silence. They resented the growing influx of Negroes as a drain on the city's economy, a threat to its peace, and, not least important, a possible source of alienation from their best customer, the South. Many of Philadelphia's prosperous, upper-class citizens were allied to the South by blood ties or marital alliances as well as by trade and commerce, and they wanted no part in the attacks upon the South which were implicit in all antislavery agitation. This was the position of the majority of the members of the Unitarian Society.

American Unitarians had not rushed into the front ranks of abolitionism. William Ellery Channing, the leader of the denomination, had first preached against slavery in 1830 and had taken up the abolitionist cause in 1835 when he published his book entitled *Slavery*, while several other members of the clergy and many illustrious Unitarian laymen as well entered the struggle. But abolitionism in the 1830's meant Garrisonianism and such activity was complete anathema to most Unitarians. Furness in March, 1835, confided in a letter to a close friend, after meeting the president of the American Anti-Slavery Society at the home of Lucretia and James Mott, "I confess I like Garrison & always had a sneaking feeling in his favour," but he added the pious hope that "His spirit I think will soften with success. Let us do him the utmost possible justice & that will soften his asperities."[2]

Garrison's American Anti-Slavery Society had been organized in Philadelphia in December, 1833, at the Adelphia Building on Fifth Street below Walnut, only five blocks from the Unitarian Church, to an accompaniment of great public disorder, but Furness had made no public comment. Anti-Negro rioting concentrated its most violent outbursts during 1833 and 1834 in the neighborhood between Sixth and Seventh and Walnut and South Streets, but still the Unitarian pastor was silent. A member of the Unitarian Society, Willis H. Blayney, a high constable of Philadelphia, helped to put down the rioting in his official capacity but he heard no reference to his difficulties from the pulpit of his church. Privately, however, Furness was already very much involved in the antislavery struggle. Lucretia Mott wrote to James Miller McKim, a leader of Philadelphia's abolitionists, on May 8, 1834, that "our dear friend, Wm. H. Furness . . . is becoming increasingly interested in the Abolition cause, and we hope it will ere long be with him a pulpit theme."[3] When Harriet Martineau, the English Unitarian reformer, visited Furness in that year, she noted that when the subject of southern slavery was mentioned, "he . . .

turned as pale as ashes," and his countenance became "ghastly."[4] However, though he admitted in March, 1835, "I have been greatly int. in this subject of late," he stated flatly, "I am not going to join any anti-Slavery Socy."[5] He still had his reservations about Garrison, also, but in May, 1837, he decided to subscribe to the *Liberator*, for even "with all its coarseness that paper is like a *living* thing."[6]

The tempo of violence in Philadelphia increased. Charles Godfrey Leland, a member of Furness' church, later said of this period:

Whoever shall write a history of Philadelphia from the Thirties to the end of the Fifties will record a popular period of turbulence and outrages so extensive as to now appear almost incredible. These were so great as to cause grave doubts in my mind whether the severest despotism, guided by justice, would not have been preferable to such republican license as then prevailed in the city of Penn. .[7]

In June, 1836, city councils passed an act providing city funds to reimburse the victims of mob violence for damages to their property and persons. The Commonwealth in 1837, however, yielded to the growing anti-Negro prejudice when the "Reform Convention" added the word "white" to the qualifications for electors in the state constitution. The Unitarian Pierce Butler was a member of this convention.[8] A climax was reached in Philadelphia in May, 1838, when a mob burned down Pennsylvania Hall, built as a meeting-place by the antislavery forces and dedicated but four days before. Furness could restrain himself no longer and on May 20 preached "A Sermon occasioned by the Destruction of Pennsylvania Hall." He still did not plead for the cause of abolition. His concern was for the perilous consequences of mob violence in general.

Whether the Abolitionists are right or wrong, is, comparatively speaking, a small question now. Your dearest liberties, the security of your property and your lives, and, above all, your sacred rights as the intelligent and accountable creatures of God, whose privilege and whose duty it is to think and speak each for himself, upon his own sure and incommunicable responsibility; these have been struck at and violated in their persons, and it is in behalf of these, our common liberties, that I would now speak.[9]

What he knew to be true for others, he soon proved to be true for himself.

When, instead of replying to a man's arguments, you put a torch to his house, or threaten his person with violence, you awaken in him a keen sense of injustice. . . . If he is right, and he feels that he is right, you are taking the surest method to inspire him with a superhuman, divine strength. As you wound his body, and annoy his outward condition, you animate the soul that is in him.[10]

The torch that ignited Pennsylvania Hall awakened Furness from "the sleep of the soul."[11] A year later he fully committed himself to the antislavery struggle and never gave it up until victory was won.

Rarely in human experience is complete unanimity of opinion achieved in group living. There are three ways of looking at everything, three answers to every question: yes, no, and perhaps. The Philadelphia Unitarian Society exhibited all three reactions to Furness' antislavery preaching. Some agreed wholeheartedly; others disagreed violently; many simply listened and waited to see what the more vocal and more assertive would do.

Joseph Todhunter had been a member of the Pennsylvania Abolition Society as early as 1829. On May 31, 1831, the church had taken up a collection for the American Colonization Society, a very unusual procedure for the Unitarians, who were temperamentally "averse to any direct appeal to their charity."[12] Sill was a member of the Pennsylvania Abolition Society from 1832 onward and enthusiastically favored emancipation, but on a gradual basis. When, in March, 1835, he listened to George Thompson, the English abolitionist brought to the United States by Garrison to lecture for the American Anti-Slavery Society, he declared that Thompson's demand for immediate, total emancipation was "unreasonable, and at variance with all the reformations that have ever been effected throughout the whole history of the world."[13]Another member of Furness' congregation, Mrs. Pierce Butler, in 1835 had written an antislavery article but had not dared to publish it in the face of extreme public disapproval. Three years later, when she visited her husband's Georgia plantation, she had recorded all of her horror and pity in her *Journal of a Residence on a Georgian Plantation in 1838–39*, which, however, also remained unpublished because of family pressure, until in 1863 it was issued as a powerful propaganda weapon for the Union cause. Sartain, another member of the congregation, declared in 1892 that he had been an abolitionist in 1835 and had suffered consequences "in various ways extremely damaging."[14]

However, when Furness preached his first sermon on the subject of slavery the Sunday before the Fourth of July in 1839, he declared: "It required all the nerve I've got—There sat P. Butler before me the possessor of some 2 or 300 slaves, Mr. Taylor who apologizes for Slavery under the authority of the N[ew] T[estament]. Mr. Vaughan who cannot bear to hear a word on the subject, & the majority of my congregation—It was not pleasant but painful."[15] Reactions ran the gamut from reverence for the status quo to fear of physical violence, from desire for public approval to anxiety over possible economic losses. Furness summed it all up in lofty terms: "I was regarded as endangering the interests of Unitarian Christianity, which, it was pleaded, had as much as it could do to bear the odium of the Unitarian name without having the added burthen of Abolitionism."[16]

The peace was preserved until January 3, 1841, when Furness' anniversary sermon took up the question of slavery. Sill found the pastor's opinions "very just and strong and independently enforced,"[17] and hoped they would be accepted by the congregation, but this hope was defeated. James Taylor, one of the venerable founders of the society and one of its principal financial pillars, "wrote Mr. Furness a note, in an arrogant tone, demanding to know how far he purposed to go with his obnoxious doctrines, and protesting solemnly against them."[18] Telling Furness that he would do well to "preach *nothing else* but 'Jesus Christ and him crucified,'" Taylor stated that he had no intention of listening to one more word on the subject of slavery and demanded that when Furness proposed to preach such a sermon he notify the congregation in advance so that they might act accordingly.[19] Furness was understandably disturbed that he had antagonized such an influential member of the society, but he was even more upset over what he considered an invasion of his personal liberty. Further, his professional pride was touched to the quick. His flock, or at least a very large part of it, was refusing to follow whither he led.

By May of that year matters had come to an open breach. Furness preached an especially outspoken antislavery sermon on May 14 and less than an hour after he got home from church he received a notice from Samuel Vaughan Merrick that he was withdrawing from the society. Joshua Tevis also publicly declared that he would never enter the church again, and, on May 20, James Taylor notified John Vaughan of his resignation. He did so as much in sorrow as in anger and he never attended another church. Stating that he disapproved of "the introduction of any political matter into the pulpit of a Christian Church," he told Vaughan: "I retire from an attendance on Mr. Furness's ministry with sincere and earnest wishes that the Church may be built up a *spiritual* house; and as my stated attendance in a church of a different faith and worship might be misconstrued, it is not my intention to frequent any other church."[20]

Sill observed in the middle of this outburst that "it is hard to convince people who are determined not to listen, and in this situation are to be found not only a majority of our Church, but a large majority of the people of this Community:—and it seems to me that they will not listen to the slightest whisper on the subject."[21] Furness began to shout. His preaching aroused so much "talk and passion," he confessed, that "really, I was almost sick," but he refused to keep silent.[22] So adept did he become in turning every possible occasion into an opportunity to preach abolitionism that even his devoted sister-in-law, Mary Jenks, asked him how he could "twist" slavery so completely out of its normal context. Furness indignantly retorted: "So far from twisting the subject out of the occasion, I could not, for the life of me, avoid it, much as I wished to avoid it."[23] When Miss Jenks pointed out that all of the family's friends in Medford agreed with her, his only reply was: "Certainly the perversion of the Northern conscience must be greater than I supposed."[24]

The Taylors and the Merricks never returned to membership in the society but Tevis did not make good his threat and returned to carry on the fight from within. A trustee from 1837 to 1843, a prosperous merchant and a man of considerable community prestige, he held a strong vantage-point from which to attack Furness. The pastor's Fourth of July sermon in 1842 "made some strong allusions to the inconsistency of our profess'd Liberty & Freedom, with the fact of holding 3 millions of beings in Slavery," whereupon "several, perhaps 5 or 6, of the Congregation suddenly arose, and left the Church," with Tevis leading the way.[25] Sill had to admit that, coming from church after the service, "10 made objections to 1 who said anything in . . . favour" of the sermon, and the following day he learned that the dissident faction was drawing up a formal protest addressed to the pastor.[26] On July 9 at a meeting of the trustees, Tevis proposed a resolution censuring Furness, but Sill countered by reading from the by-laws of the society that portion which declared that no one had the power "to control or interfere with the Minister in relation to his official duties," and the resolution was tabled. Tevis at the same time withdrew his resignation as a trustee which he had previously offered.

In the first week of August, 1842, a new wave of anti-Negro riots engulfed Philadelphia and Garrison noted that "the only Philadelphia clergyman who made this shocking outbreak the subject of a discourse was the Unitarian William H. Furness."[27] Meanwhile Tevis had asked Sill as secretary of the society to furnish him with a list of members and Sill knew that his purpose was the canvassing of the membership for signatures to the protest. Waiting for the opposition to act wore on Furness' nerves and he seriously considered resigning. Sill expressed this fear to one prominent member of the congregation, who retorted that he thought it would be better for the pastor to resign. The two men parted and strode off in opposite directions, after "other conversation of a warm nature."[28] Sill was furious. "By the folly & perversity of a few white Slaves, we shall lose the presence & services of an excellent conscientious Christian guide," he exploded in his diary.[29]

Furness was also having trouble at home. Mrs. Furness wrote to her sister in September: "I am continually uneasy & unhappy. . . . Sometimes I wish William would give all up & take a small farm in one of the New England states. I am sure we should be happy even if we did have to work very hard."[30] Sill commented on this situation when he discussed the matter of abolition with both of the Furnesses later in the month. "I was sorry to find so little unison between them on this important topic—he has trials, it seems, at home, & abroad; & needs all the support & sympathy of his friends to invigorate his convictions of truth & duty."[31]

Sill himself was attacked in *The Spirit of the Times* on September 29, when he had been appointed to serve as a juror in the damage suit being brought by the proprietors of Pennsylvania Hall, destroyed by the mob in 1838. The writer of the denunciatory article, whom Sill believed to be a member of the church, strongly objected to his appointment, declaring him "one of the most ardent disturbers of the peace of the South and the whole Country, in this matter. His views are well known to all, we presume, who attend Mr. Furness's Church; and he is represented to be the strongest supporter of the Abolitionist discourses delivered by that Gentleman."[32]

The pro-Furness party, led by Sill, John Scholefield, president of the Board of Trustees, and Jacob Snider, Jr., finally grew tired of waiting for the protest of the opposition to be delivered and decided to draw up a paper of its own, a Counter-Paper, to reassure Furness of the continuing loyalty of at least a part of his congregation. They had gathered almost fifty signatures within a few days, when the anti-Furness faction gave up the contest and on September 23 presented its handiwork to Furness. Actually the protest was extremely mild:

We whose names are hereunto subscribed, being pewholders, renters of pews, & occupants of portions of pews in the First Unitarian Church in the City of Philadelphia,—sincerely desirous of maintaining harmony in said Church would respectfully represent our deliberate opinion, before Mr. Furness & the Congregation, and we hereby declare it our conscientious conviction that in the occasional lectures by the Pastor on the subject of *Abolition of Slavery in the South* we perceive no good, present or remote, but on the contrary it sows the seeds of disunion and if continued, we earnestly believe it will greatly injure the Society as a body of Christians, creating hostile parties, where the holier bands of brotherhood should exist—And we do moreover conscientiously believe, that in the course referred to, no good can result to that portion of human beings for whom our sympathies are so earnestly required.[33]

Not Tevis but Hurlbut, strangely enough, turned out to have been the author of the Protest, although Tevis had gladly carried the main responsibility in the matter. Furness was deeply hurt by Hurlbut's defection. Tevis had long made his hostility clear but Hurlbut had given Furness to understand that he favored his position and it was this which most upset the pastor. After six weeks of solicitation, only thirty-nine names appeared on the paper, but they included some of the most influential members of the congregation. Outstanding among them were Evans Rogers, Thomas Mellon, Thomas Sully, Charles Leland, Sampson Tams, Isaac Elliott, James Crissy, and, of course, Hurlbut and Tevis. In the listing of wealthy Philadelphians made in 1845, Evans Rogers was named one of the city's seven millionaires, Tams as the possessor of $200,000, Mellon of $100,000, Crissy, Elliott, and Tevis of $50,000 each. At least seventeen of the thirty-nine signers were merchants, three were exchange brokers, five were retired gentlemen, one a printer and publisher, one a teacher, one an attorney and counsellor. Two had joined the society between 1813 and 1825, six between 1825 and 1828, nineteen between 1828 and 1839, and twelve since 1839.

The Counter-Paper, when it was delivered to Furness on November 2, held seventy-eight names, an exact doubling of the number of signatures on the Protest, which was thought a neat and fitting point at which to stop.[34] Unfortunately, the Counter-Paper has not survived, and it is not known who the faithful seventy-eight were. Furness was reassured, however, that he still had the support, if not the agreement, of a majority of his congregation and he carried on his work. In December, Mrs. Furness told her sister, "I go to church with fear & trembling every Sunday, fearing what I may hear . . . and William strong in the Lord & powerful convictions that he is right not fearing what man can do."[35]

On December 30, 1841, the Unitarian Society lost its oldest and most valued member in the death of John Vaughan, at the age of eighty-five years and eleven months. Charles Godfrey Leland later described the almost legendary character which Vaughan had assumed in the years before his death. "He was a gentle and beautiful old man, with very courtly manner and snow-white hair, which he wore in a queue."[36] He was a link with an age that had gone, keeping alive legends of Priestley, Berkeley, and Thomas Moore, delighting the younger generations with personal reminiscences of Washington, Jefferson, and all the great men of the previous half-century. Furness said of him: "He was my first friend, my first acquaintance in this city, and his first act towards me, at the moment of my arrival, was an act of common but substantial kindness. . . . From the moment that I saw Mr. Vaughan, this city ceased to be the strange place it had appeared in the distance."[37] Vaughan died one of Philadelphia's most well-known citizens. Hundreds of persons, scattered through the world, owed him their pleasantest recollections of the city. "He filled a large space."[38]

Although Vaughan had not agreed with Furness' program of antislavery preaching he had upheld the pastor's right to say what he chose and had not signed the Protest. Hurlbut, the author of that document, died on January 17, 1843, and Furness magnanimously paid a tribute to him in his sermon the following Sunday.[39] Taylor died on April 30, 1844, without ever having reconciled his differences with Furness. Since the pastor was at the time on an extended visit to New England the question of a memorial sermon was not raised but a year later Taylor's name was quietly added to the memorial tablet on the wall of the church where a place had been left for it when the tablet was originally installed in August, 1842. Taylor shared the memorial with two other founders of the society, Birch and Eddowes. Significantly, however, though Birch was cited as "The Benefactor of the Blind" and Eddowes as "A lover of civil and religious liberty," it was noted of Taylor simply that he had died.

Though many were lost to the society by natural causes or in protest against Furness' antislavery preaching, many who had left returned and accepted the course which the pastor had taken. Lucretia Mott wrote to a friend on February 18, 1843: "Wm. H. Furness was threatened for a time with loss to his Church, in consequence of his boldness for truth & right; but some of the absentees are returning to him, & those who remained are enlightened by his faithfulness."[40] Thomas Sully, whose daughter had been married to a southern plantation owner by Furness in 1838,[41] absented himself but returned on April 25, 1847, when his son's funeral service was conducted by Furness. The Merricks did not return, although they remained friends with the Furnesses, at Merrick's request. Some, like the Tevises, came and went as the pastor's sermons grew more or less controversial, and a shifting in the make-up of the congregation became a regular feature of the church's life. It is not known how many were like Sampson Tams, who ordered Sill to sell his pew in January, 1846, using "some very improper and vulgar language about Mr. Furness."[42] Tams was still a member of the society, however, in April, when Tevis, at the annual meeting, opened a direct attack on Furness, introducing a resolution of censure and moving that the pastor's salary be reduced. Tams seconded the motion, but when a vote was taken, only Tevis, Tams, and Mellon upheld the resolution. Sill dubbed them "the glorious Trinity."[43] Fifteen members were opposed, with Elliott refraining from voting.[44]

The church continued to be well filled, as new members came to take the seats left vacant by departed dissidents and many who did not formally join the society were drawn to hear the eloquent preaching of Furness. The pattern of the congregation remained what it had always been, predominantly mercantile, with at least twenty new merchant families added between 1839 and 1846. The leadership of the society was still firmly held by merchants, fifteen of whom served 78 per cent of the trustee terms between 1829 and 1846. Sill was the outstanding member of this group, his service as a trustee extending from 1831 until his death in 1854. Except for a few meetings, he served as secretary from 1831 through 1850.

A very valuable new member was an exchange broker, Enoch W. Clark, whose first recorded connection with the society was the funeral of one of his children on June 11, 1841.[45] His brother-in-law, Edward Dodge, however, had bought a pew in the church two years earlier. Born in East Hampton, Massachusetts, Clark had come to Philadelphia as a very young man and had worked for S. & M. Allen & Co., one of the most prominent banking houses of the early part of the century. Leaving this position, he returned to New England and began his own banking business in Boston, but, this having failed, he returned to Philadelphia in 1836 and in January of the following year established the firm of E. W. Clark & Co. with his brother-in-law, Dodge. The firm was soon highly successful but Clark used his profits from 1837 to 1844 to pay off the debts he had incurred in his Boston venture. Between 1844 and 1856, when he died, however, he was able to amass a considerable fortune. In 1839 he offered a position to the young Jay Cooke, who in 1843 was admitted to the firm, remaining a partner until the Panic of 1857, when he withdrew and established his own business. Clark's oldest son, Edward W., became a partner in the family firm in 1849 and the older man gradually withdrew from the business, which continued to flourish and today still holds a prominent position among the brokerage houses of the city.

Although Fanny Kemble had become a regular attendant at the Unitarian Church after she married Pierce Butler, she had simultaneously ceased to appear upon the stage, and the only other records there were of theatrical people connected with the society were the marriage in 1831 and the funeral in 1836 of James W.

Walstein, described in the church records only as "of the Chestnut Street Theatre," and the purchase of a pew in 1837 by William R. Dinmore, then treasurer of the Chestnut Street Theatre, though listed in the *City Directory* in 1839 as a "gentleman."[46] In April, 1843, however, the very celebrated actress Charlotte Cushman and her brother and sister took sittings in the Unitarian Church.[47] Unfortunately, one Mr. Schroeder, in whose pew the sittings were, refused to sit in the same pew with stage people and, when he learned of the Cushmans' presence one Sunday morning as he was about to enter the church, he stalked indignantly away down the street. His wife went on into the service but took another seat. The day after this performance Schroeder expressed to Sill his regret over the incident, explaining that he had since heard that the Cushmans were very respectable, and hoped that they would not hear of his action, but he still insisted that he wanted another pew. Sill was very much displeased with Schroeder, for he felt that stage folk should be encouraged to attend church.

Actually, Miss Cushman had all of the "proper" Unitarian connections.[48] She was born in Boston, the daughter of a shipping merchant who was a direct descendant of a Pilgrim Father. The Rev. Henry Ware was a close friend of her family and from the age of thirteen to fifteen she had sung at various times in the choirs of all the Unitarian churches in Boston. In the winter of 1842 she undertook the management of the Walnut Street Theatre in Philadelphia, which was much run down but improved greatly under her able management. She was also the leading actress of the resident company, her sister acting with her. When Macready arrived she gave up management to act and study with his company. Many years later, in November, 1874, when Miss Cushman made a farewell appearance in Philadelphia, she indicated no knowledge of the unpleasant incident which had occurred at her first appearance at the Philadelphia Unitarian Church. "In the earlier part of my professional career, Philadelphia was for some time my happy home. Here I experienced privately the greatest kindness and hospitality, publicly the utmost goodness and consideration, and

I never come to Philadelphia without the affectionate feeling that I am coming home, and to my family."[49]

Although the antislavery crusade was the major interest in Furness' life and in the life of the Unitarian Society during this period, the world continued in its regular orbit and much else happened to claim the minds and hearts of the people. Unitarians continued to be active in the American Philosophical Society, of which Furness was elected a member in 1840, in the Historical Society of Pennsylvania, the Athenaeum, the Franklin Institute, and the Academy of Natural Sciences. Elliott became a director of the Philadelphia Museum Company. Pierce Butler and Peter Hulme joined the Philadelphia Society for the Promotion of Agriculture.

In art circles Unitarians were extremely active and well represented, with members serving as directors of the Pennsylvania Academy of the Fine Arts and as members and officers of the Artists' Fund Society, the Artists and Amateurs Association, and the Art Union. Sill was an ardent collector and amateur artist himself and took delight in furthering the careers of professional artists when he could. When the young artist E. G. Leutze was encouraged to go abroad to study in 1840, only Sill and Edward L. Carey gave him advance commissions to make his trip possible, and while Leutze was still in Dusseldorf Sill ordered a picture from him. Furness also collected works of art and he and Sill were constant visitors at the home of Edward Carey to view his new acquisitions. Despite the success of his fellow Unitarian Sully, however, Sill was discouraged about the state of the arts in Philadelphia. In 1843 when he heard of the arrival of a new artist who planned to settle in the city, he declared, "I am afraid that he has come to an unprofitable place for the prosecution of his Art."[50] The topic was much on his mind and a few months later he recorded sadly in his diary: "Philadelphia is not the place for artistic success. Indeed the taste for the Arts seems to be waning away in this City; and with our Commerce we shall lose our refinement also— Something must be done to resuscitate our taste!"[51]

Sill dabbled in writing as well as painting and had at least one story published by *Godey's Lady's Book*, in two parts in October and November, 1842. Furness published a devotional work entitled *Domestic Worship* in 1840 and on the lighter side, in 1843, helped Edward Carey with the literary make-up of *The Gift*, an annual, which was merged with *The Diadem* in 1844. At the same time Furness became the chief editor of the latter, which was discontinued in 1847. Of Furness' general accomplishments in the arts, a colleague, the Rev. Dr. Charles G. Ames, declared:

He was a poetic man in a somewhat prosy city. . . . Probably no person has ever dwelt in the Quaker city since the landing of William Penn who has done so much as Dr. Furness to quicken the aesthetic sense of the community, and thus indirectly to elevate the drama, to promote a taste for the fine arts, and to stimulate an interest in the enrichment of common and household life, even among thousands who never heard his name.[52]

In the world of business Unitarians held positions of prominence, not only as successful merchants, brokers, tradesmen, and artisans but as directors of banks and insurance companies. Samuel Bradford was secretary and treasurer of Little Schuylkill Navigation, Rail Road and Coal Company, of the Philadelphia and Reading Rail Road Company, "and three other corporations." William Blackburn was president of the Washington Mining Company. Three Philadelphia hotels were operated by Unitarians during the period from 1839 to 1846, the Merchants' Hotel, the Franklin House, and the Morris House. The Unitarians were notably prosperous. Charles Godfrey Leland stated that $50,000 "constituted the millionaireism or money aristocracy of those days. On it, with a thriving business, Samuel could maintain a family in good fashion, and above all, in great comfort, which was sensibly regarded as better than fashion or style. Fifty thousand dollars entitled a man to keep a carriage and be classed as 'quality' by the negroes."[53] Of the 683 Philadelphians listed as wealthy citizens according to this classification in 1845, sixteen were of known Unitarian connection. Seven possessed the minimum $50,000, three had $75,000, three had $100,000, one had $200,000, and one was a millionaire.[54]

Unitarians continued to concern themselves with works of philanthropy, both privately and through established organizations. The Society of the Sons of St. George was still dominated by Unitarians, while the "new" German immigration was reflected in Henry Duhring's election as one of the three secretaries of the German Society for the Relief of German Immigrants. In 1841, at the suggestion of Furness, a Charitable Fund was set up at the church, which undertook to collect funds and distribute them in the form of fuel, food, and clothing to the poor of Philadelphia without any distinction. The name of this organization was changed to the Vaughan Charitable Association in 1842 in memory of the departed founder of the church. The ladies of the church organized a Ladies Sewing Circle during the winter of 1842–43 to sew for the poor, and in 1844 this was referred to as the Vaughan Sewing Circle in the annual report of the Vaughan Charitable Association. The Unitarians of those days were apparently finding that "the work of charity is a difficult work,"[55] however, with the recipients thereof not always properly grateful. The 1842–43 report of the Vaughan association admitted that "In almost all cases of poverty and distress there is a presumption at least of ignorance and improvidence, of the want of ability to economize and manage to get on in the world."[56] However, the association felt that more to blame were those wealthy men who were "answerable in a great degree for the existence of those false systems of trade, those artificial commercial arrangements, which by unduly stimulating trade, by diverting it from its natural channels, by disregarding its natural laws, create commercial convulsions and changes, whose disastrous effects fall most heavily upon the poor."[57] This gratuitous attack upon the protectionists indicated that though many of the Unitarians were Whigs, many of them also still clung to the theory of laissez faire. The Sills, meanwhile, proceeded with practical works of charity in an intensely personal way. They visited the poor regularly and the help they gave did not stop at money or good advice. On one occasion, when they found a four-year-old child dying in the home of an English weaver, they took it home with them and cared for it with the greatest tenderness until it died.[58] Another day, visiting a Scottish family living in a miserable hovel, Mrs. Sill arrived just in time to assist in the delivery of a child, who was named Jane Sill Reilly by the grateful parents.[59] Innumerable other instances of simple human goodness are recorded in Sill's diary merely as part of the day's normal activities.

At least one Unitarian was successful in local politics during this period. Elliott served as a member of the Select Council in 1840, 1842, and 1845. In March, 1844, Sill was asked to become a member of the Central Committee of the Liberty party then being organized in Pennsylvania but he refused.[60] His heart and that of many of his fellow Unitarians still belonged to Henry Clay. The author of the 1845 listing of wealthy Philadelphians identified Anderson, Crissy, Elliott, and Fales as "good Whigs," while Dr. Daniel Egbert made his sentiments clear when he named his son, baptized by Furness on November 27, 1842, Harry Clay Egbert.[61] Sill noted that Furness himself voted for Clay in 1844, the first time he had gone to the polls in three or four years.[62] The ladies of the Vaughan Sewing Circle openly declared their devotion when they presented a bouquet to Clay when he visited Philadelphia on February 24, 1848.[63]

Sill was a member of the Executive Committee of the Society for the Abolition of Capital Punishment in 1845. He was also greatly interested in Negro welfare and in October, 1842, attended a meeting at Dr. Caspar Wister's house to consider means of securing the mental and moral improvement of Philadelphia Negroes. The anti-Negro riots of August, 1842, he considered "the work of low Irishmen, who are more degraded than the Blacks themselves,"[64] and later declared that he had found Negro homes cleaner than those of the Irish and English weavers, because as servants the Negroes had learned to be tidy. He found the "rooted hatred" of "the low Irish towards our Negro population . . . almost unaccountable," but "Their conduct is certainly barbarous & blood-thirsty & deserves punishment. . . !"[65] The economic reasons for this antagonism, the necessity for the poor white immigrants to compete with the poor Negroes for the insufficient means of livelihood available at the bottom of the scale, seem to have escaped Sill. This was odd, for 1842 found Philadelphia business at a particularly low ebb and in April of that year Sill had had to borrow money for the first time in his career. When the Nativists began rioting against the Irish in Kensington in May, 1844, the Unitarian Willis H. Blayney was shot in the leg as he "was exhorting those engaged in the fight to leave the ground."[66] Sill at first blamed the Irish for the riots and believed that the native Americans had a right to protect themselves. But then, conscientious man that he was, he procured some books on Ireland and began to read about the situation, and, when the May riots culminated in the burning of St. Augustine's Church, his sympathy, with that of the rest of respectable Philadelphians, turned toward the Irish, and he denounced the Nativists as disgraceful. The rioting continued through June and July, and Sill served in November on a jury dealing with the July riots in Southwark.

Sill deplored violence in any form. He was revolted by what he considered the "brutality" of professional boxing, demonstrated in 1842 in a fight between Lilly and McCoy, which lasted over two hours and 120 rounds, finally causing McCoy's death. Sill chose happier forms of diversion. His family greatly enjoyed a menagerie on an open lot at Thirteenth and Spruce Streets in 1842. Then there was a buffalo hunt with real Indians staged in Camden in September, 1843, which Sill found very tame until one of the buffaloes escaped and ran around in the audience. It was exciting to go down to the wharf on November 5, 1843, and welcome home from the Rocky Mountains the elderly John James Audubon, who brought back with him from the wilderness a live young fawn, a badger, a fox, and many preserved specimens. Two weeks later there was the intellectual treat of listening to a lecture on American poetry by Edgar Allan Poe, whom Sill, however, found conceited, caustic, dogmatical, and censorious. Even the sober business of Sunday school, on the other hand, was rendered glamorous by the scintillating presence there of Fanny Kemble Butler. Furness was sufficiently

stimulated out of his professional imperturbability by this phenomenon to write to his sister-in-law, "Just think of her as a Sunday
School teacher!"[67]

The medical development of mid-nineteenth century generated
a great deal of heat in Sill and Furness. In 1837 the use of animal
magnetism enjoyed tremendous popularity in New England and
Furness became convinced that it held the answer to many ills of
mankind. In 1841 a Mr. Johnson captured the attention of Philadelphia with a series of lectures and exhibitions of animal magnetism at Masonic Hall, and in November the Unitarian publishers,
Kay & Brother, issued—according to the *Public Ledger*, "just in
the nick of time"—"a little volume called 'The Animal Magneti-
zer; or, The History, Phenomena and Curative Effects of Animal
Magnetism, with Instruction for Conducting the Magnetic Operations.'"[68] Furness became particularly enthusiastic about Johnson's
demonstrations and for one whole Saturday evening he subjected
Sill to a discussion of this medical treatment, trying to persuade
him to use it for his ailing oldest son, Joseph. Sill, however, dismissed the new idea as "charlatanry" and "ridiculous quackery."[69]
Two years later Furness was urging him to try the services of W.
H. Rodgers, who mixed phrenology with animal magnetism, and
by this time Sill was so desperate about his son that he had Joseph
"magnetized" several times but the boy continued uncured and
Rogers was dismissed. Sill then declared that he had never believed
in the theory anyway. His own cure for practically everything,
including a sprained leg, was a dose of magnesium and salt. In 1840
Furness believed that a cancer cure had been found when he read a
pamphlet from Leeds, England, claiming that the administration
of a mixture of two-thirds brandy and one-third salt had cured five
out of six patients who took it. Furness gave the formula to a lip
cancer victim, who became "miraculously better" and he planned
to spread the good news to other sufferers.[70]

Furness made almost a holy cause out of his devotion to homeo-
pathic medicine. In 1842 he declared: "We are still as Homeo-
pathic as ever. I acct. it a great blessing to be delivered from the

barbarities of the old school.''[71] Traditional medicine certainly was
barbarous at times, but there were many converts to homeopathy
who backslid under duress. Mrs. Snider became quite ill in 1847
and Furness wrote to his sister-in-law: "Only think Mary she
insisted upon having Dr. Meigs. Poor Mr. Snider how I do pity
him with all his other troubles to be so mortified! Only think after
he has said & done so much for Dr. Herring to have his wife do so
& after she has professed so much faith in homoe—the first time
she is really sick to send for Dr. Meigs. Is it not too bad?''[72] Mrs.
Evans Rogers, suffering from tuberculosis, in 1848 had lost one
lung completely and the other was almost gone. In October she
was confined to her room and not expected to live a week but the
following April Furness reported happily that she was "wonder-
fully well—thanks to Homoeopathy.''[73] She died in June,1852.

Sill's dentist in 1840 was not only a practitioner of animal
magnetism but also a believer in somnambulism. He was not, Sill
noted, a Unitarian but a Swedenborgian. Unfortunately he was
unable to install Sill's false teeth in his mouth so that they would
stay in place more than two months. He assured Sill that ladies
were better at holding in their plates than gentlemen were.

In December, 1845, the First Congregational Society of New
Bedford, Massachusetts, one of the wealthiest and most cultivated
Unitarian congregations in New England, privately invited Furness to become its pastor. Furness discussed the offer only with
his family and with Sill, who assured him that his usefulness was
now greater in Philadelphia than it had ever been. "It was our
opinion also that his sentiments on abolition were no longer pre-
judicial, but were generally honour'd; & that altogether he was as
much appreciated by his people as any Pastor of any denomination.''[74] Furness declined New Bedford's invitation. He preached
for them the following summer, however, and must have shown
a more receptive attitude at that time, for on September 1, 1846,
they followed the unusual procedure of writing simultaneously to
the Philadelphia Society and to Furness, rather than to him alone,
again offering him their pastorate. They openly stated that they

"thought that there might be reasons that would make it seem right to [the Philadelphia Society] that he should come."[75]

Furness put the choice before his people in a letter dated September 15.

Although I am aware that the course, which I believe it to be my duty to pursue in relation to a certain obnoxious subject, has met the disapproval of many, probably of a majority of my people, yet my confidence in the personal goodwill and friendship of those who have continued to attend on my ministry, and even of some who have withdrawn themselves from it, has continued unimpaired.[76]

He had not believed that any of his congregation wanted him to leave, but obviously rumors of such dissatisfaction must have reached New Bedford and he desired to know how matters stood. He stated plainly, "I have not the shadow of a desire to leave you."[77] At a meeting held on September 28, the congregation replied that it considered "the permanent good of this Religious Society to be intimately connected with the pastoral labours and private virtues of . . . our beloved Pastor" and asked him to decline the New Bedford offer.[78] Furness said of the printed version of these proceedings that it was "like a love letter."[79] The final vote was three hundred to three in favor of his retention, with only "the glorious trinity"—Tevis, Tams, and Mellon—in the negative. There was some question in Sill's mind as to whether Furness might have maneuvered the congregation into the position of having to vote upon the basic issue, which was not whether or not he should go to New Bedford but whether or not he should be free to continue his antislavery preaching in Philadelphia. In any case, the New Bedford episode did bring to a decisive conclusion this phase of the society's life. Thenceforward, though there continued to be occasional murmurs of disagreement, there was no serious questioning of Furness' course.

There was nothing startlingly original about Furness' antislavery arguments. As a Christian he found slavery contrary to Divine Law. As a humanitarian he deplored the physical, moral, and spiritual cruelty inflicted by slavery upon the enslaved. As a moralist he hated the degradation worked by slavery upon those who practiced it and those who tolerated its practice by others. As a patriot he was ashamed of the national hypocrisy and deceit of which the United States stood convicted in the eyes of the world when it boasted of its commitment to the ideals of freedom and at the same time permitted the continued existence of slavery within its boundaries.

Although he had initially been repelled by Garrison's "asperities," he finally became convinced that Garrison was one of those "with large and fiery hearts" who occasionally come upon the earth to lead the way to Right, and he took an atypical position for a Unitarian upon the Garrisonian approach to abolition.[80] "We may ridicule and despise enthusiasm and call it by all sorts of disparaging names," he told his congregation in 1851, "yet it is the life and hope of mankind, the central and moving power."[81] Garrison recognized in Furness a powerful ally and frequently paid eloquent tribute to him in the pages of *The Liberator*. Like Garrison, Furness considered the Declaration of Independence the basic document in the struggle for freedom, by which Americans "are irretrievably committed to the cause of universal emancipation."[82] He did not, however, follow Garrison to the point of advocating anarchy and as a clergyman he naturally disagreed with Garrison's decision to scrap religion altogether.

Furness believed that abolitionism was "a profoundly religious movement"[83] but he was never identified with the Theodore Weld group of abolitionists. In 1863 he said that he had once listened to Weld "with the greatest delight" and thought him "a high style of man,"[84] but there is no record that they had any other contact and Furness clearly despised the revivalistic spirit which Weld personified. When Philadelphia was seized by an evangelical outburst in 1858, sponsored by the newly organized Young Men's Christian Association, Furness excoriated the revivals as a paroxysm, "wasting the religious feeling of this generation," and prayed that "God, in his mercy, may bury it deep beyond the possibility of a resurrection."[85] He opposed Weld's program of political action, furthermore, as thoroughly as he disliked his revivalistic religion. In 1844 he refused to become a member of the Central Committee of the Liberty party then being organized in Pennsylvania on the grounds of his opposition to political measures for abolition. "Legislation in this country can do little or nothing," he insisted, "if the governing spirit among all classes is hostile to it,"[86] and he was convinced that the Garrisonians had the best program for the arousing of public opinion in favor of emancipation.

Actually, however, in spite of their differences in philosophy and program, Furness was more like Weld than he was like Garrison. Like Weld, Furness was endowed with overwhelming personal charm and even those who disagreed with him usually liked him, while Garrison, on the other hand, had a particular genius for making enemies and alienating friends. Furness never indulged in invective, of which Garrison was a master. Furness gave the soft answer which turned away wrath. He preached more and more to the already converted, for those whom he most earnestly wanted to reach to convince them of their wrong thinking and action in regard to slavery removed themselves from the congregation and did not return. One exception was Evans Rogers, but his singularity was apparently so notable that a memorial tablet was erected to him in the church by the pastor's son Horace, because he had "in the dark days of slavery and with ties binding him to the South, steadfastly upheld the unrestricted Liberty of Speech in the Pulpit, whereby a moral support of rare value was afforded to the Minister."[87]

Though it may be doubted that Furness converted any slaveholders to the cause of abolition, he enjoyed a tremendous personal success with the like-minded and his devoted followers continued to increase in numbers. It is reasonably certain that his antislavery preaching rather than Unitarianism was the key to much of this growth, for Furness' religion never shared his outstanding popularity in Philadelphia. The Rev. Dr. Joseph Belcher in a history of *The Religious Denominations in the United States*, published in Philadelphia in 1864, said of the Philadelphia Society: "Its congregation is highly respectable; but if the high classical attainments, and general amiable disposition of the Rev. W. H. Furness, D.D., its pastor, could insure a congregation, it would be very much larger than it is. Unitarianism never flourished greatly in Philadelphia."[88]

NOTES

CHAPTER VII

[1]Adams, IX, 279.

[2]Furness to Lucy Osgood, March 30, 1835: OSGOOD CORR.

[3]Hallowell, p. 119.

[4]Harriet Martineau, *Autobiography* (Boston, 1877), I, 340.

[5]Furness to Lucy Osgood, March 30, 1835:OSGOOD CORR.

[6]Furness to Lucy Osgood, May 16, 1837: OSGOOD CORR.

[7]Leland, p. 216.

[8]Kemble, *Records of Later Life*, p. 71.

[9]W. H. Furness, *A Sermon occasioned by the Destruction of Pennsylvania Hall, and delivered . . . May 20, 1838* , . . (Philadelphia, 1838), p. 5.

[10]Furness, *Sermon occasioned by the Destruction of Pennsylvania Hall*, pp.8–9.

[11]Furness, *Sermon occasioned by the Destruction of Pennsylvania Hall*, p.10.

[12]Sill, II, 45.

[13]Sill, I, 396–97.

[14]Sartain, p. 229.

[15]Furness to Lucy Osgood, July 7, 1839: OSGOOD CORR.

[16]Furness, *Robert Collyer and His Church*, p. 6.

[17]Sill, II, 326.

[18]Sill, II, 334–35.

[19]Sill, II, 335.

[20]Taylor to Vaughan, May 20, 1841: MSS, APS.

[21]Sill, III, 51.

[22]Furness to Mary Jenks, May 24, 1841: COLL. CORR. II.

[23]Furness to Mary Jenks, June 2, 1841: COLL. CORR. II.

[24]Furness to Mary Jenks, June 2, 1841: COLL. CORR. II.

[25]Sill, IV, 32.

[26]Sill, IV, 34, 37.

[27]Wendell Phillips Garrison and Francis Jackson Garrison, eds., *William Lloyd Garrison, 1805–1879* (Boston, 1885), III, 45.

[28]Sill, IV, 73.

[29]Sill, IV, 73.

[30]Letter to Mary Jenks, September 2, 1842: COLL. CORR. II.

[31]Sill, IV, 110.

[32]*Spirit of the Times*, September 29, 1829; Sill, IV, 108.

[33]The Protest was given to the First Unitarian Church by Furness' daughter, Mrs. Caspar Wister, shortly after his death. The signers were: James Allen, William V. Anderson, William H. Bernard, S. H. Carpenter, E. W. Clark, E. L. Colcord, Thomas Cook, Charles S. Cope, James Crissy, George F. Croft, Edward Dodge, Isaac Elliott, Hugh English, James English, William H. Evans, Samuel, C. Ford, Isaac Heylin, David Hill, William T. Howell, M. L. Hurlbut, Charles Leland, Z. Lathrop, Robert McGregor, Thomas Mellon, R. B. Parkinson, Algernon S. Roberts, William E. Rogers, Thomas Sully, Sampson Tams, Joshua Tevis, Charles J. Thomas, Jacob Thomas, Joseph M. Thomas, Charles Toppan, John Towne, Daniel C. Wharton, George W. A. Williams, John Yarrow.

[34]Sill, IV, 138.

[35]Letter to Mary Jenks, December 20, 1842: COLL. CORR. II.

[36]Leland, p. 4.

[37]W. H. Furness, *A Discourse delivered on the occasion of the Death of John Vaughan,* . . . *January 16, 1842* . . . (Philadelphia, 1842), p. 3.

[38]Furness, *Discourse on the Death of John Vaughan,* p. 14.

[39]Sill, IV, 227.

[40]Hallowell, p. 241.

[41]Ellen Sully married Colonel Wheeler, whose slaves were to be involved in the Passmore Williamson case in Philadelphia in 1855. Furness to Lucy Osgood, November 4, 1855: OSGOOD CORR.

[42]Sill, VI, 469.

[43]The official account of this meeting appears in RECS & MINS, pp. 142–43, but Sill's account in his "Diary," VII, 58–59, tells the "inside" story, with thumbnail sketches and Sill's opinions of his fellow Unitarians. Furness stopped at Sill's store the morning after the meeting to get the details of the previous night's "strange and mortifying occurrences," which upset him greatly.

[44]Those upholding Furness were: Allen, Robert H. Beresford, Bernard, Bradford, George Fletcher, Hamilton, Haseltine, Simon P. Hastings, Walter R. Johnson, Lewis Moore, Porter, Sill, Snider, Jacob Thomas, Toppan, and Wood.

[45]REG I, [208]. Sketches of Clark's life are in Scharf and Westcott, III, 2100-101, and Oberholtzer, *City History,* II, 189.

[46]REG I, 99, [206]; UNNAMED, p. 28.

[47]Sill, IV, 305–6.

[48]This account is based on Emma Stebbins, ed., *Charlotte Cushman, Her Letters and Memoirs of Her Life* (Boston, 1878).

[49]Stebbins, p. 267.

[50]Sill, V, 98.

[51]Sill, V, 198.

[52]Ames, p. 3. Ames was pastor of the Germantown Unitarian Society in Philadelphia, 1872–77, and of the Spring Garden Society, 1880 and 1888.

[53]Leland, pp. 33–34.

[54]*$50,000:* Estate of Astley, William P. Bryan, Crissy, Elliott, Gill, Patten, Tevis; *$75,000:* Anderson, Fellowes, Estate of Taylor; *$100,000:* Fales, Mellon, Stone; *$200,000:* Sampson Tams; *millionaire:* Evans Rogers.

[55]RECS & MINS, p. 125.

[56]RECS & MINS, p. 126.

[57]RECS & MINS, p. 127.

[58]Sill, VI, 113–31.

[59]Sill, VI, 138–39.

[60]Sill, V. 194.

[61]REG I, 18.

[62]Sill, V, 431.

[63]Sill, VII, 131.

[64]Sill, IV, 60.

[65]Sill, IV, 61.

[66]*A Full and Complete Account of the late Awful Riots in Philadelphia* (Philadelphia, 1844), pp. 15, 19.

[67]Furness to Lucy Osgood, April 18, 1844, 1844: OSGOOD CORR.

[68]Philadelphia *Public Ledger,* November 1, 1841.

[69]Sill, III, 182.

[70]Furness to Lucy Osgood, December 14, 1840: OSGOOD CORR.

[71]Furness to Mary Jenks, July 24, 1842: COLL. CORR. II.

[72]Furness to Mary Jenks, December 19, 1847: COLL. CORR. II.

[73]Furness to Mary Jenks, April 18, 1849: COLL. CORR. II.

[74]Sill, VI, 431.

[75]*Proceedings of a Meeting of the Members and Pew-Holders . . . Held on the 28th September, 1846* (Philadelphia, 1846), p. 7.

[76]*Proceedings . . . 28th September, 1846,* p. 8.

[77]*Proceedings . . . 28th September, 1846,* p. 9.

[78]*Proceedings . . . 28th September, 1846,* p. 13.

[79]Furness to Lucy Osgood, February 8, 1847: OSGOOD CORR.

[80]W. H. Furness, *The Moving Power. A Discourse delivered . . . February 9, 1851 . . .* (Philadelphia, 1851), p. 6.

[81]Furness, *The Moving Power,* p. 8.

[82]W. H. Furness, *Two Discourses occasioned by the Approaching Anniversary of the Declaration of Independence. Delivered June 24, . . . and July 2, . . . 1843* (Philadelphia, 1843), p. 16.

[83]W. H. Furness, *A Discourse occasioned by the Boston Fugitive Slave Case* (Philadelphia, 1851), p. 13.

[84]Furness to Lucy Osgood, October 10, 1863: OSGOOD CORR.

[85]W. H. Furness, *The Revivals. A Discourse delivered . . . April 11, 1858* (Philadelphia, 1858), pp. 9, 14.

[86]W. H. Furness, *A Discourse delivered . . . January 19, 1840 . . . Occasioned by the Loss of the Lexington* (Philadelphia, 1840,) p. 5.

[87]*Church Memorials,* p. 6. Horace Howard Furness had married Rogers' daughter Helen Kate on June 12, 1860: REG I, 117.

[88]P. 761.

VIII

The Eminent Allies

WITH THE BEGINNING OF THE MEXICAN WAR, FURNESS ADDED A new theme to his sermons and began preaching against the evils of war as well as slavery. He found it "a fact clear, unquestioned, unquestionable" that the waging of war and the extension of slavery were in direct disobedience to the commandments of Christ and he declared that the nation's yielding to the demands of the slaveholders in the war on Mexico was "flat rebellion against Heaven . . . downright atheism."[1] He deplored the "national corruption" which had made the war possible and regretted "the curse of [the] victories which provoke the appetite for conquest."[2] In November, 1847, he varied his annual Thanksgiving Day attack on slavery by presenting to his congregation at the end of his sermon a memorial to Congress, protesting against the war. He invited all those who wished to sign the petition to come to the pulpit and do so. Twenty answered the call but the petition then bore a total of one hundred and twenty names, as Sill had been obtaining signatures for it the day before at Furness' request.

For Furness these were days of "political degeneracy" and for politics and professional politicians he had nothing but contempt. "There is not a man of any intelligence and observation," he declared, "who does not see what poor things our political parties are, by what self-seeking management they are ruled, and how their zeal is inflamed by the forgetfulness of truth, and by the most ruthless mutual denunciations."[3] When John Quincy Adams died, he bestowed upon him the supreme accolade when he said that "no party could ever depend on him."[4] The Unitarian Society hastened to offer its church as a resting-place for Adams' body on its journey home but this was declined in favor of Independence Hall.

"The politicians, like the monkey in the fable," Furness told his congregation in 1849, "take the oyster and give the shells to the country."[5] He held them responsible for hurling the nation into the Mexican War, "that abyss of blood and wrong,"[6] and he was delighted when the Free Soilers in 1849 were able to halt the machinery of the national government by preventing the election of a speaker in the House. For him this meant simply that "a right principle has become strong enough in its councils to prevent its moving any longer in a wrong direction."[7]

Furness never joined an antislavery society and it was not until December 19, 1849, that he made his first speech to an antislavery meeting, addressing on that occasion the Pennsylvania Anti-Slavery Society. In May the following year he was one of the scheduled speakers at the Annual Meeting of the American Anti-Slavery Society in New York and shared the platform with such abolitionist leaders as Garrison, Wendell Phillips, Edmund Quincy, Isaac Hopper, Francis Jackson, and Frederick Douglass. Furness later looked back upon this meeting as the most memorable and moving of his antislavery experiences. A hostile press presented the meeting in a ridiculous light and its participants were made to look like fools, but Furness considered this "a cheap price to pay for the privilege of witnessing such a triumph."[8] His friends in Philadelphia, however, were "all greatly mortified at my being mixed up with Garrison, Phillips & Douglas, etc."[9] and many stayed away from church for several Sundays following. Furness "had hardly given a thought to the effect at home, so full was I of the interest and glory of the occasion,"[10] but he decided that the excitement of the New York meeting had been too much for him. "It won't do . . . for me to participate in such scenes," he wrote to a friend on May 20. "I am just getting over the terrible headaches (a new complaint for me) which that occasion caused. I cannot talk long, I can't preach without bringing on a pain in my

head which is very severe."[11] During that summer his physical and
mental tension was commented upon by a total stranger, the
Swedish writer Fredrika Bremer, who occupied a cottage next to
his at Cape May, New Jersey. "Mr. F. . . . is the minister of a
Unitarian congregation in Philadelphia, one of the noblest, purest
human beings whom God ever created, true, fervent, and full of
love, but so absorbed by his anti-slavery feelings that his life and
mind suffer in consequence. . . ."[12]

Philadelphia's proslavery sympathizers grew increasingly vocal.
A "Great Union Meeting" was held in the large salon of the
Chinese Museum on November 21, 1850, "under a call signed by
upwards of 5,000 citizens."[13] John Sergeant presided and the
speakers included George M. Dallas, who denounced the "imported fanaticism" of the abolitionists, Josiah Randall, who pleaded
for "our Southern friends," and James Page, who bluntly suggested
that the North mind its own business. At least eight men of Unitarian connection signed the call: George Fales, Isaac Elliott, Jr.,
Charles Desilver, George W. Fairman, Kay & Brother, Sampson
Tams, and Jacob Snider, Jr. During the same year Philadelphia
publishing distinguished itself by refusing the manuscript of *Uncle
Tom's Cabin* and Godey ejected "Grace Greenwood" from his list
of contributors because of her antislavery views. *Graham's Magazine*, in a vituperative review of *Uncle Tom's Cabin*, declared that
"The shelves of booksellers groan under the weight of Sambo's
woe done up in covers! . . . We hate this niggerism, and hope it
may be done away with."[14] Charles Godfrey Leland said of this
period in Philadelphia that "everything Southern was exalted and
worshipped."[15]

The Fugitive Slave Law of 1850 provoked Furness to new extremes of protest. In October he announced from the pulpit his intention to oppose the law, regardless of what happened to him as a result,
and called upon all Christians to do the same. This sermon offended
many and there were new absences from the congregation as a
result. Furness carried his threat into action, however, and became
exceedingly concerned in the operations of the Underground

Railroad. William Still, the corresponding secretary of the Vigilance Committee of the Railroad, testified that "In the operation of the Vigilance Committee [Furness] took the liveliest interest. Though not in form a member he was one of its chief co-laborers. He brought it material aid continually, and was one of its main reliances for outside support."[16] As one of the main stations in the network created to assist escaping slaves, Philadelphia was hard hit by the Fugitive Slave Law. Furness wrote to Mary Jenks in April, 1851: "You can have no idea of the suffering which the Fugitive Slave Law is producing among the colored people in this neighborhood. Case after case has occurred of black persons kidnapped & dragged away in the night without even a form of law."[17] At the trials which were held Furness became a familiar figure among the anti-slavery workers in the area, who always attended in full force. On August 25, 1852, he was among the "eminent divines" who wrote to Charles Sumner, congratulating him for his speech in the Senate against the Fugitive Slave Act.[18]

Sill noted in February, 1854, that many strangers seemed to be coming to church on Sunday. The pews were always well filled and the congregation gave Furness its rapt attention. Continuing the pattern established by the founders and maintained down through the years, the leaders of the society were well-to-do, upper middle-class citizens, prominent in business, patrons of the arts, distinguished for good works. They supported the Society of the Sons of St. George and the Pennsylvania Institution for the Blind, traditionally major interests of the Unitarians, and served in various capacities the House of Refuge, the County Prison, and the Office of the Guardians of the Poor. They assisted in the founding of the Rosine Association in 1847, established "to rescue from vice and degradation that class of women who have forfeited their claims to the respect of the virtuous."[19] They joined the Athenaeum, the Philadelphia Society for the Promotion of Agriculture, the Pennsylvania Horticultural Society, the Academy of Natural Sciences, the Franklin Institute. At the American Philosophical Society an old Unitarian tradition was re-established in 1858, when a member of the Philadelphia fellowship was elected Librarian, the post held for almost forty years by Vaughan.

As befitted men of strongly intellectual temperament, several Unitarians held positions of importance in the field of education, one a professor in the city's high school, two directors of Girard College, one the treasurer of the Female Medical College of Philadelphia, two professors at the University of Pennsylvania. Three were engaged in scientific activity of great importance, two publishing outstanding works before 1861, while the pastor of the society continued to gain fame for his theological writings and began publishing translations from the German. Furness was one of the first American scholars to study and translate German literature, assisting Frederick H. Hedge in the preparation of *Prose Writers of Germany*, published in 1849. In recognition of his leadership in this field, when the centennial of Schiller's birth was celebrated in Philadelphia in 1859, with fireworks and illuminations and a torchlight parade by the German population of the city, the Unitarian pastor was chosen to deliver the English oration at the climax of the festivities at the Academy of Music.

Unitarianism in Philadelphia, however, was distinguished by no "flowering" of the creative arts such as had been coincident with the prospering of Boston Unitarianism. Philadelphia Unitarians were patrons of the arts, not creative artists. Illustrious exceptions were Sully, at this time considered the leading portrait painter in the United States, Childs and the Sartains, father and son, distinguished engravers, but the congregation at Tenth and Locust Streets in the pre-Civil War years contained no other artists, no poets, no novelists, no creative musicians of first stature. The young William Henry Furness, Jr. was showing promise as a portrait painter but was still a novice. His father also painted and wrote occasional verses and hymns which were pleasant and "elevating" but little more. Sill produced a few tales, ground out labored doggerel, most of which remained mercifully hidden in the pages of his diary, and ploddingly executed portraits of his family. But the real creative strength of the Philadelphia Unitarians lay elsewhere. They were pre-eminently men of action in the business world and in this world they held conspicuous places. Seventeen were directors of banks, eleven of insurance companies. Several took an active part in the development of Pennsylvania's coal and iron resources, established steamship companies, promoted the extension of the Commonwealth's canal system. Participating in the burgeoning growth of rail transportation, two Unitarians were railroad presidents, one a secretary and treasurer, one a general superintendent, four directors. Unitarians were also more actively concerned in practical politics during the prewar years than they had been previously. One of them served six terms on the Select Council of the city, another four. Three served on the Common Council, one of them as president in 1854. Philadelphia's most prominent Unitarian in politics at this time, however, was William D. Kelley, who was beginning to rise in the new Republican party and in 1860 started a spectacular congressional career in Washington.

The English tradition of Philadelphia Unitarianism was stoutly maintained. Many native Englishmen in the society still lived in two worlds, closely bound to England by family and business ties while they made their way in America. In April, 1846, Sill objected violently to the suggestion made at a meeting of the Society of the Sons of St. George that the President of the United States be toasted before the Queen of England and noted regretfully, "We have got very little loyalty left among us."[20] Even Furness, however, a third-generation American and native of Boston, was strongly Anglophile and believed that, "so far as mere blood goes, the most promising fact in the history of our own country is, that we are sprung from Englishmen."[21]

The New England element in the congregation also continued to wax strong but in 1846 Furness declared that the church was "made up to an unusual degree out of the native population of this vicinity."[22] A further comment upon the nature of the congregation at this time was made by William D. Kelley, a new member himself, who called attention to the number of young men who were attending the evening services, "young men of other congregations, freed from family restraint, who gather into our Church in the evening, to be warmed into hope and life by the glowing truths that fall from our Pastor's lips."[23] Kelley himself had been reared in the Calvinistic faith but had left it when he felt that its teachings were false to the joyous truths of American life. For many years he had been without a church home but had finally accepted Unitarianism as the faith congenial to his spirit. He had travelled the path trod by Taylor fifty years before and it is probable that he had company on his journey.

Apparently the atmosphere of Philadelphia had mellowed somewhat in the half-century since the Unitarian Society had first met, for it was felt feasible to invite the national Unitarian Convention to meet there in October, 1846, the minds of the people "from various causes [being] favorably disposed towards the reception of the simple truths of Christianity as promulgated in the precepts and the practices of Unitarian Christians."[24] When the Convention met there were five hundred persons present at the collation offered on October 10, including twenty-five clerical delegates but representatives from many other religious denominations in the city as well.

In 1852 and 1853 the existence of a Second Unitarian Church at Locust and Schuylkill Eighth Streets was noted in the *City Directory* but no further information concerning it has been located. There had been earlier attempts to found a second Unitarian Society in Philadelphia. In 1835 a group had planned to gather every Sunday afternoon for Unitarian worship in a room over the Northern Liberties Reading-Room. Two years later "some twenty individuals, worthy good people," were gathered together by a Rev. Mr. Holland, seemingly without any connection with the 1835 organization.[25] Mr. Holland's expenses had been paid by the American Unitarian Association, but, according to Mrs. Furness, his people tired of him and he decided to leave Philadelphia. The meetings continued with the Rev. Mr. Sweat, "under whose ministrations the Society increased, and had good promise of permanent success,"[26] but unfortunately Mr. Sweat was called back to New England. He was succeeded by a Rev. Mr. Eustice, who continued about a year, at the end of which time the society had so diminished that it was disbanded. It had lasted about four years.

In 1859 another attempt was made to establish a second society, meetings of substantial size being held at Handel and Haydn Hall at Eighth and Green Streets. The Rev. John K. Karcher was called in 1860 to be its pastor for one year but, according to the only available source of information, Karcher "was not an attractive preacher and unfortunately had no ability or stability."[27] There was a rapid decrease in the attendance and at the end of eleven months Karcher left. The society was continued, however, with supply preachers sent from New England by the American Unitarian Association. During the winter of 1861 the Rev. T. T. Stone and the Rev. Frederick K. Frothingham each preached there for three months, and in September, 1862, William L. Chaffin, after preaching in the spring as a candidate for settlement, was installed as pastor. Meetings were then held in Washington Hall at Eighth and Spring Garden Streets. It is not certain how long this group survived, but "The congregation never made any progress,"[28] and, when the Rev. Charles G. Ames began his efforts in 1876 which led to the establishment of the Spring Garden Society, the project was spoken of as a new undertaking.

In the parent society itself by 1860 there were seventy-five families and fifty-seven individuals regularly contributing to its support. Continuing the congregation's tradition, at least twenty-five of those who became affiliated with the society between 1846 and 1861 were merchants. Of the thirty-nine men who served a total of 112 terms as trustees between 1846 and 1861, twenty-nine were merchants, who served eighty-one terms or 72 per cent of the total.

Second generation Philadelphia Unitarians assumed positions of importance in the community in their own right during this period. Samuel Sartain, son of John Sartain, born in Philadelphia on October 8, 1830 and baptized by Furness the following month, began the practice of engraving on his own account in 1851.[29] Having studied under his father and at the Pennsylvania Academy of the Fine Arts, he came to be considered the leading portrait engraver in Philadelphia, both in mezzotint and line engraving on steel, his best work being done after Sully, Peale, and Neagle. By the end of the century it was said that he had probably engraved more portraits on steel than all other engravers combined, especially for the biographical encyclopaedias of the preceding twenty-five years.

Fairman Rogers, son of Evans and Caroline Fairman Rogers, grandson of Gideon Fairman, was a descendant of Philadelphia Unitarians on both sides of his family.[30] Born in 1833, the only son of the millionaire retired hardware merchant, he led a charmed life, possessing not only wealth and good looks but an attractive personality and intelligence of a high order as well. The Rogers family had a long Pennsylvania ancestry and Fairman was one of the few Philadelphia Unitarians of this period to matriculate at the University of Pennsylvania,[31] from which he graduated in 1853. He married a Philadelphia Unitarian, Rebecca H., daughter of John F. Gilpin of the society. In 1855 he was made professor of civil engineering and survey at the University of Pennsylvania, becoming in addition, in 1859, dean of the Faculty of the Department of Mines, Arts, and Manufactures, which he remained, through a series of reorganizations of the division and a change in its name, until his resignation in June, 1871. He was elected a trustee in May, 1871, serving his alma mater actively in that capacity until his resignation in March, 1876. In 1878 he gave a magnificent library to the university in memory of his father. In 1880, when Provost Stillé resigned, Rogers was offered the provostship but declined. Always devoted to the university, Rogers was one of the original promoters of the Saturday Club, a gathering which developed the idea of the Union League, and at which, it was reported jokingly, "half the affairs of the University were transacted."[32]

When Rogers was elected to membership in the American Philosophical Society at the age of twenty-four, he was the youngest member ever to have been elected. In 1861 he did three months' duty with the First City Troop, of which he was made a captain after the Civil War, and he served as a volunteer engineer officer with the Pennsylvania militia during the Antietam and Gettysburg campaigns. He was one of the fifty original members of the National Academy of Sciences when it was founded in 1863 and in 1871 was elected a director of the Pennsylvania Academy of the Fine Arts, in which latter capacity he served for twelve years. From 1855 to 1864 he lectured on mechanics at the Franklin Institute, and was connected with the United States Coast and Geodetic Survey at various times during his career. A voluminous writer on engineering and mechanical subjects, his *Treatise on Terrestrial Magnetism and on the Magnetism of Iron Vessels*, published in 1877, was used as a text book at the United States Naval Academy for many years. An avid devotee of riding and coaching, he published in 1899 his *Manual of Coaching*, still another proof of the great diversity of his interests and talents.

Another Philadelphia Unitarian became a professor at the University of Pennsylvania during the pre-Civil War decade. J. Peter Lesley was born in Philadelphia on September 17, 1819, of the third generation of his family to be born there, the family having originally come from Scotland.[33] Like Rogers, Lesley attended the University of Pennsylvania, graduating in 1838. The following year his appointment as a sub-assistant to Professor Henry D. Rogers in the First Geological Survey of Pennsylvania started him on the career for which he became famous. He held the title of Assistant State Geologist of Pennsylvania from 1839 to 1841. Raised in a highly religious Presbyterian home, he decided to enter the ministry and spent three years at the Princeton Divinity School, being licensed as a minister by the Philadelphia Presbytery in 1844. He spent the next year studying at the University of Halle in Germany and the following year as a colporteur for the American Tract Society in the hinterland of Pennsylvania. He returned to his geological work with a year in Boston again assisting Professor Rogers, and again turned to theology, undertaking parish work for the First Evangelical Church of Milton, Massachusetts, from 1848 to 1851.

Lesley's father was much concerned about his son's spiritual welfare from the beginning of his stay in "the cold Unitarian atmosphere of Boston,"[34] but, even though the son preached one Sunday in June, 1847, for James Freeman Clarke, he assured his father that there was nothing to fear. In 1849, however, he was married by a Unitarian minister, Rufus Ellis, to Susan Lyman, daughter of Judge Joseph Lyman of Northampton, an ardent Unitarian herself and the inheritor of a tradition of staunch devotion to that faith. As late as October, 1850, Lesley continued to reassure his father, nonetheless, that he could never become a Unitarian, because "I never come into close contact with Unitarians, but I am chilled and repelled."[35] It is assumed that this did not include his wife or her family, nor could it have included the Furness brothers, William Henry and James, who were among the first friends the Lesleys had in their new home when Lesley brought his wife to Philadelphia to live in 1852.

By 1851 Lesley had finally decided, after much alternating between his two vocations, that he preferred geology to the ministry and resigned his pastorate at Milton. Within a decade he established his reputation as a working geologist of the first rank and thereafter devoted himself to a series of geological projects, in the most famous of which, the Second Geological Survey of Pennsylvania, he was engaged up until the time of his last illness. He was made the state geologist of Pennsylvania, heading the survey, in 1884.

In 1856 Lesley was elected a member of the American Philosophical Society and two years later was elected librarian, the position held by Vaughan from 1803 to 1841. Lesley retained this post until 1885, served as a secretary from 1859 to 1886, and as a vice-president from 1887 to 1897. In 1859 he was appointed professor of mining at the University of Pennsylvania, relieving Fairman Rogers of one of his assignments, and in 1872 this title was changed to professor of geology and mining, which he remained until 1885, when he became an emeritus professor. In 1872 he added to his professorship the position of dean of the Department of Science, which was named the Towne Scientific School in 1875, after it became the residuary legatee of the estate of John H. Towne. Towne had been a partner of Samuel Vaughan Merrick and a member of the Unitarian Society, but the last record of his connection with the society had been his signature on the antislavery Protest in 1842.

Extant sources do not indicate the exact date when Lesley began his active participation in the affairs of the Philadelphia Unitarian Society. His wife was an enthusiastic member from the beginning of her residence in the city and by 1857 her husband's letters indicate a close familiarity with its people. By 1859 at the latest he was paying pew rent. When, in 1876, their close friend, the Rev. Charles G. Ames, then minister of the Germantown Unitarian Church, began the series of Sunday evening lectures out of which was to develop the Spring Garden Unitarian Society, both of the Lesleys threw themselves into the new enterprise with enthusiasm. They were among the eleven signers of the petition for a charter for the new society, which was granted June 18, 1881. Although they never completely gave up their association with the First Church because of their friendship with Furness and his successor, the Rev. Joseph May, they gradually turned to the Spring Garden Society as their own, Mrs. Lesley serving as a member of its Board of Trustees for many years.

Another famous geologist, Richard C. Taylor, was connected with the Philadelphia Unitarian Society during this period, according to Sill, who referred to Taylor when he died in Philadelphia in 1851 as having been a member of the church.[36] Taylor was born in either Suffolk or Norfolk, England, in 1789, and had won a reputation as a geologist in his native land before emigrating to the United States with his wife and four daughters in 1830. Among his various studies he surveyed the coal regions of Pennsylvania and elsewhere, and his chief work, *Statistics of Coal*, published in Philadelphia in 1848, won great praise from all over the world.

One of the most outstanding new members of the society was William D. Kelley, who referred to himself as a "junior member" in 1846.[37] Kelley became nationally, if not internationally, famous as the outstanding defender of protectionism in the national House of Representatives, where his devotion to the cause earned him the nickname of "Pig-Iron" Kelley. A man of great dignity and seriousness, he "cheerfully accepted the sportive nickname," said Vermont Senator Justin S. Morrill in eulogizing him, "bestowed upon him by those unable otherwise to meet his arguments, and he used the epithet as a club furnished by his foes to win for himself greater reknown."[38] Kelley was born in Philadelphia in 1814, his Irish ancestors having settled in Delaware in 1662 and his French Huguenot forebears being early settlers of New Jersey. Both grandfathers had fought in the American Revolution. His father had been one of the leading watchmakers and jewellers of Philadelphia but had been ruined in the War of 1812 and had died in 1816, leaving his family in poor circumstances. Kelley attended the congregational school of the Second Presbyterian Church until he was eleven and had then gone to work at a variety of occupations, finally becoming apprenticed to a jeweller in 1827. When he was twenty, unable to find work in Philadelphia, he went to Boston, where he worked at enamelling and in his leisure time wrote for the press and gained a reputation as a lecturer and debater. In 1838 he returned to Philadelphia and began reading law, finally being admitted to the bar in 1841. In 1845 he was appointed prosecutor of the pleas for Philadelphia and two years later became judge of the Court of Common Pleas, Oyer and Terminer and Quarter Sessions. Always an antislavery man, Kelley left the Democratic party after the repeal of the Missouri Compromise and eventually became one of the founders of the Republican party. In 1856 he resigned his judgeship to run for Congress on the Republican ticket but was defeated and resumed his legal practice. Four years later he was elected to Congress from the Fourth Pennsylvania District and was subsequently re-elected fourteen times from the same district, a record at the time of his death in office in 1890, when he was referred to as "the

Father of the House." Although he had originally been a free
trader, Kelley changed his position as a result of his observation
of English laboring conditions and the developments leading up to
the Panic of 1857 in the United States, and by 1866 he had become
a leader of the protectionists, regarded as the best orator on the
Republican side of the House. A close friend of Henry C. Carey and
a regular attendant at Carey's Vespers, he was the most able and
ardent of Carey's promoters in Washington. Charles H. Cramp,
another friend of Carey declared:

Mr. Carey always referred in the highest terms to what he owed to the
great ability and high character of statesmanship of the Hon. William D.
Kelley. He frequently stated to me that protection owed more to Judge
Kelley in its defense in Congress than the efforts of any other party there.
In this Judge Kelley was supereminent and no one crossed his path nor
interrupted his remarks with successful results.[39]

When Kelley died in Washington he was accorded the highest
national honors, his body being brought into the House for a
special funeral service attended by both houses, with many laudatory addresses made by leaders of both parties and a real respect
and affection for the deceased apparent beneath the oratorical flam-
boyance usual on such occasions. His body was given an official
escort back to Philadelphia, where Furness conducted the funeral
service in the Unitarian Church.

One of the notable new members from New England was Henry
Winsor, born in Duxbury, Massachusetts, who came to Philadelphia in 1852 to take charge of a steamship line to be established
between that city and Boston.[40] He rented a pew in the Unitarian
Church in 1857 and two years later was elected a trustee of the
society, which office, with the exception of only a few years, he
held until 1882. His steamship line was incorporated as the Boston
and Philadelphia Steamship Company in 1872, at which time he
was made president, and in the same year the company added a
line between Philadelphia and Providence. Ten years later a third
line, to Fall River, was established. Winsor became a leading

citizen of Philadelphia, holding directorships in several large corporations. He was serving as a vice-president of the Board of Trade when he died in 1889.

Another prominent citizen of New England origin who joined the Philadelphia Unitarian Society before the Civil War was Barnabas H. Bartol.[41] Born in Freeport, Maine, in 1816, Bartol moved to New York City with his parents when he was thirteen. Three years later he entered the West Point foundry as an apprentice and before he reached the age of twenty-one he had superintended the construction of machinery in Virginia, New Orleans, and Cuba. He came to Philadelphia in 1842 as superintendent of the Southwark foundry, continuing there until 1867, when he resigned to devote his time to the Grocers' Sugar Refinery which he had established with Alfred Kusenberg in 1859. Using a centrifugal process, this was the first plant to manufacture a high grade sugar from molasses. Elected a trustee of the Unitarian Society in 1861, Bartol served almost continuously in that capacity for twenty-five years, resigning in 1886 because he felt it "advisable that younger men should come into the management."[42] When he died two years later the church Register recorded that he had been "for forty-five years a member of this Church and one of its most active faithful, and liberal supporters—a citizen universally respected."[43]

The tremendous growth of railroads in the middle of the century was reflected in the coming into the society of such new members as Samuel Morse Felton and Enoch Lewis. Felton, born in West Newbury, Massachusetts, July 17, 1809, of an old and influential family, had struggled with poverty in his youth, his father having been financially ruined in the War of 1812.[44] The son nonetheless, by dint of much labor and saving, managed to put himself through Harvard College, where he obtained a Bachelor's degree in 1834 and a Master's degree in 1837. After teaching for a brief period he took up railroad work, in which he was engaged for the rest of his life. He was president of the Philadelphia, Wilmington and Baltimore Railroad Company, one of the four divisions of the Pennsylvania Railroad, from 1851 until he resigned because of ill health in 1865, regarded as the most prominent of the company's presidents, "having brought the corporation up from the depths of almost financial ruin and placed it on a sound and paying basis."[45] First noted in the Pew Register of the Unitarian Society in 1855, he was described as one of the oldest, most generous and constant members of the church when he died in 1889.[46] Lewis, whose first recorded connection with the church was his payment of pew rent in 1858, was the general superintendent of the Pennsylvania Railroad through the crucial years 1860 to 1865.[47] Elected a trustee of the Unitarian Society in 1869, he was re-elected almost continuously until 1896.

Although the society was gaining strong new members it suffered a sad loss, and Furness lost one of his closest friends, when Joseph Sill died suddenly on November 2, 1854, at the age of fifty-three. "He was our hand and our heart," Furness declared in his memorial sermon.[49] "My confidence in him was entire. . . . His help and sympathy were always at my command, and they knew no stint." As a tribute to Sill, their president at the time of his death, the members of the Society of the Sons of St. George expressed a wish to attend the Unitarian Church services in a body on Sunday, November 12. The trustees arranged to meet them in the vestry and escorted them into the church, the occupants of the first twenty pews on the middle aisle having relinquished their places to accommodate the guests, and Furness preached a special sermon honoring Sill.

The Passmore Williamson trial in 1855 was of particular interest to the Philadelphia Unitarian Society. Williamson, a secretary of the Pennsylvania Abolition Society, had told Jane Johnson, a slave brought to Pennsylvania by her southern master, that she was free under the laws of the Commonwealth and he had been thrown into prison under the provisions of the federal law. The southern master was Colonel John H. Wheeler, who had been married by Furness to Ellen, daughter of Thomas Sully, in 1838.

The struggle between North and South was drawing to a climax in May, 1856, when Furness' good friend, Charles Sumner, United

States senator from Massachusetts, was beaten into insensibility at his desk in the Senate by Preston Brooks, member of Congress from South Carolina. A large and vociferous meeting was held in the Philadelphia District Court-Room on June 6 to express public indignation over this outrage, and prominent among those who denounced the "slave-power" were Furness and Kelley. A month later Sumner, still suffering acutely from the effects of Brooks's attack, came to Furness' home on Pine Street to recuperate, placing himself under the care of Dr. Caspar Wister, who in June, 1854, had married Furness' daughter Annis.[49] Sumner's presence in Philadelphia was supposed to be a secret but it was an open one, for Susan Lesley was told about it by Rosa Hopper and the word was thus passed along to others.[50] As the summer progressed the patient unfortunately grew no better and, it having been suggested that the seashore air might be beneficial, Sumner went to Cape May for several weeks as the guest of James Furness, the pastor's brother.[51] When the sea air brought no relief, however, he moved to Cresson in the Allegheny Mountains, where the pastor visited him several times. In September Sumner returned to Philadelphia to the James Furness home, still very ill and deeply depressed by his condition. He confided in Mrs. Lesley that he wished he had died during Brooks's attack for he felt that nothing he could accomplish in the future with his damaged health could be as valuable to the abolition cause as his martyrdom would have been.[52] Actually, he was already considered a martyr by his Philadelphia friends and was accorded the homage that was felt to be his due. When he returned to Boston in late October to vote in the fall elections, his Philadelphia hostess declared that in her home after his departure "The little library was like an empty chapel, and the old friendly sofa had a monumental air."[53]

Furness fared better in the whole Sumner episode than did another Philadelphia clergyman, the Rev. Dudley Atkins Tyng, rector of the Episcopal Church of the Epiphany, who was forced to resign his charge when he preached an antislavery sermon based on the Brooks attack on Sumner.[54] Furness did, however, become the object of federal scrutiny during this period, as he continued to preach against the Fugitive Slave Act and to defy its enforcement in every possible way short of armed rebellion. His son Horace later reported that during one of President Buchanan's cabinet meetings there had been a discussion as to whether or not Furness should be indicted for treason and the case had been dropped only because of the strong opposition of John K. Kane, United States district judge of Pennsylvania, to whom the matter was referred.[55] Kane had been a close friend of Furness at one time but had become estranged from him because of Furness' antislavery activity, which made Kane's defense of the pastor the more noteworthy. Ironically, in October, 1855, Furness commented on Kane's judicial activities in Philadelphia's fugitive slave trials: "The wrong which K—— has done, is not done, but doing, swelling out & belittling Neapolitan despotism."[56]

John Brown's raid on Harper's Ferry in November, 1859, precipitated a new outburst of activity by Furness. At the church service on Sunday morning, November 27, he told his congregation that he would receive contributions for Brown's family. On December 2, the day of Brown's execution, "the friends of impartial freedom" called a public meeting in National Hall, which was opened with prayer by Furness.[57] The pastor then delivered a eulogy of Brown to the accompaniment of deafening hissing from a group of southern medical students in the rear of the hall. These students had come to be a standard feature of all antislavery meetings and were sufficiently numerous to constitute a real nuisance. On the eve of the Civil War approximately two hundred out of four hundred and fifty students at the Medical School of the University of Pennsylvania were southerners while nearly four hundred out of six hundred and thirty at Jefferson Medical College came from the South.[58]

In Virginia, after his execution, Brown's body was hurried northward by train as quickly as possible, without any preparation for burial, to avoid the possibility of mob violence. The train was to enter Philadelphia at the Broad and Prime Streets Station, where the body was to be removed, taken to an undertaking establishment, prepared for burial, and then placed on the train again for its journey back to Brown's home at North Elba, New York. A large crowd, both white and Negro, gathered at the station long before the train was due there but only Mayor Alexander Henry, the chief of police, the abolitionist leader Miller McKim, and the Unitarian pastor Furness and his son Horace were admitted to the platform.[59] The train was an hour late and by the time it had arrived tension in the crowd had mounted so high that the mayor decided not to risk taking the body to the undertaker but to move it on immediately out of the crowd's reach. A box of tools made to simulate the coffin was taken from the train, placed upon a cart and driven off to lure the crowd away and when they had gone the body was quickly taken down to Walnut Street Wharf and ferried over to New Jersey to resume its journey.

Brown's execution and its attendant circumstances filled the front pages of Philadelphia's newspapers for several days and Furness' name appeared prominently in most of the stories. He was mentioned specifically at the "Great Union Meeting" held on December 7, 1859, to "rebuke" the National Hall demonstrators.[60] The organizers of the Great Union Meeting hastened to set the record straight as to their attitude toward Brown sympathizers. "Our patriotic and conservative citizens," they declared, "were even more alarmed than their Southern brethren at such a display of fanaticism," and they quite openly stated their main reason for their attitude.[61] "Philadelphia has always been loyal to the Union. Her business relations with all sections of the country are such as to interweave her interests with those of the South as well as the North. Her prosperity is dependent upon domestic peace and harmony."[62] All classes were included in the audience of over 6,000 persons who crowded into Jayne's Hall on Chestnut Street below Seventh, but "The business men were strongly represented" and especially enthusiastic.[63] "The Voice of the Great Union Meeting," composed especially for the occasion, set the tone of the proceedings in song:

The South shall have her rights—O'er her
Our eagle spreads its wings—
The treason plotters, *brown* or white,
Shall on the gallows swing.[64]

Colonel Page, one of the speakers, declared himself in favor of forthwith hanging or shooting on the spot all "abolitionists of the John Brown stamp."[65] Charles Ingersoll, Esq., referred to his fellow Americans of antislavery convictions as "these animals . . . come among us to splash with . . . venom all that is sacred. . . ."[66] The Honorable Josiah Randall admitted, however, that Philadelphians "have no power to prevent the Rev. Mr. Furness and Mrs. Lucretia Mott from disseminating their sceptical disunion doctrines," though he steadfastly reiterated that "the people at large . . . have no part nor lot with them. . . ."[67] Furness dismissed this attack several months later when he referred in a sermon to "persons from whose education and position better things were to be expected," concluding that they must have been the victims of "some black art practised, some charm employed, more potent than ether or chloroform, made out of cotton or gold."[68]

On December 15, 1859, George William Curtis arrived at Furness' house to stay while giving an address at National Hall on "The Present Aspect of the Slavery Question."[69] Public excitement was intense and tremendous crowds gathered around the hall as the hour for the lecture approached. Mayor Henry called out the police to keep order but an earnest plea was delivered to Curtis, in the interest of public safety, not to deliver his speech. Curtis consulted Furness, who declared, "If it costs the lives of all of us, we ought to go on." The meeting proceeded as scheduled, but not before the police had arrested the ringleaders of the mob, including two Georgia medical students, both armed with loaded revolvers. All were placed in the cellar of the hall as a deterrent to the rioters' firing the building. A year later, when Curtis was invited to speak again in Philadelphia, the lessee of Concert Hall refused to permit its use for that purpose and the mayor agreed with his decision, so inflamed was public opinion in Philadelphia against all antislavery activity.

On January 3, 1861, representatives of the "mercantile interests" held a meeting at the rooms of the Board of Trade to petition the state legislature to repeal any legislation which "might be deemed unfriendly to our Southern brethren."[70] The following day one hundred and fifty "leading citizens" met in the same place to discuss means for getting the South back into the Union. On January 7 a meeting of citizens "opposed to war" and in favor of giving guarantees to the South was held at Barr's Hotel, followed by another meeting at the same place three days later at which the right of secession was admitted and Pennsylvania was asked to decide, in the event of secession, whether to go "with fanatical New England or with the South, whose sympathies are ours."[71] At a mass meeting held at National Hall on January 16, "anti-coercionists" passed resolutions asking the South not to leave them to "the despotism of a sectional party flushed with victory," and William B. Reed pleaded for peace and conciliation, claiming that he spoke for "all of Pennsylvania, except those who, as technical abolitionists, I count as outlaws."[72]

In February, 1861, the Philadelphia Unitarian Society became intimately involved in the foiling of a purported plot against the life of President-elect Lincoln, who was scheduled to visit Philadelphia on his way to his inauguration in Washington.[73] Samuel Morse Felton, president of the Philadelphia, Wilmington and Baltimore Rail Road, had heard rumours a month before that an attempt would be made to assassinate Lincoln on the train between Baltimore and Washington and he had hired Allen Pinkerton, the detective, to investigate the matter. An elaborate counterplot was organized with the aid of innumerable Pinkerton operatives, both male and female, who hovered over Lincoln from the moment he landed in Philadelphia on February 21, through the flag-hoisting ceremonies at the State House the following morning at dawn, the trip to Harrisburg and the meeting with the governor and the legislature, and the subsequent journey to Washington. Enoch Lewis, general superintendent of the Pennsylvania Railroad and also a member of the Philadelphia Unitarian Society, with two others personally escorted Lincoln from Harrisburg.

The threat of violence hung over the Unitarian Society in the last days before the war. Furness never yielded an inch before the verbal attacks which constantly battered at his seemingly inexhaustible reserves of physical strength and moral courage. Some of his friends, however, were not as impervious as he to the signs of the times and they worried about the possibility that the increasingly violent pro-southern faction in Philadelphia would express its fear and hatred in physical terms. Furness himself fully anticipated that such an attack would be made upon him and declared that he would never fight back but many of his friends in the congregation quietly armed and constituted themselves a defensive phalanx around the pulpit on Sunday mornings.

The climax occurred, without violence, on April 26, 1861, two weeks after the firing on Fort Sumter. Furness opened his sermon with the words "The long agony is over!"[74] Crowded into every available space in the church and standing outside, crammed together at the doors and windows, so as not to miss a single word uttered by the eloquent preacher, was the largest congregation ever assembled in that place for that purpose. Furness had won his fight. His most powerful ally had been the natural course of human events, for the tide of human freedom was rising throughout the world and it was inevitable that Philadelphia would some day be engulfed.

NOTES

CHAPTER VIII

[1] W. H. Furness, *Doing Before Believing. A Discourse delivered at the Anniversary of the Derby Academy in Hingham, May 19, 1847* (New York, 1847), p. 19.

[2] W. H. Furness, *The Son of Man Cometh. A Discourse preached before the Society of Cambridgeport Parish . . . May 30, 1847* (Boston, 1847),p. 19.

[3] W. H. Furness, *An Address delivered before a meeting of the Members and Friends of the Pennsylvania Anti-Slavery Society during the Annual Fair, December 19, 1849* (Philadelphia, 1850), p. 14.

[4] W. H. Furness, *The Memory of the Just . . . A Discourse delivered . . . February 27, 1848* (Philadelphia, 1848), p. 11.

[5] Furness, *Address before the Pennsylvania Anti-Slavery Society*, p. 16.

[6] Furness, *Address before the Pennsylvania Anti-Slavery Society*, p. 15.

[7] Furness, *Address before the Pennsylvania Anti-Slavery Society*, p. 8.

[8] Furness, *Fiftieth Annversary*, p. 35.

[9] Furness to Lucy Osgood, May 20, 1850: OSGOOD CORR.

[10] Furness, *Fiftieth Anniversary*, p. 35.

[11] Furness to Lucy Osgood, May 20, 1850: OSGOOD CORR.

[12] Fredrika Bremer, *The Homes of the New World* (New York, 1854), I, 529–30.

[13] *Proceedings of the Great Union Meeting, held . . . 21st of November, 1850* (Philadelphia, 1850).

[14] "Black Letters; or Uncle Tom-Foolery in Literature," *Graham's Magazine*, XLII (February 1853), 209.

[15] Leland, p. 136.

[16] William Still, *The Underground Rail Road* (Philadelphia, 1872), p. 659.

[17] Letter of April 14, 1851: COLL. CORR. II.

[18] Edward L. Pierce, ed., *Memoirs and Letters of Charles Sumner* (Boston, 1894), III, 309.

[19] Scharf and Westcott, II, 1454.

[20] Sill, VII, 53–54.

[21] W. H. Furness, *Discourse on the Sunday Morning following the Interment of Joseph Sill, November 12, 1854* (n.p. n.d.), p. 20. The first American-born Furness was the pastor's grandfather, Jonathan, born in Boston, September 16, 1731.

[22] *Proceedings of the Regular Autumnal Convention of Unitarian Christians: Held in the City of Philadelphia, October 20, 1846* (Philadelphia, 1846), p.6.

[23] *Proceedings . . . 28th September, 1846, p. 6.*

[24] RECS & MINS, p. 145.

[25] Furness to Lucy Osgood, March 31, 1837: OSGOOD CORR. The only other available sources of information are a letter from Furness to Lucy Osgood, May 16, 1837: OSGOOD CORR.; an account signed by John A. McAllister, April, 1864: CHURCH MSS; a letter from Mrs. Furness to Mary Jenks, August, 1837: COLL. CORR. II; and a reference in Sill's "Diary," III, 242.

[26] McAllister MS.

[27] In a letter dated March 8, 1881, to the Rev. Joseph May, McAllister further stated that Karcher had been a Lutheran or a Methodist, and after leaving Philadelphia renounced Unitarianism and went to Minnesota where he was ordained to the

Episcopal ministry. In less than a year he left that church and became a Roman Catholic.

[28]McAllister letter of March 8, 1881.

[29]This account was based on DAB, XVI, 372–73; Scharf and Westcott, II, 1060–62; Fielding, p. 317; and *Philadelphia and Popular Philadelphians* (Philadelphia, 1891), p. 230.

[30]An excellent sketch of Rogers' life was written by Horace Howard Furness, F[airman] R[ogers], *1833–1900* (Philadelphia, 1903) and there is also a brief sketch in University of Pennsylvania, *Biographical Catalogue of the Matriculates of the College, . . . 1749–1893* (Philadelphia, 1894), p. 184.

[31]Dr. Isaac Heylin's son, Rowland P., took an A.M. degree in 1821 (University of Pennsylvania, *Biographical Catalogue*, p. 63); John and Thomas Mease, sons of Dr. James Mease, entered in 1820, the former taking an A.M. degree in 1823, while the latter did not graduate (pp. 69–70); Thomas Harper, Jr. graduated in 1825 (p. 72); Peter Lesley, Jr. in 1838 (p. 112); and Henry Augustus Duhring, son of Henry Duhring, took an A.M. degree in 1852 (p. 179).

[32]H. H. Furness, F[airman] R[ogers], *p.* 15.

[33]The sources for this account were: Mary Lesley Ames, ed., *Life and Letters of Peter and Susan Lesley* (New York, 1909), 2 vols.; DAB, XI, 183–84; and University of Pennsylvania, *Biographical Catalogue*, pp. 112–13. Lesley, baptized "Peter, Jr.," disliked his first name and placed the "J." for "Jr." in front of it, dropping the "Jr." at the end.

[34]Ames, *Peter and Susan Lesley*, I, 146.

[35]Ames, *Peter and Susan Lesley*, I, 232.

[36]Sill, IX, 459–60.

[37]This account is based largely on DAB, X, 299–300, and *Memorial Addresses on the Life and Character of William D. Kelley, Delivered in the House of Representatives and the Senate* . . . (Washington 1890).

[38]*Memorial Addresses on the Life and Character of William D. Kelley*, p. 82.

[39]Cramp, "Carey's 'Vespers.' "

[40]Scharf and Westcott, III, 2170–71.

[41]Scharf and Westcott, III, 2284; obituary notice in REG II, 157.

[42]Letter of resignation, April 22, 1886, inserted in RECS & MINS, p. 290.

[43]REG II, 156.

[44]William Bender Wilson, *History of the Pennsylvania Railroad Company* . . . (Philadelphia, 1895), II, 280–82, supplied these data.

[45]Wilson, II, 280.

[46]REG II, 157.

[47]Wilson, I, 191.

[48]W. H. Furness, *A Tribute to the Memory of Joseph Sill* (n.p., n.d.), p. 4. Delivered at Sill's funeral, November 5, 1854.

[49]Pierce, III, 487.

[50]Ames, *Peter and Susan Lesley*, I, 333.

[51]Pierce, III, 505, 507.

[52]Ames, *Peter and Susan Lesley*, I, 339.

[53]Pierce, III, 507.

[54]Russell E. Francis, "The Religious Revival of 1858 in Philadelphia," *Pa. Mag. of Hist. & Biog.*, LXX (January 1946), 56.

[55]Horace Howard Furness, *Historical Address delivered in Connection with the Installation of the Reverend Charles E. St. John as Minister of the First Unitarian Church of Philadelphia, 12th of January, 1908* (Philadelphia, 1908), p. 12.

[56]H. H. Furness, *Records of a Lifelong Friendship*, p. 108.

[57]Scharf and Westcott, I, 732. Furness shared the platform with James and Lucretia Mott, Mary Grew, Theodore Tilton and Robert Purvis.

[58]Frederick P. Henry, ed., *Standard History of the Medical Profession of Philadelphia* (Chicago, 1897), p. 219.

[59]This account is taken from the younger Furness' report of it in his *Historical Address . . . 12th of January, 1908*, pp. 16–18, and the *North American and U.S. Gazette*, December 5, 1859. *The Anti-Slavery History of the John Brown-Year, . . . the Annual Report of the American Anti-Slavery Society* (New York, 1861), p. 130, stated that "one of the noblest men that [Philadelphia] holds, Rev. Wm. H. Furness," protested in the public press against the mayor's not allowing Brown's body to rest for a few hours in the city. Furness believed that the whole city should have been at the station, headed by civil, ecclesiastical, and military authorities, to do honor to Brown, and he felt that the mayor exceeded his authority in ordering the body moved on immediately.

[60]*Great Union Meeting, Philadelphia, December 7, 1859* (Philadelphia, n.d.).

[61]*Great Union Meeting*, p. 3.

[62]*Great Union Meeting*, p. 3.

[63]*Great Union Meeting*, p. 4.

[64]*Great Union Meeting*, p. 6.

[65]*Great Union Meeting*, p. 45.

[66]*Great Union Meeting*, p. 43.

[67]*Great Union Meeting*, p. 26.

[68]W. H. Furness, *Put Up Thy Sword. A Discourse delivered before Theodore Parker's Society at the Music Hall, Boston . . . March 11, 1860* (Boston, 1860), pp. 9–10.

[69]This incident and that of the following year were related by Isaac H. Clothier in an article in the Philadelphia *Public Ledger*, December 14, 1902, "Philadelphia in Slavery Days." Clothier was chairman of the Committee on Arrangements and an active participant in the two episodes.

[70]Scharf and Westcott, I, 740–41.

[71]Scharf and Westcott, I, 746–47.

[72]Scharf and Westcott, I, 747.

[73]An account of this episode is given in Norma B. Cuthbert, ed., *Lincoln and the Baltimore Plot, 1861* (San Marino, Calif., 1949) and in Wilson, I, 314–17.

[74]Still, p. 665.

IX

Conclusion

UNITARIANISM AS A PHILOSOPHY OF LIFE WAS ADMIRABLY SUITED TO the Philadelphia scene in the years before the Civil War. It embraced the positive values of American civilization in its conviction that all good things were possible for all men, that man's road led ever upwards, that perfection was attainable in this world. It emphasized what have been described as the middle-class American virtues of sobriety, industry, and frugality. It upheld the supreme importance of practicality and common sense, in religion as in everything else in life. In addition to all of these purely ideological attractions, however, Philadelphia Unitarianism was blessed by the inspiring leadership of William Henry Furness, one of the most forceful and attractive human beings ever to preach any gospel anywhere. How, then, can one explain the failure of Philadelphia Unitarianism to grow beyond one large congregation and one small, struggling fellowship by 1860? Its ranks included many of the finest men and women in the city, outstanding leaders in its cultural life, in business, in the professions, in government, and in philanthropy; yet, though Philadelphia's population increased from 70,000 in 1800 to 568,034 in 1860, and the number of its churches increased from 27 in 1796 to 327 in 1860, not until 1859 were the Unitarians able to sustain even a second congregation for more than a few years.

Priestley had commented upon the static quality of English Unitarianism long before he came to Philadelphia:

One cause certainly is, that though Unitarian Dissenters are not apt to entertain any doubt of the truth of their principles, they do not lay so much stress upon them as other christians do upon theirs. Nor, indeed, is there any reason why they should, when they do not consider the holding of them to be at all *necessary* to *salvation*, which other christians often do with respect to theirs. They, therefore, take much less pains to make proselytes, and are less concerned to inculcate their principles upon their children, their servants, and their dependents in general.

Furness, preaching at the dedication of the new church edifice in Philadelphia in 1828, noted the same phenomenon but declared himself untroubled by it.

So far from considering it an objection to Unitarianism that its influence is not very perceptible, we should be seriously concerned if we saw it followed by rapid and striking effects. We should begin to doubt whether it is that pure system of truth which we believe it to be.If it readily affected the minds of the generality of those whose previous self-regulation has been in no wise remarkable, we might suspect that it purchased its success by yielding something to the lower tendencies of our nature. History points us to those religions which were more or less earthly in their character, as having produced the greatest *visible* effects. The greatest apparent triumphs of the Christian faith were wrought at the period when it was most corrupted.[2]

Yet Unitarianism did flourish in Boston during this period with a notable lack of corruption both in theory and in practice. Why did the Philadelphia church not do the same?

Philadelphia Unitarianism was at the beginning an English growth, without roots in the American soil, and this alone would explain much of its difference from New England Unitarianism, which, with the single exception of King's Chapel, Boston, originally an Episcopal church, evolved out of native Congregationalism. There were widespread, well-developed family traditions of church membership in New England which only had to change their label to come into the Unitarian fold, bringing with them the accumulated strength and prestige of many generations. Philadelphia, on the other hand, seems to have had more than its share of nonbelievers and scoffers at religion. The prevalence of infidelity greatly disturbed Priestley when he arrived in the city in 1794. Thirty years later, Furness, coming from pious New England, found the lack of religion in his new home alarming. Furthermore, he observed, "Unitarianism is certainly not the cause for there is very little of it here and in Boston where it prevails there is little or no infidelity."[3] At the same time, for those who were church members, their membership was strongly hereditary in origin and extremely conservative in character. Philadelphians were born into their church affiliation as they were born into their political allegiance, and gentlemen changed neither. The orthodox were cool when they were not actively hostile toward theological liberalism and Philadelphia Unitarianism had to begin from the beginning, with no already established base from which it could grow.

Membership in the Philadelphia Unitarian Church was, for the most part, a matter of conscious choice. There was some family continuity, with marriages taking place between the members and between the children of members, with their children in turn carrying on the Unitarian tradition, but it was obvious from the large size of the individual families and the relatively stationary numbers in the congregation that there must have been a steady movement out of the church which kept pace with the movement into it. Many of its children married non-Unitarians, and, since the Philadelphia church under the leadership of Furness not only never attempted to inspire a strong denominational spirit but actually discouraged it, many of these persons turned toward the more positive demands of their new partners' non-Unitarian faith. Also, since blood relationship does not guarantee the inheritance of personality traits, many children of Unitarian parents did not feel drawn to the faith of their fathers and, being free from proscription, they sought a congenial home elsewhere.

It must also have been true of some Philadelphia Unitarians in the middle of the nineteenth century, as it had been true of many English Unitarians at the end of the eighteenth century, that the controversial theological issues on which the denomination had been founded "no longer seemed alive or did not seem sufficiently alive to make the younger generation think it worthwhile to pay the price of isolation."[4] Some may have left the relatively lonely, minority position of Unitarianism for the larger fellowship of other denominations for the sheer comfort of numbers. Others may have felt that their growing affluence required a more elite setting than that provided by Unitarianism. Many are believed to have gone into the Episcopal Church for reasons of social, political, or economic prestige. For others the changing over to the Episcopal or Presbyterian Church represented only a final return to their original church home after a period of wandering.

The exodus was sometimes reversed. Unitarianism attracted some Calvinists who had given up that faith because they felt its insistence upon the vanity of all earthly pleasures did not reflect the happier truths of the American experience. It offered a new church home to many dissident Quakers who felt that the main body of the Society of Friends was departing from its original teachings and who found Unitarianism congenial to their spirit. Some new members joined because they felt that some sort of church connection was necessary in order for them to be considered respectable by their churchgoing neighbors and who found the formal requirements of membership in the Unitarian Society less irksome than those of other churches. Some of its converts were middle-aged persons who had been so busy making their way in the world that they had had no time for religion but, once having their temporal prosperity assured, were free to worry about their spiritual welfare. They chose the Unitarian Society because there was "less nonsense" about it than there was about other churches. For many the choice of Unitarianism represented a phase of intellectual growth which made imperative a new religious outlook based on intellectual as well as spiritual conviction.

Priestley had counselled his coreligionists in 1785: "Let us not, therefore, be discouraged, though, for the present, we should see no great number of churches professedly unitarian. It is sufficiently evident that unitarian principles are gaining ground every day. Every attempt to suppress them by writing, or otherwise, has hitherto been favourable to their spread, and we may be confident it ever will be so."[5]

Furness arrived at a similar conviction: "All the real moral worth exhibited under any and every form of Christianity, all the real moral advancement made even by those who oppose us most violently, we can trace to the operation of those simple truths which *we* maintain as the vital doctrines of Christianity, and which enter into the composition of every system of Christian faith."[6]

Orthodox Philadelphians by the middle of the nineteenth century found it difficult to maintain their initial hostility to the Unitarians. Theologically they continued to regard them as suspect, when they were not simply incomprehensible, in their insistence upon the Unity of God. There was no denying the fact, however, that the Unitarians were people who "got on" in life. Universal acceptance of the Protestant ethic pointed to but one conclusion. Those whom the Lord loved prospered. Temporal prosperity was a certain proof of virtue.

Not even the most sanguine could have claimed for Unitarianism a great triumph in Philadelphia but by 1861 it had definitely won a respected place in the life of the city. Unitarians went quietly about their business, imperturbable, self-assured. Furness spoke for them when he said:". . . We know that . . . this is God's own world, and that He loves every atom of it, and that not a single soul is there on the face of the broad earth that He is not caring for. . . . We can afford to wait patiently upon God."[7]

NOTES

CHAPTER IX

[1]Joseph Priestley, "A Prefatory Discourse Relating to the present State of those who are called Rational Dissenters," Prefaced to "A Sermon preached at the New Meeting, Birmingham, November 3, 1782," in *Discourses on Various Subjects, Including Several on Particular Occasions* (Birmingham, England, 1787), p. 95.

[2]W. H. Furness, *A Discourse preached at the Dedication of the First Congregational Unitarian Church,* . . . *November 5, 1828* (Philadelphia, 1828), pp.26–27.

[3]Furness to Mrs. Jenks, December 5, 1825: COLL. CORR. I.

[4]Raymond V. Holt, *Unitarian Contribution to Social Progress in England,* p. 330.

[5]Joseph Priestley, "The Importance and Extent of Free Inquiry in Matters of Religion: A Sermon Preached Before the Congregations of the Old and New Meeting of Protestant Dissenters at Birmingham. November 5, 1785," in *Discourses on Various Subjects,* pp. 184–85.

[6]Furness, *Discourse preached at the Dedication* . . . *November 5, 1828,* p. 27.

[7]W. H. Furness, *Ecclesiastical Organizations. A Discourse delivered* . . . *March 19, 1865* (Philadelphia, 1865), p. 12.

TABLE OF ABBREVIATIONS

RECORDS OF THE FIRST UNITARIAN CHURCH OF PHILADELPHIA

CASH II	General Cash Account No. 2. Treasurer's records, 1811–50.
CHURCH MSS	Manuscript collection of the First Unitarian Church.
COLLS	Collections. Subscriptions to the Octagon Church of 1813.
GEN RECS	General Records Book. Miscellany, including lists of subscribers, pew rents, burial notices, etc.
PEW REG	Pew Register [1854–61]. No page numbers. Numbered by pews.
PROC	Proceedings [June 12, 1796—January 20, 1823].
RECS & MINS	Records and Minutes [of Annual Meetings, Financial Reports, and Societies of the Church, January 20, 1823 to February 7, 1907].
REG I	Register, Vol. I. Births, baptisms, marriages, and burials, prior to January 12, 1876.
REG II	Pastor's Register, Vol. II. Births, baptisms, marriages, and burials, from January 12, 1876 to 1907.
TRUSTS III	Minutes of Trustees, Vol. III, 1828–82.
UNNAMED	Unnamed journal, untitled and without date. Scattered items of historical interest, lists of subscribers to various projects, etc.

FURNESS CORRESPONDENCE

COLL. CORR. I	Letters written chiefly by Dr. William H. Furness, with a few written by Mrs. Furness, to the Jenks family, Mrs. Furness' mother and sister, from January, 1820 to May, 1832.

Table of Abbreviations

COLL. CORR. II   Continuation of the Jenks letters from June, 1832 to January, 1852.

OSGOOD CORR.   Letters written by Dr. Furness to Miss Lucy Osgood from August 3, 1824 to November 28, 1867.

OTHER SOURCES

ACAB   *Appletons' Cyclopaedia of American Biography*

APS   American Philosophical Society

CD   Philadelphia *City Directories*

DAB   *Dictionary of American Biography*

HSP   Historical Society of Pennsylvania

APPENDIX A

OFFICERS OF THE SOCIETY

READERS (1796–1800)
Six elected every six months to serve for six months.

	Dates of Election	*Occupation*
Allport, William	February, 1797	Unknown
Birch, William Young	August, 1796–May, 1800	Bookseller and stationer
Darch, Edmund	November, 1797	Unknown
Eddowes, Ralph	August, 1796–May, 1800	Merchant
Gales, Joseph	August, 1796–May, 1799	Journalist
Jarvis, John	February, 1797	Scrivener
Leishman, William	August, 1796, November, 1797–November, 1798	Unknown
Taylor, James	August, 1796–May, 1800	Merchant
Thomas, Nathaniel	August, 1796–May, 1800	Scrivener and merchant
Turner, John	February, 1797–March, 1797	Unknown
Woodman, William	May, 1799	Teacher

COMMITTEE OF MANAGEMENT (1807–11)
Five members elected annually to serve for one year.

Astley, Thomas	1808–10	Merchant
Boult, Peter	1807–10	Merchant
Eddowes, Ralph	1807–10	Merchant
Taylor, James	1807–10	Merchant
Trendel, Thomas	1807	Teacher
Turner, William	1810	Unknown
Vaughan, John	1807–10	Merchant

Appendix A

COMMITTEE OF ORDER (1812)
Five members elected annually to serve for one year. Called trustees after incorporation, January 18, 1813.

Astley, Thomas	Merchant
Eddowes, John	Merchant
Eddowes, Ralph	Merchant
Turner, William	Unknown
Vaughan, John	Merchant

TRUSTEES (1813–61)
Five elected annually, 1813–24, seven thereafter, only five of whom were eligible for re-election.

Allen, James	1843	Plasterer
Astley, Thomas	1814–17	Merchant
Bailey, Lewis	1828	Merchant
Barnes, Joseph	1834, 1835	Judge
Bartol, Barnabas H.	1861	Engineer
Bernard, William H.	1844, 1850	Merchant
Binder, George	1831	Carpenter
Birch, William Young	1818–32	Gentleman
Blackburn, William	1833, 1834	Merchant
Bradford, Samuel	1846, 1847	Railroad official
Clark, Edward W.	1855–59	Broker
Clark, Enoch W.	1847–49	Broker
Colladay, Samuel R.	1860, 1861	Merchant
Cowperthwaite, Edwin	1851	Merchant
Coxe, Charles W.	1856–61	Merchant
Duhring, Henry	1845, 1846	Merchant
Eddowes, John	1813	Merchant
Eddowes, Ralph	1813–22	Merchant
Elliott, Frank	1851	Unknown

247

Elliott, Isaac	1830–36, 1841–46, 1854, 1855, 1858	Conveyancer
Fales, George	1841, 1842, 1849	Merchant
Farnham, Benjamin A.	1847	Merchant
Finch, Francis	1852	Unknown
Fletcher, Charles	1828	Jeweller
Fletcher, Thomas	1824–26, 1838, 1839, 1845, 1855, 1856	Jeweller and merchant
Ford, John	1823, 1824, 1826	Merchant
Furness, James T.	1849, 1850	Merchant
Galvin, Thomas P.	1858, 1859	Merchant
Gilpin, John	1850, 1851, 1857	Broker
Griffith, Eli	1850–54	Merchant
Hamilton, Charles	1853, 1854	Merchant
Harper, Thomas	1815–17, 1823–25, 1827	Merchant
Hastings, Simon	1856	Merchant
Haven, Charles Chauncey	1835–38	Merchant
Haven, Thomas	1832, 1833, 1842–44	Merchant
Heylin, Isaac	1840	Physician
Hill, David	1836	Merchant
Hill, William	1856–59	Actuary
Hulme, Peter	1851	Unknown
Hurlbut, Martin L.	1838	Teacher
Johnson, Walter R.	1828, 1829	Teacher
Jones, Thomas	1813, 1814, 1818	Unknown
Lea, Joseph	1852–54	Merchant
Leland, Charles	1841	Gentleman
Lesley, James Jr.	1857	Merchant
Lincoln, E.	1844	Merchant
Mason, James S.	1849, 1859, 1860	Blacking manufacturer

248

McFarland, James B.	1848, 1859, 1860	Merchant
Mellon, Thomas	1839, 1840	Gentleman
Merrick, Samuel Vaughan	1835	Engine manufacturer
Merrill, George	1842, 1843	Merchant
Moore, Marmaduke	1845, 1848 1857, 1858	Merchant
Morgan, Thomas W.	1829, 1830, 1833, 1834, 1850–53	Merchant
Morrison, William	1837–39	Unknown
Patten, John W.	1830, 1857, 1858	Merchant
Potts, Robert T.	1832	Merchant
Roberts, Algernon S.	1845, 1846	Merchant
Rogers, Evans	1847–49, 1851, 1852, 1855, 1856, 1860, 1861	Gentleman (Retired merchant)
Scholefield, John	1840–48	Gentleman
Shippen, Charles	1824	Accountant
Sill, Joseph	1831–54	Merchant
Small, Abraham	1825, 1829	Bookseller and printer (1825); gentleman (1829)
Small, Robert H.	1852, 1853	Bookseller and printer
Somers, Chalkley	1854–56	Merchant
Soule, Horace H.	1861	Merchant
Sully, Thomas	1819–22, 1834–37	Artist
Taylor, James	1814, 1815	"Unitarian minister"
Tevis, Joshua	1837–42	Merchant
Thomas, Jacob	1836, 1837, 1839, 1840, 1843, 1844	Unknown
Thomas, Joseph M.	1848	Merchant

Thomas, Samuel H.	1824–31	Merchant
Todhunter, Joseph	1827–33	Merchant
Turner, William	1813–27	Unknown
Vaughan, John	1813, 1816–41	Merchant
Wetherill, Edward	1860, 1861	Unknown
Winsor, Henry	1859–61	Merchant
Wood, George A.	1845, 1846, 1849, 1850, 1853–55	Merchant

APPENDIX B

OCCUPATIONS OF MEMBERS

Only those members are listed below whose occupations are known for the period during which they made their first recorded connection with the society. In many cases these occupations were subsequently changed. Dates following addresses refer to the *City Directory* for that year. Other references are to other items in the Bibliography.

	Address	First recorded connection with the society
ACCOUNTANT		
Birnie, William	1 Farmer's Row, E. of 43 Dock (1825)	Paid pew rent, Dec. 16, 1826 (CASH II, 15)
Foulke, William	Cor. n. 11th & Hunter's Court (1825)	Contrib. May 6, 1826 (CASH II, 13)
Hill, Thomas C.	80 Market, h. 178 S. 9th (1856)	Married by Furness June 10, 1856 (REG I, 114)
Howell, William T.	52 High (1830)	Married by Furness Nov. 6, 1828 (REG I, 98)
Merino, John	13 Walnut, h. 78 N. 11th (1855)	Paid pew rent 1855 (PEW REG, # 60)
Shippen, Charles	Near Callowhill & Ridge Rd. (1823)	Signed records Jan. 17, 1820 (PROC, 114)
ACTRESS		
Butler, Fanny Kemble (retired)	Butler Farm, Old York Road (Kemble, *Records of Later Life*, 2)	Regular attendance noted by Furness Oct. 1, 1834 (COLL. CORR. I)
Cushman, Charlotte	Manager, Walnut St. Theatre (Stebbins, *Charlotte Cushman*, 53)	Rented 3 pew sittings in April, 1843 (Sill Diary, IV, 305–6)
ACTUARY		
Hill, William B.	Pa. Co. for Ins. on Lives, etc., 66 Walnut, h. 178 S. 9th (1856)	Elected trustee April 21, 1856 (RECS & MINS, 168)

251

AGENT

Parker, Francis	912 Cherry (1860)	Paid pew rent 1857 (PEW REG, # 161)
Scott, Thomas	192 High, d. 343 Mulberry (1828)	Paid pew rent Jan. 13, 1827 (CASH II, 15)

ARCHITECT

Furness, Frank H.	1426 Pine (1860)	Son of pastor, born 1837 (Jayne, *Letters of Horace Howard Furness*, xviii)

ARMY OFFICER (RETIRED)

Davis, Col. Samuel B.	266 Walnut (1828)	Contrib. Aug. 18, 1827 (CASH II, 19)

ARTIST

Bridport, Hugh	N.E. cor. 5th & Chestnut (1830)	Married by Furness May 26, 1830 (REG I, 99)
Furness, William H., Jr.	1426 Pine (1859)	Son of pastor, born May 21, 1828 (ACAB, II, 566)
Peale, Rembrandt	Not listed in *City Directories*	Paid pew rent Dec. 24, 1825 (CASH II, 2)
Sully, Thomas	Philosophical Hall, 5th St. (PROC, 81)	Signed records April 9, 1815 (PROC, 81)

ATTORNEY

Barnes, Joseph	11 Sansom (1829)	Furness noted recent membership April, 1829 (COLL. CORR. I)
Brewster, Francis E.	5 Little George (above 6th) (1825)	Paid pew rent Sept. 29, 1825 (CASH II, 1)
Cadwallader, John	88 S. 4th (1831)	Bought part pew Nov. 17, 1831 (UNNAMED, 27)
Cope, Charles S.	Deputy clerk of Orphans Court, h. 22 N. 7th (1839)	Bought pew April 6, 1839 (UNNAMED, 28)

Furness, Horace Howard	520 Walnut, h. 1426 Pine (1860)	Son of pastor, born Nov. 2, 1833 (DAB, VII, 78)
Grimshaw, William	Spruce above 12th (1828)	Contrib. May 10, 1828 (CASH II, 35)
Hambleton, David M.	51 N. 6th (1858)	Paid pew rent 1858 (PEW REG, # 129)
Hubbell, Ferdinand Wakeman	Walnut below 3rd (1828)	Paid pew rent May 1, 1828 (CASH II, 34)
Kelley, William Darrah	5th & Library, h. 14 Sansom (1846)	Present at meeting Oct. 20, 1846 (COLL. CORR. II)
Smukler, Samuel M.	252 N. 12th (1859)	Held one sitting 1859 (PEW REG, # 115)
Warriner, H. Ryland	16 N. 7th, h. 227 Jacoby (1859)	Paid pew rent 1859 (PEW REG, # 42)

BAKER

Smiedel, Charles	137 S. 10th (1817)	Two children baptized Sept. 1, 1817 (REG I, 6)

BANKER

Dodge, Edward	25 S. 3rd, h. 76 S. 4th (1839)	Bought pew June 26, 1839 (UNNAMED, 28)

BLACKSMITH

English, James	25 Filbert (1825)	Contrib. May 6, 1826 (CASH II, 13)
English, Robert	219 N. 15th (1859)	Paid pew rent 1859 (PEW REG, # 138)

BLACKING MANUFACTURER

Mason, James Servetus	95 Callowhill (1835)	Child buried Nov. 27, 1835 (UNNAMED, 209–10)

BOARDING HOUSE PROPRIETOR

Eaton, Mrs. Olivia	9 S. 9th (1825)	Son baptized April 3, 1825 (REG I, 9)

BOOKSELLER, PRINTER, PUBLISHER

Beresford, Robert G.	Unknown	Infant son buried June 9, 1834 (REG I, 204)
Beresford, Robert H.	16 Swanwick (1829)	Married by Furness July 25, 1829 (REG I, 98)
Birch, William Young	17 S. 2nd (1797)	Founder June 12, 1796 (PROC, 5)
Blanchard, William A.	S.E. cor. Chestnut & 4th, h. 20 N. 11th (1839)	Bought pew April 30, 1839 (UNNAMED, 28)
Carey, Henry C.	114 Walnut (1833)	Paid pew rent Feb. 21, 1833 (UNNAMED, 33–34)
Cogan, Edward	48 N. 10th (1858)	Paid pew rent 1858 (PEW REG, # 130)
Crissy, James	4 Minor, h. 12 Montgomery Square (1840)	Daughter married by Furness, Jan. 1840 (REG I, 105)
Dalling, James	S.E. cor. 8th & Chestnut (1845)	Infant son baptized June 1, 1845 (REG I, 19)
Desilver, Robert P.	225 High, h. Chestnut above Schuylkill 7th (1837)	Wife buried Aug. 18, 1837 (REG I, 206)
Desilver, Thomas Jr.	Race, 3rd door below 10th (UNNAMED, 209–10)	Bought pew Nov. 17, 1834 (UNNAMED, 30)
Gould, Marcus T. C.	6 N. 8th (1831)	Agreed to extra payment to Furness Oct. 26, 1831 (UNNAMED, 290)
Harrison, Appollos W.	8½ S. 7th, h. 431 Walnut (1850)	Infant buried July 10, 1850 (REG I, [216])
Kay, James, Jr.	209 Sassafras (1828)	Paid pew rent Jan. 1, 1826 (CASH II, 2)
Kay, John	209 Sassafras (1828)	Paid pew rent Jan. 1, 1826 (CASH II, 2)

Mortimer, John	61 & 74 S. 2nd (1825)	Infant son buried July 7, 1825 (REG I. 195)
Pugh, Thomas B.	205 Chestnut, h. 149 S. 10th (1857)	Paid pew rent 1857 (PEW REG, # 27)
Small, Abraham	112 Chestnut (1817)	Infant daughter baptized April 27, 1817 (REG I, 6)
Small, Robert H.	165 Chestnut (1828)	Paid pew rent Dec. 15, 1827 (CASH II, 21)
Webster, James	24 S. 8th (1825)	Paid pew rent Nov. 7, 1825 (CASH II, 2)

BOOT AND SHOE MANUFACTURER

Bedford, John	296 Market (1816)	Signed records April 9, 1815 (PROC, 81)
Burns, John M.	121 S. 9th (1817)	Infant son buried Feb. 9, 1817 (REG I, 192)
Fox, Samuel	40 Filbert (1837)	Wife buried Sept. 9, 1837 (REG I, 206)
Hastings, James	138 Cedar (1825)	Contrib. May 6, 1827 (CASH II, 17)
Hill, James	154 S. 11 (1828)	Paid pew rent Sept. 11, 1827 (CASH II, 19)
Palmer, Robert	182 S. 2nd (1842)	At meeting April 18, 1842 (RECS & MINS, 117)
Snider, Jacob	5 N. 8th (1814)	Signed records April 9, 1815 (PROC, 81)

BRASSFOUNDER

Homer, Benjamin	24 Strawberry (1833)	At meeting April 15, 1833 (RECS & MINS, 94)
Homer, Henry	92 Callowhill (1839)	Married by Furness April 8, 1834 (REG I, 101)
Houghton, John	Germantown Road above 1st gate (1820)	Child baptized May 8, 1820 (REG I, 7)

BRICKLAYER

Evans, Josiah	60 New & 63 **N.** 6th (PROC, 81)	Signed records July 12, 1807 (PROC, 12)

BRICKMAKER

Homer, James	Bank & Federal (1855)	Paid pew rent 1855 (PEW REG, # 11)

BROKER

Barker, Abraham	28 S. 3rd, h. 1118 Spruce (1859)	Paid pew rent 1859 (PEW REG, # 124)
Bicknell, Robert T.	26 S. 4th (1828)	Held part pew Nov. 12, 1828 (UNNAMED, 301)
Clark, Edward W.	25 S. 3rd (1854)	Elected trustee Nov. 1, 1854 (TRUSTS III)
Clark, Enoch W.	25 S. 3rd, h. Pine above 9th (1841)	Infant daughter buried June 11, 1841 (REG I, [208])
Colcord, Enoch L.	17 S. 5th, d.h. 171 S. 5th (1829)	Held pew Nov. 12, 1828 (UNNAMED, 307)
Gilpin, John F.	67 Dock, h. Broad below Spruce (1850)	Elected trustee April 15, 1850 (RECS & MINS, 159)
Harper, Thomas	101 S. 2nd & 72 S. 5th (1811)	Member of committee May 5, 1811 (PROC, 93)
Nevins, J. West	68 S. 3rd, Spruce west of Broad (1844)	Married by Furness May 20, 1844 (REG I, 107)

CABINETMAKER

Edson, Nathan	Mary & Green (W.P.) (1855)	Paid pew rent 1855 (PEW REG, #50)

CARPENTER

Binder, George	Coates above 7th (1831)	At meeting April 18, 1831 (RECS & MINS, 81)

Broome, William	3 Carter's Alley, d.h. 62 S. 2nd (1826)	Daughter married by Furness May 11, 1826 (REG I, 97)

CARPET MANUFACTURER

Scholefield, John	176 Cedar (1825)	Paid pew rent Sept. 29, 1827 (CASH II, 21)

CHAIR ORNAMENTER

Haydon, William	George above 10th (1825)	Paid pew rent Dec. 17, 1825 (CASH II, 2)

CLERGYMAN

Christie, William	Unknown	Signed records July 12, 1807 (PROC, 12)
Furness, William H.	9 S. 9th (1825)	Elected pastor Sept. 15, 1824 (RECS & MINS, 33)
Hurlbut, Martin L.	Unknown	Paid pew rent Aug. 16, 1826 (CASH II, 14)
Priestley, Joseph	Northumberland, Penna.	Signed records Jan. 8, 1797 (PROC, 11)

CLERK

Dodson, William A.	N.W. cor. 2nd & Market, h. 179 S. 11th (1856)	Paid Pew rent 1856 (PEW REG, ♯91, ♯123)
Dyer, Olney	111 Chestnut, h. 136 S. 6th (1860)	Paid pew rent 1859 (PEW REG, ♯67)
Fairman, George W.	U.S. Bank, 435 Chestnut (1831)	At meeting Sept. 7, 1831 (RECS & MINS, 83–84)
Furness, James T.	11th near Chestnut (Oct. 12, 1829, COLL. CORR. I.)	Living with pastor, his brother (Oct. 12, 1829, COLL. CORR. I)

COACHMAKER

Crees, Thomas C.	Juniper Lane, d.h. 81 S. 11th (1828)	Paid pew rent Sept. 27, 1827 (CASH II, 21)

| Harvy, Peter | Near 58 S. 4th (1807) | Signed records July 12, 1807 (PROC, 12) |
| Haskell, Ebenezer | 332 S. 6th (1837) | Married by Furness Aug. 27, 1838 (REG I, 104) |

COACH-TRIMMER

| Copia, Jacob | 183 Pine (1819) | Infant buried Aug. 29, 1819 (REG I, 193) |

CONFECTIONER

| Parkinson, George | 174 Chestnut (1833) | Bought pew June 29, 1833 (UNNAMED, 28) |
| Parkinson, R. B. | 180 Chestnut (1842) | Signed antislavery Protest, 1842 (CHURCH MSS) |

CONVEYANCER

Canby, William J.	S.W. cor. 7th & Arch (1858)	Paid pew rent 1858 (PEW REG, #49)
Elliott, Isaac	82 Chestnut (1828)	Paid pew rent Oct. 1, 1827 (CASH II, 21)
Thackara, Samuel W.	S.E. cor. 3rd & Walnut (1829)	Held part pew Nov. 12, 1828 (UNNAMED,304)

CORDWAINER

| Fryer, George | 1 Ellet's Ave. (1848) | Married by Furness May 4, 1848 (REG I, 110) |

CURRIER

Esherick, Frederick	67 Cherry (1825)	Contrib. May 6, 1826 (CASH II, 13)
Espy, George	110 Sassafras (1825)	Paid pew rent Jan. 8, 1826 (CASH II, 2)
Mogridge, Thomas	65 Chestnut (1823)	Married by Taylor April 12, 1823 (REG I, 96)
Warren, James C.	10 S. Broad (1811)	Signed records Dec. 23. 1810 (PROC, 81)

Appendix B

DAGUERREOTYPIST

Collins, Simeon	110 Chestnut, h. 5 N. 11th (1855)	Paid pew rent 1855 (PEW REG, ♯ 10)

DENTIST

Townsend, Elisha	90 Walnut (1833)	At meeting April 15, 1833 (RECS & MINS, 94)

DRUGGIST

Holloway, William	376 High (1850)	Married by Furness April or May, 1850 (REG I, 111)
Roberts, Algernon S.	76 S. 2nd (1842)	Signed antislavery Protest, 1842 (CHURCH MSS)
Saltmarsh, Seth	Cor. Schuylkill 7th & Filbert (1837)	Married by Furness Sept. 19, 1835 (REG I, 102)

ENGINEER

Bartol. Barnabas H.	276 S. 10th (1855)	Paid pew rent 1855 (PEW REG, ♯13)
Eddowes, Joshua	101 Wood (1855)	Infant son buried July, 1855 (REG I, [220])

ENGRAVER

Carpenter, Samuel A.	Unknown	Agreed to pay extra compensation to Furness Oct. 20, 1831 (UNNAMED 289)
Childs, Cephas G.	54 Sansom, d.h. 200 Chestnut (1828)	Paid pew rent March 12, 1828 (CASH II, 23)
Fairman, Gideon	47 Sansom above 8th, d.h. 200 Chestnut (1825)	Member when Furness came in 1825 (COLL. CORR. I, Nov. 3, 1825)
Lovett, Robert	1 Carpenter's Court, h. Townsend's Court (1823)	Infant buried Aug. 20, 1823 (REG I, 195)

Pease, Joseph Ives	S.W. cor. 7th & Sansom (1841)	Married by Furness Dec. 8, 1841 (REG I, 106)
Sartain, John	S. 9th below Cedar (1831)	Infant son baptized Nov. 18, 1830 (REG I, 12)
Sartain, (Kenneth) Samuel	28 Sansom (1853)	Baptized Nov. 18, 1830 (REG I, 12)
Saulnier, Henry E.	181 N. 8th (1846)	Baptized as child Sept. 1, 1817 (REG I, 6)
Spencer, Asa	d.h. 48 Sansom above 8th (1825)	Contrib. June 19, 1826 (CASH II, 14)
Toppan, Charles	30 S. 7th (1829)	Infant son baptized Nov. 27, 1829 (REG I, 11)
Tucker, William E.	Cor. 4th & Library (1828)	Paid pew rent Nov. 12, 1828 (UNNAMED, 302)

ENVELOPE MANUFACTURER

Tobey, Samuel	233 S. 5th, h. 1903 Chestnut (1858)	Paid pew rent 1858 (PEW REG, #37)

FIRE ENGINE MANUFACTURER

Merrick, Samuel Vaughan	Pearson's Court back of St. James's Church (1823)	Signed records Jan. 21, 1823 (PROC, 114)
Towne, John Henry	Prime below 5th, off. 32 Walnut (1841)	At meeting April 19, 1841 (RECS & MINS, 114)

GENTLEMAN

Butler, Pierce	Butler Farm, Old York Rd. (Kemble, *Records of Later Life*, 2)	Birth (as "Pierce Mease" on March 23, 1810) registered in 1814 (REG I, 4)
Butler, Thomas	Not in *City Directories*, 1817–20	Birth of three children recorded in 1817 (REG I, 7)
Connell, George	Schuylkill 4th & Chestnut (1845)	Member of committee Dec. 1, 1845 (RECS & MINS, 139)

Emery, Samuel	256 High (1825)	Paid pew rent Oct. 9, 1825 (CASH II, 1)
Fellowes, Caleb	Clinton above 10th (1846)	Thanked for Communion silver April 20, 1846 (RECS & MINS, 141)
Gill, William	55 S. 12th (1845)	Member of committee Dec. 1, 1845 (RECS & MINS, 139)
Hulings, William E.	138 Pine (1807)	Subscriber July 13, 1807 (CHURCH MSS)
Hulme, Thomas	371 High (1822)	Daughter married by Taylor Nov. 28, 1822 (REG I, 96)
Logan, Zaccheus	19 S. 10th (1829)	Held pew Nov. 12, 1828 (UNNAMED, 305)
McIlhenney, William, Jr.	49 Old York Road (1825)	Paid pew rent April 22, 1826 (CASH II, 12)
Russell, William	319 High (1797)	Founder, summer 1796 (PROC, 5)

GEOGRAPHER

Melish, John	371 High (1817)	Wife buried Feb. 2, 1817 (REG I, 192)

GEOLOGIST

Lesley, J. Peter	N.E. cor. 8th & Walnut, h. 411 Blackstone (1859)	Paid pew rent 1859 (PEW REG, #17)
Taylor, Richard C.	Unknown	Sill declared him member when he died Oct. 27, 1851 (Sill, Diary, IX, 459–60)

GOLD LEAF MANUFACTURER

Carvill, Henry	59 Dock (1822)	Married by Taylor Nov. 28, 1822 (REG I, 96)

GUN MAKER

Miles, John	500 N. 2nd, Northern Liberties (1798)	Signed records March 19, 1797 (PROC, 11)
Miles, John Jr.	500 N. 2nd, Northern Liberties (1798)	Signed records June 3, 1798 (PROC, 11)

HOTEL PROPRIETOR

Renshaw, William	Washington Hotel, 122 S. 3rd (1816)	Three young children baptized Nov. 6, 1816 (REG I, 5)
Sanderson, Joseph M.	Merchants Coffee House, S. 2nd cor. Bank Alley (1829)	Paid pew rent Jan. 28, 1829 (UNNAMED, 30)

JEWELLER

Fletcher, Charles	N.E. cor. Chestnut & 3rd (1825)	Contrib. Feb. 27, 1826 (CASH II, 3)
Fletcher, George	139 Chestnut (1825)	Contrib. May 6, 1826 (CASH II, 13)
Fletcher, Thomas	325 Chestnut (1823)	Elected member Nov. 16, 1823 (RECS & MINS, 7)
Gardiner, Sidney	130 Chestnut (1825)	Paid pew rent Sept. 24, 1825 (CASH II, 1)
Mansfield, Samuel A.	20 N. 2nd, h. 729 N. 10th (1860)	Paid pew rent 1860 (PEW REG, #21)
Masson, Charles	18 N. 8th (1830)	Held half pew Nov. 11, 1828 (UNNAMED, 308)

JOURNALIST

Gales, Joseph	145 S. 2nd (1797)	Founder June 12, 1796 (PROC, 5)

JUDGE

Barnes, Joseph	Presiding Judge, U.S. District Court (1826)	Furness noted he had recently joined society April, 1829 (COLL. CORR. I)

| Kelley, William Darrah | Court of Common Pleas (1847) | New member Oct. 20, 1846 (COLL. CORR. II) |

LEATHER WORKER

| Hunt, Paul | 11 Marshall's Alley (1823) | Infant son buried June 9, 1822 (REG I, 194) |

MACHINIST

| Chapman, Jonathan | 517 N. 10th (1860) | Paid pew rent 1860 (PEW REG, #115) |
| Lewis, Enoch | 614 N. 16th (1858) | Paid pew rent 1858 (PEW REG, #71) |

MERCHANT

Aldrich, Lyman D.	3 and 5 Bank, h. 182 S. 3rd (1837)	Infant son buried March 12, 1838 (UNNAMED, 211–12)
Anderson, William V.	25 N. Water, d. h.152 N. Front (1828)	Rented pew Nov. 12, 1828 (UNNAMED, 315)
Astley, Thomas	Cor. 3rd & Spruce (1808)	Elected member Dec. 25, 1808 (PROC, 88)
Bailey, Lewis	30 S. Wharves (1828)	Contrib. May 6, 1826 (CASH II, 13)
Bargh, William	52 Commerce, h. 259 N. 11th (1855)	Paid pew rent 1855 (PEW REG, #66)
Bernard, William H.	169 High, d. 29 N. 5th (1833)	Paid pew installment Nov. 30, 1832 (UNNAMED, 33–34)
Birch, William Young	See under "BOOK-SELLER, etc."	
Blackburn, William	2 Church Alley (1828)	Paid pew rent Sept. 28, 1827 (CASH II, 21)
Blackwell, George	206 N. 2nd (1797)	Signed records Dec. 18, 1796 (PROC, 11)
Boggs, James	201 High (1830)	Young daughter baptized July 25, 1830 (REG I, 12)

Boult, Peter	150 S. 6th (1807)	Signed records July 12, 1807 (PROC, 12)
Bowlby, Richard W.	D.h., 4th above Willow (1833)	Young daughter buried April 9, 1832 (REG I, 201)
Bridges, Edwin N.	30 S. Wharves, d.h. 104 S. 9th (1828)	Bought pew Nov. 12, 1828 (UNNAMED, 24)
Bryan, Guy	223 Mulberry (1811)	Donated to Building Fund 1811 (COLLS, I)
Bryan, Timothy M.	225 High (1816)	Registered by father 1814 (REG I, 2)
Bryan, William P.	225 High (1816)	Registered by father 1814 (REG I, 2)
Bulkeley, Charles	130 Chestnut, h. 44 Prune (1840)	Infant son buried Aug. 6, 1840 (REG I, [208])
Burril, George	87 S. Front (1829)	Paid pew installment Dec. 19, 1828 (CASH II, 27)
Cabot, Frederick	175 Market, d.h. 163 S. 9th (1837)	Infant daughter baptized June 9, 1833 (REG I, 14)
Carter, George	55 N. Front (1797)	Founder Sept. 11, 1796 (PROC, 5)
Cheever, Benjamin R.	17 S. Front (1823)	Contrib. Jan. 5, 1826 (CASH II, 2)
Churchman, Charles W.	30 S. Front, h. 5 mile stone (Gtn.) (1855)	Paid pew rent 1855 (PEW REG, #14)
Coffin, Hector	28 S. Front (1825)	Paid pew rent Jan. 31, 1826 (CASH II, 3)
Colladay, Samuel R.	140 High, h. 9 Jacoby (1843)	At meeting April 17, 1843 (RECS & MINS, 120)
Conrad, J. Hicks	21 E. 3rd & Dock (1857)	Married by Furness Feb. 26, 1857 (REG I, 115)
Conway, Thomas	S.E. cor. 6th & High, h. 100 Union (1848)	Married by Furness May 4, 1848 (REG I, 110)
Cowperthwaite, Edwin	6 Commerce, h. 10th above Mulberry (1851)	Married by Furness Jan. 1851 (REG I, 111)

Coxe, Charles W.	12 Chestnut, h. 65 N. 11th (1855)	Elected trustee April 16, 1855 (RECS & MINS, 167)
Creighton, James	11 Strawberry, h. 522 Walnut (1860)	Paid pew rent Aug. 1, 1859 (PEW REG, #97)
Croft, Samuel	53 Commerce (1845)	Member of committee Dec. 1, 1845 (RECS & MINS, 139)
Davis, David M.	82 High, d.h. 165 Pine (1830)	Infant daughter buried Aug. 3, 1830 (REG I, 19)
Davy, William	141 S. Front (1797)	Signed records March 19, 1797 (PROC, 11)
Deland, Thorndike	46 S. Front (1831)	Agreed to extra payment to Furness Oct. 26, 1831 (UNNAMED, 289)
Duhring, Henry	53 N. 3rd, d.h. city hotel (1828)	Paid pew rent Dec. 16, 1827 (CASH II, 22)
Dummig, Charles	207 Chestnut & 33 N. 8th, h. 26 N. 7th (1854)	Paid pew rent 1854 (PEW REG, #30)
Eddowes, John	27 N. 3rd (1807)	Signed records July 12, 1807 (PROC, 12, 59)
Eddowes, Ralph	67 N. 3rd (1797)	Founder June 12, 1796 (PROC, 5)
Eddowes, Ralph, Jr.	1 Church Alley (PROC, 81), 27 N. 3rd (1807)	Signed records July 12, 1807 (PROC, 12, 59)
Eliot, Frank A.	40 N. Front, h. Broad below Walnut (1855)	Paid pew rent 1855 (PEW REG, #31)
English, Hugh	4½ N. 6th (1825)	Present at election of Furness Sept. 15, 1824 (RECS & MINS, 33)
Evans, Whitten	7 Walnut (1853)	Married by Furness Oct. 11, 1853 (REG I, 112)
Evans, William H.	34 N. 2nd (1842)	Signed antislavery Protest 1842 (CHURCH MSS)

Fales, George	17 S. Front, d.h. 127 S. Front (1825)	Contrib. Dec. 31, 1825 (CASH II, 2)
Farnham, Benjamin A.	8 S. Front, h. 66 S. 6th (1837)	Married by Furness Oct. 26, 1837 (REG I, 103)
Farnsworth, Jacob	134 Chestnut, d.h. 6 Sansom (1833)	At meeting April 15, 1833 (RECS & MINS, 94)
Fay, Charles M.	13 Commerce, h. 68 Franklin (1847)	At meeting April 20, 1847 (RECS & MINS, 148)
Fletcher, Thomas	See under "JEWELLER"	
Ford, John	206 High, d.h. 8 N. 7th (1822)	Elected member March 31, 1822 (PROC, 181)
Ford, Samuel C.	24 N. Front, h. W. Penn Square (1837)	Bought pew Oct. 28, 1837 (UNNAMED, 28)
Galvin, Thomas P.	15 N. Delaware Ave., h. 258 Marshall (1855)	Paid pew rent 1855 (PEW REG, #5)
Gardiner, Baldwin	98 Chestnut, h. 172 S. 4th (1825)	Contrib. May 6, 1826 (CASH II, 13)
Gardiner, Sidney	See under "JEWELLER"	
Godley, Jesse	53 High, d.h. cor. Arch & 11th (1833)	Bought pew Feb. 2, 1832 (UNNAMED, 28)
Griffith, Eli	S.E. cor. 11th & Chestnut (1840)	At meeting April 20, 1840 (RECS & MINS, 113)
Griffiths, Thomas	185 Chestnut (1844)	Baptized Jan. 6, 1822 (REG I, 8)
Gummey, John M.	5 N. 6th (1828)	Rented half pew Nov. 12, 1828 (UNNAMED, 304)
Ham, Joseph W.	11 S. Water (1841)	Married by Furness Sept. 5, 1841 (REG I, 105)
Hamilton, Charles C.	Broad below Locust, h. 153 S. 11th (1844)	Elected to committee Nov. 14, 1844 (RECS & MINS, 133)
Harrison, Appollos W.	See under "BOOK-SELLER"	
Harrold, Alfred	17 N. Commerce (1839)	Bought pew June 30 1839 (UNNAMED, 28)

Harrold, Frederick W.	Not in *Directories*, 1825–31	Contrib. Dec. 14, 1826 (CASH II, 15)
Harrold, William	Not in *Directories*, 1825–31	Paid pew rent Jan. 1, 1826 (CASH II, 2)
Haseltine, Ward B.	10 S. Wharves, h. 19 Clinton (1846)	At meeting April 20, 1846 (RECS & MINS, 141)
Hastings John	111 Chestnut (1828)	Bought pew Nov. 12, 1828 (UNNAMED, 23)
Hastings, Jonas	111 Chestnut, h. Chestnut above 13th (1828)	Paid pew rent Oct. 19, 1827 (CASH II, 21)
Hastings, Simon P.	Not in *Directories*, 1834–36	Married by Furness Sept. 29, 1835 (REG I, 102)
Haven, Charles C.	68 High (1830)	Furness noted arrival Oct. 30, 1829 (COLL. CORR. I)
Haven, Charles E.	41 S. Wharves, h. 400 Mulberry (1847)	Infant buried Dec. 26, 1847 (REG I, 215)
Haven, Charles Howard	34 Church Alley (1841)	Bought pew Sept. 26 1840 (UNNAMED, 29)
Haven, Thomas	91 S. Front, d.h. cor. Walnut & 13th (1830)	Infant buried Oct. 26, 1829 (REG I, 199)
Hill, David	S.W. cor. Chestnut & S. Wharves, d.h. 38 N. 8th (1831)	Infant buried Jan. 4, 1831 (UNNAMED, 205–6)
Hinchman, Benjamin M.	18 Church Alley, d.h. 76 S. 11th (1831)	At meeting April 16, 1832 (RECS & MINS, 92)
Hobson, Richard H.	147 Chestnut (1828)	Contrib. May 6, 1826 (CASH II, 13)
Homer, Timothy	174 Chestnut (1845)	Member of committee Dec. 1, 1845 (RECS & MINS, 139)
Hoopes, Bernard	h. 37 N. Front (1828)	Held pew Nov. 12, 1828 (UNNAMED, 303)
Irwin, William C.	41 N. 3rd, h. 11th above Market (1855)	Paid pew rent 1855 (PEW REG, #44)

Jacobs, Thomas H.	19 Dock (1825)	Married by Furness Oct. 27, 1825 (REG I, 96)
Jennings, John	36 N. Front, d.h. Chestnut below 12th (1828)	Bought pew Dec. 2, 1828 (CASH II, 27)
Johnson, Roland	4 N. Wharves, h. 6 Comptroller (1837)	Daughter buried May 18, 1837 (UNNAMED, 211–12)
Justice, Warner W.	N.W. cor. 8th & Parrish (1857)	Paid pew rent 1857 (PEW REG, #117)
Kimber, Samuel	236 N. 3rd, h. 4th below Green (1837)	Married by Furness May 28, 1835 (REG I, 102)
Landis, Henry D.	59 High, h. 11th above Walnut (1847)	Married by Furness Feb. 11, 1847 (REG I, 109)
Lea, Joseph	32 Chestnut, h. Spruce near Schuylkill 7th (1852)	Elected trustee April 19, 1852 (RECS & MINS, 164)
Lea, Thomas	32 Chestnut, h. 12th & Walnut (1844)	Married by Furness Nov. 12, 1844 (REG I, 108)
Leland, Charles	78 High, d.h. 85 Chestnut (1825)	Paid pew rent Sept. 23, 1825 (CASH II, 1)
Lentz, Henry	236 N. 2nd (1825)	Contrib. May 6, 1826 (CASH II, 13)
Lesley, James Jr.	243 Market (1855)	Two young sons baptized June 25, 1855 (REG I, 22)
Lewis, F. Mortimer	N.E. cor. 3rd & Walnut, h. 9 Belmont Place, Spruce (1852)	Married by Furness March 2, 1852 (REG I, 112)
Lincoln, E. Jr.	33 S. Wharves (1828)	Paid pew rent June 28, 1826 (CASH II, 14)
Lorenz, Ferdinand	2 Chestnut, h. Pine above 10th (1852)	Infant son baptized 1852 (REG I, 21)
Lothrop, Z.	6 S. Front, h. 19 S. 10th (1839)	Bought pew May 30, 1839 (UNNAMED, 28)
Lukens, Milton J.	102 High, h. 113 S. 3rd (1855)	Rented half pew 1855 (PEW REG, #7)

Lunt, Martin P.	cor. 2nd & Race, d.h. City Row Chestnut (1835)	Bought pew Nov. 23, 1835 (UNNAMED, 33–34)
Lyman, Charles A.	16 Dock, h. 48 S. 18th (1856)	Owned pew 1856 (PEW REG, #107)
Lyman, N. Parker	31 Commerce, h. 100 S. 3rd (1855)	Rented pew 1855 (PEW REG, #107)
Lyon, Walter T.	95 Market, h. 81 Wood (1855)	Rented half pew 1855 (PEW REG, #87)
Martin, Jacob	287 N. 3rd (1825)	Young daughter buried Sept., 1825 (REG I, 195)
McFarland, J.B.	105 High, h. 147 N. 4th (1845)	Member of committee Dec. 1, 1845 (RECS & MINS, 139)
McGregor, Robert	172½ High, h. 310 Walnut (1842)	Signed antislavery Protest 1842 (CHURCH MSS)
Mellon, Thomas	79 Pine (1828)	Bought pew Sept. 6, 1828 (CASH II, 27)
Merrill, George	11 S. Wharves, d.h. S.E. cor. Library & 5th (1831)	"Younger Member" Sept. 7, 1831 (RECS & MINS, 84)
Mitchell, James H.	13 S. Front, h. 439 Walnut (1841)	Infant buried Dec. 24, 1841 (UNNAMED, 211–12)
Moore, Bloomfield H.	24 E. North, h. 19th & Arch (1855)	Three children baptized May 17, 1855 (REG I, 22)
Moore, Lewis S.	224 Chestnut, h. George above Broad (1846)	At meeting April 20, 1846 (RECS & MINS, 141)
Moore, Marmaduke	195 High, h. 122 N. 10th (1839)	Bought part pew April 30, 1839 (UNNAMED, 28)
Morgan, Thomas W.	4 N. Wharves (1827))	Paid pew rent Sept. 14, 1827 (CASH II, 19)

Morris, Lewis S.	37 S. Wharves, h. 136 Chestnut (1842)	At meeting April 18, 1842 (RECS & MINS, 117)
Natt, Thomas	134 High (1825)	Paid pew rent July 11, 1826 (CASH II, 14)
Newhall, Gilbert Jr.	113 Walnut, h. 915 Pine (1860)	Paid pew rent 1855 (PEW REG, #72)
Newhall, Joseph H.	113 Walnut, h. 236 N. 12th (1860)	Paid pew rent 1855 (PEW REG, #39)
Nidda, Frederick K.	12 N. 3rd (1814)	Signed records April 9, 1815 (PROC, 81)
O'Brien, John, Jr.	154 High (1828)	Paid pew rent April 1, 1827 (CASH II, 16)
Palmer, Robert	182 S. 2nd (1842)	At meeting April 18, 1842 (RECS & MINS, 117)
Papegay, Miss F.	151 Walnut (1825)	Contrib. May 6, 1826 (CASH II, 13)
Patten, John W.	166, d.h. 163 N. 3rd (1825)	Married by Furness Oct. 15, 1826 (REG I, 97)
Peabody, Edward G.	159 High (1841)	Married by Furness Jan. 21, 1841 (REG I, 105)
Potts, Robert T.	105 High (1830)	Bought pew April 17, 1830 (UNNAMED, 27)
Pratt, Dundas T.	80 High, h. 128 Pine (1848)	Married by Furness April 27, 1848 (REG I, 110)
Reed, Charles D.	164 Market, h. 241 Vine (1855)	Paid pew rent 1855 (PEW REG, #18)
Robertson, William H.	20 Walnut, h. Locust near Schuylkill 8th (1842)	Signed antislavery Protest 1842 (CHURCH MSS)
Rogers, Evans	52 High (1828)	Bought pew Dec. 1, 1828 (CASH II, 27)
Rogers, William E.	52 High (1828)	Bought pew Dec. 1, 1828 (CASH II, 27)
Saulnier, John Joseph Mary	299 High (1817)	Eight children baptized Sept. 1, 1817 (REG I, 6)

Shute, John	106 High (1796)	Founder June 12, 1796 (PROC, 5)
Sill, Joseph	177 Chestnut (1828)	Married by Furness Oct. 16, 1825 (REG I, 96)
Snider, Jacob, Jr.	28 Walnut, d.h. 10 Castle (1835)	Married by Furness Dec. 19, 1832 (REG I, 100)
Somers, Chalkley	120 Market, h. 437 W. Walnut (1854)	Elected trustee April 17, 1854 (RECS & MINS, 169)
Soule, Horace H.	32 N. Front, h. 1100 Walnut (1861)	Elected trustee April 15, 1861 (RECS & MINS, 174)
South, George W.	98 Chestnut, d.h. 202 S. 4th (1829)	Paid pew installment June 17, 1829 (CASH II, 27)
Stanbridge, John C.	N. 4th, d.h. 5 S. 9th (1828)	Paid pew rent Sept. 1827 (CASH II, 18)
Stavers, William	44½ N. 2nd, h. 13 Branch (1844)	Infant son buried Nov. 29, 1844 (UNNAMED, 213–14)
Stone, Dexter	43 N. Water, Perot's Wharf, h. 9 S. 9th (1825)	Contrib. Dec. 27, 1825 (CASH II, 2)
Stone, John	41 S. 2nd (1837)	Married by Furness July, 1837 (REG I, 103)
Stotesbury, Thomas P.	71 S. Front, h. 427 Callowhill (1856)	Paid pew rent 1856 (PEW REG, #72)
Sweeney, Thomas W.	333 Market, h. 1226 Chestnut (1860)	Paid pew rent 1860 (PEW REG, #68)
Tams, James	243 High (1828)	Bought pew Nov. 12, 1828 (UNNAMED, 24)
Tams, Sampson	243 High (1828)	Bought pew Nov. 12, 1828 (UNNAMED, 24)
Taylor, James	28 N. 3rd (1797)	Founder June 12, 1796 (PROC, 5)
Tevis, Joshua	14 Church Alley, h. Walnut near Broad (1837)	Elected trustee April 17, 1837 (RECS & MINS, 105)

Thayer, Ziptheon	210 High, h. 9 Sergeant (1837)	Two children baptized Aug. 8, 1836 (REG I, 16)
Thomas, Charles J.	177 High, h. 164 N. 8th (1842)	Signed antislavery Protest 1842 (CHURCH MSS)
Thomas, Joseph M.	253 High, h. 11 Montgomery Square (1842)	Signed antislavery Protest 1842 (CHURCH MSS)
Thomas, Moses	87 Chestnut, d.h. Walnut above 11th (1831)	Held pew Nov. 11, 1828 (UNNAMED, 304)
Thomas, Samuel H.	107 and h. 246 Walnut (1823)	Signed records Jan. 21, 1822 (PROC, 114)
Todhunter, Joseph	54 S. 2nd (1824)	Wife buried Dec. 10, 1824 (REG I, 195)
Todhunter, William	2 N. 4th, d.h. 123 Chestnut (1830)	Paid pew rent Sept. 1827 (CASH II, 18)
Tredrick, Thomas	S.W. cor. Market & 9th, d.h. S.W. cor. 13th & George (1833)	Infant daughter buried Aug. 3, 1833 (UNNAMED, 207–8)
Trott, George, Jr.	45 Dock, h. 389 Walnut (1842)	Present at meeting April 18, 1842 (RECS & MINS, 117)
Tucker, James	Cor. South & 4th (1797)	Founder June 12, 1796 (PROC, 5)
Vaughan, John	107 S. Front & Chestnut above 8th (1798)	Signed records June 3, 1798 (PROC, 11)
Veron, Lewis	98, d.h. 130 Chestnut (1828)	Contrib. Jan. 5, 1826 (CASH II, 2)
Veron, Timothy	100 Chestnut, d.h. 3 Jefferson Row (1835)	At meeting Sept. 7, 1831 (RECS & MINS, 84)
Warren, William	385 S. 2nd (1811)	Signed records Dec. 23, 1810 (PROC, 81)
Weaver, William	77 High, h. 4th above Callowhill (1839)	Bought pew June 30, 1839 (UNNAMED, 28)

Wharton, Daniel C.	6 S. Front, h. 108 S. 3rd (1839)	Bought pew June 11, 1839 (PEW REG, #105)
Whittle, Robert	15 S. 2nd (1809)	Signed records Dec. 24, 1809 (PROC, 81)
Winsor, Henry	81 S. Delaware Avenue, h. 439 Spruce, below Broad (1857)	Paid pew rent 1857 (PEW REG, #89)
Wood, George A.	25 S. Wharf, h. 9 Belmont Place, Spruce (1844)	Member of committee April 15, 1844 (RECS & MINS, 130)
Wood, James	Cor. Front & Chestnut (1813)	Paid pew rent March 8, 1813 (CHURCH MSS)
Yarrow, John	127 High (1839)	Bought pew April 30, 1839 (UNNAMED, 28)

ORGAN-BUILDER

Stanbridge, J. C. B.	Factory, 22nd below Spruce, h. 2107 Chestnut (1859)	Paid pew rent 1859 (PEW REG, #65)

PAINTER (HOUSE)

Jewell, John B.	72 Chestnut (1828)	Paid pew rent Nov. 1, 1828 (UNNAMED, 35)
Thomas, Richard	Back of 13 German (1825)	Paid pew rent Feb. 19, 1826 (CASH II, 3)
Wheeler, John	12 Combs Alley (1796)	Signed records Sept. 11, 1796 (PROC, 10)

PHYSICIAN

Blayney, Arthur	158 S. 3rd (1796)	Founder June 12, 1796 (PROC, 5)
Brookfield, Joseph	Juniper & Filbert (1851)	Daughter baptized Sept. 29, 1851 (REG I, 21)
Egbert, Daniel	N.E. cor. 12th & Filbert (1842)	Three children baptized Nov. 27, 1842 (REG I, 18)

Green, Jonas   79 Walnut (1828)   Paid pew rent April 7, 1828 (CASH II, 33)

Heylin, Isaac   Palmyra Square (1824)   At meeting Nov. 9, 1824 (RECS & MINS, 33)

Mifflin, Charles   322 Walnut (1836)   Infant daughter baptized Feb. 8, 1836 (REG I, 16)

Neihardt, Charles   239 Spruce (1842)   Married by Furness Sept. 16, 1842 (REG I, 106)

Patterson, Henry   92 Arch (1854)   Young son buried 1854 (REG I, 219)

PLASTERER

Allen, James   216 Cherry (1839)   Bought half pew June 30, 1839 (UNNAMED, 28)

Evans, Josiah   101 N. 6th (1807)   Became member July 12, 1807 (PROC, 59)

RAILROAD OFFICIAL

Bradford, Samuel   10 Belmont Place, s. side Spruce below Broad (1837)   Infant son buried June 30, 1837 (UNNAMED, 211–12)

Felton, Samuel Morse   President, Phila., Wilm. & Balto. RR., h. (Chester) (1860)   Paid pew rent 1860 (PEW REG, #125)

Steele, J. Dutton   224 S. 4th (1860)   Paid pew rent 1859 (PEW REG, #91)

REAL ESTATE BROKER

McCay, Alexander   186 S. 5th (1831)   Infant son baptized July 4, 1830 (REG I, 11)

SACKING-BOTTOM MAKER

Murphy, William N.   285 N. 6th (REG I, 101)   Married by Furness March 18, 1834 (REG I, 101)

SALESMAN

Creighton, Hugh   10 S. Front (1855)   Paid pew rent May, 1855 (PEW REG, #21)

Appendix B

SCRIVENER

Jarvis, John	126 N. 3rd (1797)	Signed records Jan. 8, 1797 (PROC, 11)
Thomas, Nathaniel	186 or 168 S. 3rd (1796)	Founder June 12, 1796 (PROC, 5)

SHOEMAKER

Jordan, Thomas	Morgan's Court (1823)	Married by Eddowes April 17, 1823 (REG I, 96)
Owen, John	12 Pear (1797)	Signed records Nov. 6, 1796 (PROC, 11)
Ward, John	306 S. Front (1807)	Became member July 12, 1807 (PROC, 59)

SILK DYER

Newnham, Thomas	145 N. 2nd (1796)	Signed records Sept. 11, 1796 (PROC, 5)

SILVERPLATER

Armitage, George	438 Sassafras (1817)	Contrib. Sept. 1, 1817 (CASH II, 11)
Pinchin, William	Jacoby St. (1820)	Two children baptized Feb. 28, 1820 (REG I, 7)

STEREOTYPE FOUNDER

Fagan, John	19 St. James, h. W. Penn Square (1848)	Took pew in 1848 (COLL. CORR. II, Sept. 9, 1848)
Johnson, Lawrence	17 Cypress Alley, d.h. 47 Spruce (1825)	Married by Furness May 3, 1825 (REG I, 96)

STONECUTTER

Napier, Alexander	399 High (1807)	Became member July 12, 1807 (PROC, 59)

TAILOR

James, Jeremiah	212 High (1828)	Paid pew installment Dec. 4, 1829 (CASH II, 27)

Royston, George	John St. between Broad & Coates (1797)	Founder June 12, 1796 (PROC, 5)
Young, William	153 South (1797)	Signed records Sept. 11, 1796 (PROC, 10–11)

TEACHER

Espy, James P.	150 Mulberry (1825)	Contrib. May 6, 1826 (CASH II, 13)
Howard, Daniel W.	120 Cherry (1856)	Paid pew rent 1856 (PEW REG, #83)
Hurlbut, Martin L.	See under "CLERGYMAN"	
Johnson, Walter R.	9 S. 7th, d.h. 127 (1829)	Contrib. April 29, 1827 (CASH II, 16)
Lesley, J. Peter	See under "GEOLOGIST"	
Rogers, Fairman	University of Penna., h. Washington Square & Locust (1856)	Born Nov. 15, 1833; both parents members of society.
Trendel, Thomas	229 Mulberry (1807)	Signed records July 12, 1807 (PROC, 12)
Woodman, William	Cooper's Court (PROC, 11)	Signed records May 20, 1798 (PROC, 11)

THEATRE

Dinmore, William R.	191 S. 9th (1837)	Bought pew April 11, 1837 (UNNAMED, 28)
Walstein, James W.	Chestnut St. Theatre (REG I, 206)	Married by Furness June 19, 1831 (REG I, 99)

TIN-PLATE WORKER

Porter, Samuel T.	N.W. cor. 13th & Filbert (1820)	Signed records Jan. 24, 1819 (PROC, 114)

UPHOLSTERER

Alder, Caleb	119 S. 3rd (1796)	Founder June 12, 1796 (PROC, 5)

Appendix B

WAREHOUSE OPERATOR

Worrall, John	19 S. 2nd (1819)	Child buried by Furness July 20, 1819 (REG I, 193)

WATCHMAKER

Quandale, Lewis	92 High, d.h. 107 Chestnut (1831)	Contrib. Oct. 26, 1831 (UNNAMED, 291)
Townsend, Charles	21 and h. 138 S. 10th (1841)	At meeting April 19, 1841 (RECS & MINS, 114)

WIRE FENDER AND CAGE MAKER

Cluley, John	34 S. 3rd (1807)	Became member July 12, 1807 (PROC, 59)

APPENDIX C

ORGANIZATIONAL ACTIVITIES OF MEMBERS

Data are fragmentary. Where no dates are given, they were not available.

Elected Member		Held Office
ACADEMY OF NATURAL SCIENCES		
Birch, William Y.	1823	
Felton, Samuel M.	1860	
Haseltine, Ward B.	1859	
Hoopes, B. A.	1856	
Johnson, Walter R.	1827	Auditor, 1832–35; Curator, 1835–37; Corresponding Secretary 1841–48
Lesley, J. P[eter]	1853	
Merrick, Samuel V.	1853	
Rogers, Fairman	1854	
Rotch, Thomas	1816	
Tryon, George W. Jr.	1859	Curator, 1869–76
Vaughan, John	1822	Curator, 1825–27

ACCOUNTANTS' SOCIETY OF PENNSYLVANIA

Mogridge, Thomas D.   Committee of Charity, 1822

AGRICULTURE, SOCIETY FOR THE PROMOTION OF

Butler, Pierce	1844	
Butler, Thomas	1805	
Childs, Cephas G.	1858	
Eddowes, Ralph, Sr.	1809	
Eddowes, Ralph, Jr.	1813	

278

Fairman, Gideon   1819

Harper, Thomas   1806

Hulme, Peter   1844

Merrick, Samuel V.   1854

Rogers, Evans   1860

Vaughan, John   1785   Vice-President, Committee of Correspondence, 1819

AMERICAN (and HEALTH) INSURANCE CO.

Kelley, William D.   Trustee, 1854

AMERICAN BENEFICIAL SOCIETY

Snider, Jacob   President, 1820, 1823

AMERICAN FIRE INSURANCE CO.

Bryan, Guy   President, 1813–15; Director, 1813–25

AMERICAN PHILOSOPHICAL SOCIETY

Carey, Henry C.   1833

Espy, James P.   1835

Furness, William H.   1840

Lesley, J. Peter   1856   Librarian, 1858–85; Secretary, 1859–86; Vice-President, 1887–97

Merrick, Samuel V.   1833

Priestley, Joseph   1785

Rogers, Fairman   1857

Vaughan, John   1784   Secretary, 1789–91; Treasurer, 1791–1841; Librarian, 1803–41

ARTISTS AND AMATEURS ASSOCIATION

Sill, Joseph   Chairman, Board of Managers, 1841–43

ARTISTS' FUND SOCIETY OF PHILADELPHIA

Bridport, Hugh	1835	Controller, 1835
Furness, William H.	1842*	
Sartain, John	1835	Controller, 1836; Treasurer, 1841–42
Sill, Joseph	1843*	
Snider, Jacob, Jr.	*	
Sully, Thomas	1843**	
Sully, Thomas, Jr.	1835	
Toppan, Charles	1836	
Vaughan, John	1838*	

Donors ($50 or more)

Sully, Thomas

Towne, John

Life Subscribers ($25)

Natt, Thomas J.

Sartain, John

Sill, Joseph

Snider, Jacob, Jr.,

Toppan, Charles

ATHENAEUM OF PHILADELPHIA

Shareholders

Anderson, William V.	
Barnes, Joseph	1836–?
Birch, William Y.	1816–38
Blanchard, William A.	1834–61
Bryan, Guy, Jr.	1819–20

*Honorary Amateur Member
**Honorary Professional Member

Burril, George	1835–?
Butler, Pierce	1848–54
Churchman, Charles West	1834–61
Cope, Charles S.	1832–46
Eddowes, John	1816–20
Eddowes, Ralph	1820–33
Fagan, John	1827–74
Fairman, Gideon	1816–19
Fales, George	1830–46; 1851–?
Fellowes, Caleb	1825–28; 1835–41
Gilpin, Charles	1835–71
Harrold, William	1825–45
Haven, Thomas A.	1833–48
Haseltine, Ward B.	1851–52
Heylin, Isaac	
Hinchman, Benjamin M.	1845–58
Hobson, Richard H.	1821–27
Johnson, Walter R.	1826–49
Kay, James	1848–69
Roberts, Algernon S.	1820–24
Rogers, Evans	1824–68
Rotch, Thomas	1816–21; 1828–41
Scholefield, John	1846–48
Sill, Joseph	1833–59
Small, Robert H.	1868–69
Spencer, Asa	
Sully, Thomas	1818–22

Taylor, James   1816–45

Thomas, Moses   1816–25;
1831–33

Thomas, Samuel H.   1816–43;
1845–58

Todhunter, Joseph, Jr.   1827–37

Trott, George   1850–?

Vaughan, John   1816–42   Director, 1819–42;
Vice-President,1819, 1823 1824, 1836–41.

Wyeth, John   1832–69

ATHENIAN INSTITUTE

Carpenter, Samuel H. 1838

Childs, C. G.

Espy, James P.   Counsellor, 1838–39

Furness, James

Furness, William H.   Counsellor, 1838–44

Haven, Charles C.

Rogers, Evans

Sartain, John

Saulnier, Henry C.

Sill, Joseph   Counsellor, 1838–40;
Secretary, 1841–44

Snider, Jacob, Jr.

Toppan, Charles   Counsellor, 1838–44

Vaughan, John   Counsellor, 1839–41

BANK OF COMMERCE

Deland, Thorndike   Director, 1848–49, 1852–53

BANK OF THE NORTHERN LIBERTIES

Childs, Cephas G.   Director, 1849, 1852–54

Stone, Dexter   Director, 1844–46

BANK OF PENNSYLVANIA

Anderson, William V.   Director, 1843–44, 1848

BLIND, PENNSYLVANIA INSTITUTION FOR THE INSTRUCTION OF THE

Birch, William Y.   Vice-President, 1834, 1837

Elliott, Isaac   Treasurer, 1834;
                                        Secretary, 1847;
                                        Manager, 1850–59

Merrick, Samuel V.   Secretary, 1845

Rogers, Evans   Manager, 1847–50

Snider, Jacob, Jr.   Recording Secretary, 1834–38;
                                        Manager, 1835

Vaughan, John   Treasurer, 1834 (3 mos.);
                                        Manager, 1834;
                                        President, 1837–41

CAPITAL PUNISHMENT, SOCIETY FOR THE ABOLITION OF

Sill, Joseph   Executive Committee, 1845

CHELTENHAM & WILLOW GROVE TURNPIKE COMPANY

Fletcher, Thomas   Director, 1813–14;
                                        Manager, 1819–20

COLUMBIAN SOCIETY OF ARTISTS

Fairman, Gideon   Secretary, 1819–20

COMMERCIAL BANK OF PENNSYLVANIA

Fales, George   Director, 1841–42, 1845–46,
                                        1848–49, 1852–53, 1857–60

Gill, William   Director, 1844 ,1846

Haseltine, Ward B.   Director, 1846, 1848, 1852

COMPANY FOR THE IMPROVEMENT OF THE VINE

Vaughan, John   Manager, 1802

CONSOLIDATED INSURANCE COMPANY

Thomas, Jacob   Director, 1859

COUNCILS, CITY

Common Council

Godley, Jesse	1849
Harper, Thomas	1822
Small, Abraham	1820–22
Tevis, Joshua	1848
Yarrow, John	1852 President, 1854

Select Council

Elliott, Isaac	1840, 1842, 1845, 1846, 1848, 1849
Thomas, Joseph M.	1852–55

FARMERS' AND MECHANICS' BANK

Farnham, Benjamin A.   Director, 1845–46, 1853–54, 1857, 1860

FEMALE MEDICAL COLLEGE OF PENNSYLVANIA

Moore, Marmaduke   Treasurer, 1856, 1858–59

FIRST-DAY OR SUNDAY SCHOOL SOCIETY

Eddowes, John   Secretary, 1813–14

Taylor, James   Vice-President, 1807

FIVE PER CENT SAVING FUND, DEPOSIT AND LOAN COMPANY

Fletcher, Thomas   President and Director, 1856–57

FRANKLIN FIRE INSURANCE COMPANY

Blanchard, William A.   Orig. stockholder

Carey, Henry C.		President, 1834–37; Director, 1829–37
Fales, George	Orig. stock-holder	Director, 1856–79; Vice-President, 1867–79

FRANKLIN INSTITUTE

Birch, William Y.	1825	
Carvill, Henry	1825	
Childs, C[ephas] G.	1825	
Crissy, James	1825	
Desilver, Robert	1825	
Espy, James P.	1825	
Fairman, Gideon	1825	
Fales, George	1825	
Fletcher, Thomas	1825	Treasurer, 1824–26; Recording Secretary, 1825; Manager, 1826–27, 1855–61; Vice-President, 1825–53
Gardiner, Sidney	1825	
Jewell, John B.		
Johnson, Lawrence		Manager, 1855–59
Johnson, Walter R.		(Committee on Inventions, 1830)
Merrick, Samuel V.	Founder	Manager, 1825–40; 1855–61; Curator, 1825–26; Treasurer, 1828–30; President, 1841–54
Roberts, A[lgernon] S.		(Committee on Premiums and Exhibits, 1829); Auditor, 1848–56
Rogers, Evans		Manager, 1854–61
Sill, Joseph	1825	
Spencer, Asa	1825	
Thomas, Jacob	1825	
Todhunter, Joseph	1825	

Toppan, Charles   Manager, 1831–32
Towne, John   Manager, 1841–57
Vaughan, John   1825

GERMAN SOCIETY FOR THE RELIEF OF GERMAN IMMIGRANTS

Duhring, Henry   Secretary, 1843–45

GIRARD COLLEGE

Roberts, Algernon S.   Director, 1855, 1860
Yarrow, John   Director, 1855–56

GUARDIANS OF THE POOR, OFFICE OF THE

Gilpin, John F.   Member for City of Philadelphia, 1849

HIGH SCHOOL

McMurtrie, Henry   Professor of Anatomy & Physiology & Natural History, 1853–60

HISTORICAL SOCIETY OF PENNSYLVANIA

Vaughan, John   Executive Council, 1829–42

HOUSE OF REFUGE

Rogers, Evans   Manager, 1859

INSURANCE COMPANY OF DELAWARE

Vaughan, John   Director, 1812

INSURANCE COMPANY OF NORTH AMERICA

Astley, Thomas   Director, 1809–39
Vaughan, John   Director, 1794–98

LANCASTER AND PHILADELPHIA TURNPIKE COMPANY

Taylor, James   Director, 1813–14; Manager, 1819–20

Appendix C

MECHANICS' BANK

Leland, Charles   Director, 1840, 1842–44, 1848, 1852, 1855–56

MERCHANTS' COFFEE HOUSE

(*Subscribers to Green Room*)

Anderson, William V.   1834–46

Bryan, William P.   1835

Farnham, B[enjamin]   1843

MUSICAL FUND SOCIETY OF PHILADELPHIA

Anderson, William V.

Birch, William Y.   Manager, Trustee, 1820

Blanchard, William A.   1852

Blayney, Miss

Bulkeley, Charles

Butler, John   1847

Butler, Pierce   1826   Director

Carey, Henry C.

Crissy, James   1827   Manager

Deland, T[horndyke]

Desilver, Miss E.   1822

Desilver, Robert

Desilver, Thomas   1821

Duhring, Henry   1830

Fletcher, Charles   1824

Fletcher, Thomas

Gardiner, Sidney

Harper, Charles   1835

Harrold, F[rederick]

Haven, Charles C.   1833
Haven, T[homas] A.
Heylin, Isaac
Jennings, John
Johnson, Walter R.
Kay, James, Jr.   Manager
Jewell, John B.
Moore, Marmaduke   1843
Morgan, Thomas W.
Nevins, J. West   Manager
Sanderson, Joseph M.   1825
Small, Robert H.
Snider, Jacob   1831
Spencer, Asa   1827
Standbridge, J. C. B.   Director
Sully, Thomas   1820   Director of Music, 1820
Thomas, Moses
Thomas, Samuel H.
Towne, John H.   1849
Vaughan, John
Veron, T[imothy]   1832

NEW ENGLAND, SOCIETY OF SONS OF, OF PHILADELPHIA

Bradford, Samuel   Treasurer, 1846
Cheever, Benjamin R.   Treasurer, 1823
Furness, William H.   Chaplain, 1846
Towne, John H.   Director, 1846

PENNSYLVANIA ACADEMY OF THE FINE ARTS

Childs, Cephas G.   Director, 1830–45
McMurtrie, James   Director, 1813–16

Peale, Rembrandt	Director, 1811–13
Sartain, John	Director, 1855–59, 1866–77; Secretary, 1857–58; Corresponding Secretary, 1863–68; Secretary, 1868–77
Sully, Thomas	Director, 1816–31, 1842
Towne, John	Director, 1844–50
Vaughan, John	Director, 1816–20, 1822–42

PENNSYLVANIA HORTICULTURAL SOCIETY

Rogers, Fairman	1860 (Life)
Rotch, Thomas	(Council member, 1833–36)
Vaughan, John	(Council member, 1829–30)

PENNSYLVANIA HOSPITAL

Elliott, Isaac	Manager, 1841–42

PENNSYLVANIA INFIRMARY FOR DISEASES OF THE EYE AND EAR

Merrick, Samuel V.	Manager, 1822
Vaughan, John	Manager, 1822

PENNSYLVANIA RAILROAD COMPANY

Godley, Jesse	Director, 1847–48
Mellon, Thomas	Director, 1856–64
Thomas, Joseph M.	Director, 1859
Yarrow, John	Director, 1849–55

PENNSYLVANIA SOCIETY FOR THE PROMOTION OF PUBLIC ECONOMY

Vaughan, John	Member, Library Committee, 1817–20

PENNSYLVANIA STEAMSHIP COMPANY

Godley, Jesse	Among incorporators in 1851

PHILADELPHIA BANK

Yarrow, John   Director, 1852–56

PHILADELPHIA, BRANDYWINE TURNPIKE COMPANY

Harvy, Peter   Director, 1813–14

PHILADELPHIA CLUB

Anderson, William V.	1849–58	
Bryan, Timothy M.	1836–64	President pro tem, Oct.–Nov., 1847 (Mexican War)
Butler, John	1834–38	
Rotch, Thomas	1834–38	
Thomas, Moses	1857–65	

PHILADELPHIA DISPENSARY

Green, Jonas   Attending physician and surgeon, 1833

PHILADELPHIA INSURANCE COMPANY

Johnson, Lawrence   Director, 1854–56

Moore, Marmaduke   Director, 1854–58

Reed, Charles D.   Director, 1855–56

PHILADELPHIA MUSEUM COMPANY

Elliott, Isaac   Director, 1840–43

PHILADELPHIA REAL ESTATE, SAVINGS AND LOAN COMPANY

Fletcher, Thomas   President, 1856; Director, 1856–60

PHILADELPHIA SAVING FUND SOCIETY

Vaughan, John   Incorporator, 1819; Manager, 1818–20

PHILADELPHIA SOCIETY FOR THE INFORMATION AND ASSISTANCE OF PERSONS EMIGRATING FROM FOREIGN COUNTRIES

Birch, William Y. — Committee of Conference and Correspondence, 1796

Blayney, Arthur — Physician, 1796; Committee of Conference and Correspondence

Newnham, Thomas — Treasurer, 1796; Committee of Conference and Correspondence

PREMIUM SOCIETY

Birch, William Y. — Manager, 1812–13

Small, Abraham — Manager, 1812–13

PRISON, BOARD OF INSPECTORS OF THE COUNTY

Rogers, Evans — 1860

RELIANCE MUTUAL INSURANCE COMPANY

Hinchman, B[enjamin] M. — Secretary, 1845–53

RIDING CLUB

Rogers, Evans — 1854 — Incorporator, 1868

Rogers, Fairman — 1854 — Incorporator, 1868

ROSINE ASSOCIATION

Furness, Mrs. William H. — One of founders, 1847

SCHUYLKILL FISHING COMPANY OF THE STATE IN SCHUYLKILL

Tams, James — 1846–48

Thomas, Joseph M. — 1853–?

SONS OF ST. GEORGE, SOCIETY OF THE

Astley, Thomas	1801	Steward, 1812–22
Birch, William Y.	1816	Steward, 1822–29, 1831–33
Bowlby, Edward	1808	
Darch, Samuel	1810	
Davy, William	1797	
Harvy, Peter	1810	
Kay, James, Jr.	1831	
Mellor, George	1840 (Hon.)	
Merrick, Samuel V.	1831	
Natt, Thomas	1823	
Renshaw, William	1807	
Sartain, John	1840	
Scholefield, John	1840	Steward, 1841; Secretary 1842–47
Sill, John T.	1851	Steward, 1853
Sill, Joseph	1829 (Life Contrib.)	Steward, 1832–33; Secretary, 1834–41 Vice-President, 1842–47; President, 1848–54
Small, Abraham	1817	
Sully, Thomas	1818	
Tams, James	1830 (Associate)	
Tams, John	1847	
Tams, Sampson	1830 (Associate) 1832 (Regular)	Steward, 1844
Taylor, James	1796	
Todhunter, John	1848 (Life Contrib.)	

Todhunter, Joseph		Steward, 1825–26; Secretary, 1827–33
Todhunter, William	1834	Treasurer, 1835–36
Vaughan, John	1789	Steward, 1791–99; President, 1840–41
Wood, James		Steward, 1816–26

UNION BENEVOLENT ASSOCIATION

Espy, Mrs.	1831	Secretary, 1831
Fairman, Mrs.	1831	
Furness, Mrs.	1831	

UNION INSURANCE COMPANY

Bryan, Timothy M.	Director, 1840–44

UNION MUTUAL INSURANCE COMPANY

Churchman, Charles W.	Director, 1855–59

WALNUT STREET THEATRE

Desilver, Robert	Subscriber, 1820
Desilver, Thomas	Subscriber, 1820
Renshaw, William	Subscriber, 1820

WESTERN BANK

Blanchard, William A.	Director, 1842–60

WESTERN SAVING FUND SOCIETY

Elliott, Isaac	Manager, 1848–59

WISTAR ASSOCIATION

Merrick, Samuel V.	1835
Vaughan, John	1818 (A founder)

BIBLIOGRAPHY

MANUSCRIPTS

Records of the First Unitarian Church of Philadelphia

Collections.
> Subscriptions to the Octagon Church opened in 1813.

Eddowes, Ralph. "Proceedings on laying the first Corner-Stone of the New Unitarian Church, 10th fronting on Locust Street, Philadelphia, 25th March, 1828, with a Brief Account of the Rise and Progress of the Society."

General Cash Account No. 2.

Treasurer's records, 1811–50.

General Records Book.
> A miscellaneous collection, including charters, lists of subscribers to the Octagon Church, burials, pew rents, etc.

Historical Notes.
> Includes "Some notices of Rev. James Taylor of Phila'da extracted from a Memoir by himself."

Minutes of Trustees, Vol. III [1828–1882].

Miscellaneous Collection
> Letters, notes, deeds to church properties, and various memorabilia.

Pew Register [1854–61].

Proceedings [1796 to January 20, 1823].

Register, Vol. I.
> Births, baptisms, marriages, and burials prior to January 12, 1876.

Register, Vol. II.
> Births, baptisms, marriages, and burials from January 12, 1876 to 1907.

Records and Minutes [of annual Meetings, financial reports, and societies of the church, January 20, 1823 to February 7, 1907].

Unnamed Journal.
> Untitled and without date. Scattered items of historical interest.

General

Archives, American Philosophical Society.

Cramp, Charles H. "Carey's 'Vespers.'" Edward C. Gardiner Collection, Historical Society of Pennsylvania.

Eddowes, Ralph. "Occurrences During a passage from Liverpool to Philadelphia from 1st August to 1st Novr. 1794." First Unitarian Church of Philadelphia.

Thomas Fletcher Papers. Historical Society of Pennsylvania.

Benjamin Franklin Papers. American Philosophical Society.

Furness, William H. Collected Correspondence with the Jenks Family, 2 vols., given to the author by Horace Howard Furness Jayne.

Furness, William H. Osgood Correspondence, given to the author by Horace Howard Furness Jayne.

History of the Shares. Athenaeum of Philadelphia.

Manuscripts [*sic*]. American Philosophical Society.

Miscellaneous Manuscript Collection. American Philosophical Society.

Pennsylvania Society for promoting the Abolition of Slavery, for the relief of Free Negroes, unlawfully held in Bondage, and for improving the condition of the African Race:

> Minutes, Volume III, 1825–47; Volume IV, 1847–1916.

> Committee for the Improvement of Colored People—Minutes, 1847–53.

> Historical Society of Pennsylvania.

Joseph Priestley Papers. American Philosophical Society.

Record of Strangers, 1814–1956. 5 vols. Athenaeum of Philadelphia.

Ronaldson Cemetery Records:

> Record of Interments . . . from 1827. 2 vols.

> Lot Books. 4 vols.

> Photostatic copies. Historical Society of Pennsylvania.

Sill, Joseph. "Diary [1831–1854.]" 10 vols. Historical Society of Pennsylvania

University of Pennsylvania. Minutes of Trustees, Volume V [1791–1811].

Benjamin Vaughan Papers. American Philosophical Society.

PRINTED WORKS

Books and Pamphlets

UNITARIANISM

Allen, Joseph Henry. *Historical Sketch of the Unitarian Movement Since the Reformation*. New York, 1894.

Ames, Charles G. *Unitarian Christianity*. Tract No. 96, American Unitarian Association. Boston, December, 1906.

Church Memorials. A pamphlet printed by the First Unitarian Church of Philadelphia. Philadelphia, n.d.

Constitution of the First Society of Unitarian Christians in the City of Philadelphia; Adopted, August 23, 1807. Philadelphia, 1807.

Cooke, George Willis. *Unitarianism in America.* Boston, 1902.

Emerton, Ephraim. *Unitarian Thought.* New York, 1911.

Furness, Horace Howard. *Historical Address delivered in Connection with the Installation of the Reverend Charles E. St. John as Minister of The First Unitarian Church of Philadelphia, 12th of January, 1908.* Philadelphia, 1908.

Holt, Raymond V. *The Unitarian Contribution to Social Progress in England.* London, 1938.

Laying the Corner Stone of the Third Church Edifice of the First Unitarian Society of Philadelphia on . . . March 25, 1885. . . . Philadelphia, 1885.

May, Joseph. *A Farewell to an Old Home. . . . A Sermon preached in the First Unitarian Church, corner of Tenth and Locust Streets, on the occasion of the last meeting in that house before its abandonment by the Society, 1885.* Philadelphia, 1885.

Scholefield, Harry B. (ed.). *Unitarianism: Some Past History and Present Meanings.* Boston, 1950.

————*A Pocket Guide to Unitarianism.* Boston, 1954.

Sermons, Addresses and Essays delivered at the Celebration of the One Hundredth Anniversary of the Foundation of the First Unitarian Church of Philadelphia. Philadelphia, 1896.

Ware, Henry, Jr. *A Sermon delivered at the Ordination of the Rev. William Henry Furness as Pastor of the First Congregational Unitarian Church in Philadelphia, January 12, 1825. . . .* Philadelphia, 1825.

Wilbur, Earl Morse. *A History of Unitarianism.* 2 vols. Cambridge, Mass., 1946–52.

Wright, Conrad. *The Beginnings of Unitarianism in America.* Boston, 1955.

INDIVIDUALS

Adams, Charles Francis (ed.). *The Works of John Adams.* 10 vols. Boston, 1856.

McCuskey, Dorothy. *Bronson Alcott, Teacher.* New York, 1940.

Sanborn, F[ranklin] B. and Harris, William T. *A. Bronson Alcott, His Life and Philosophy.* 2 vols. Boston, 1893.

Binns, John, *Recollections of the Life of John Binns.* Philadelphia, 1854.

Bibliography

Bradford, Samuel. *Some Incidents in the Life of Samuel Bradford, Senior, by his Son. Also, the Autobiography or a Brief Narrative of the Life of Samuel Bradford, Junior, to January 1, 1879.* Philadelphia, 1880.

Breck, Samuel. *Recollections of Samuel Breck.* Philadelphia, 1877.

Bremer, Fredrika. *The Homes of the New World.* 2 vols. New York, 1854.

Butler, Frances Anne. *Journal.* 2 vols. Philadelphia, 1835.

Pierce Butler vs. Frances Anne Butler, Libel for Divorce with Answers and Exhibits, in Court of Common Pleas, Philadelphia. N.p., n.d.

Mr. Butler's Statement, originally prepared in aid of his professional counsel. N.p., n.d.

A Statement of James Schott, Jr. N.p., 1844.

Kemble, F[rances] A[nn], *Journal of a Residence on a Georgian Plantation in 1838–39.* New York, 1863.

——. *Records of a Girlhood.* New York, 1883.

——. *Records of Later Life.* New York, 1883.

Armstrong, Margaret. *Fanny Kemble, A Passionate Victorian.* New York, 1938.

Elder, William. *A Memoir of Henry C. Carey.* Philadelphia, 1880.

Green, Arnold W. *Henry Charles Carey, Nineteenth Century Sociologist.* Philadelphia, 1951.

Channing, William Ellery. *Slavery.* Boston, 1835.

Chadwick, John W. *William Ellery Channing.* Boston, 1903.

Christie, William. *Dissertations on the Unity of God.* Philadelphia, 1808.

——. *Select Psalms, Christmas Hymns, and Other Devotional and Sentimental Pieces.* Philadelphia, 1821.

Cobbett, William. *Porcupine's Works: Containing Various Writings and Selections, Exhibiting a faithful picture of the United States of America.* 12 vols. London, 1801.

Stebbins, Emma (ed.). *Charlotte Cushman, Her Letters and Memoirs of Her Life.* Boston, 1878.

Dewey, Orville. *Autobiography and Letters,* ed. Mary E. Dewey. Boston, 1883.

Eddowes, Ralph. *Sermons.* Philadelphia, 1817.

Rusk, Ralph L. (ed.). *The Letters of Ralph Waldo Emerson.* 6 vols. New York, 1939..

——. *Ralph Waldo Emerson.* New York, 1949.

David, Richard Beale (ed.). *Jeffersonian America. Notes on the United States of America Collected in the years 1805–6–7 and 1811–12 by Sir Augustus John Foster, Bart.* San Marino, Calif., 1954.

Jayne, Horace Howard Furness (ed.). *The Letters of Horace Howard Furness*. 2 vols. Boston, 1922.

Furness, William Henry. *Sermons, Addresses, Articles* (1825–1869). 5 vols. Individually printed works, collected and bound by his family. N.p., n.d.

Additional sermons cited in the text:

Robert Collyer and His Church. A Discourse delivered . . . November 12, 1871. Philadelphia, n.d.

Recollections upon the Forty-Eighth Anniversary . . . January 19th, 1873. N.p., n.d.

. . . Discourse delivered . . . January 12, 1875, on the Occasion of the Fiftieth Anniversary of His Ordination. Philadelphia, 1875.

———. *Remarks on the Four Gospels.* Philadelphia, 1836.

———. *Jesus and His Biographers.* Philadelphia, 1838.

———. *Domestic Worship.* Philadelphia, 1840.

———. *Mirror of Nature.* Translated from the German of G. H. Schubert. Philadelphia, 1849.

———. *A History of Jesus.* Boston, 1850.

———. *Gems of German Verse.* Philadelphia, 1851.

———. *Julius and Other Tales from the German.* Philadelphia, 1856.

———. *Julius and The Parsonage of Rodolphe Toepffer.* N.p., 1856.

———. *Thoughts on the Life and Character of Jesus of Nazareth.* Boston, 1859.

———. *The Veil Partly Lifted and Jesus Becoming Visible.* Boston. 1864.

———. *The Character of Jesus Portrayed.* Translated from the German of Dr. Daniel Schenkel. 2 vols. Boston, 1866.

———. *The Voice in Singing.* Translated from the German of Emma Seiler. Philadelphia, 1868.

———. *The Unconscious Truth of the Four Gospels.* Philadelphia, 1868.

———. *Jesus.* Philadelphia, 1871.

———. *The Voice in Speaking.* Translated from the German of Emma Seiler. Philadelphia, 1875.

———. *The Power of the Spirit Manifest in Jesus of Nazareth.* Philadelphia, 1877.

———. *Jesus, the Heart of Christianity.* Philadelphia, 1879.

———. *The Story of the Resurrection of Christ Told Once More.* Philadelphia, 1885.

———. *The Story of the Resurrection of Jesus Told Once More.* Philadelphia, 1886.

———. *Verses; Translations from the German and Hymns.* Boston, 1886.

———. *Pastoral Offices.* Boston, 1893.

Bibliography

Furness, H[orace] H[oward] (ed.). *Records of a Lifelong Friendship, 1807–1882. Ralph Waldo Emerson and William Henry Furness.* Boston, 1910.

Garrison, Wendell Phillips and Garrison, Francis Jackson (eds.). *William Lloyd Garrison, 1805–1879.* 4 vols. Boston, 1885.

Hale, Edward E. Jr. *The Life and Letters of Edward Everett Hale.* 2 vols. Boston, 1917.

Hurlbut, Henry H. *The Hurlbut Genealogy.* Albany, 1888.

Johnson, Robert Winder, Sr. and Morris, Lawrence Johnson, *The Johnson Family and Allied Families of Lincolnshire, England. Being the Ancestry and Posterity of Lawrence Johnson of Philadelphia, Pennsylvania.* Philadelphia, 1934.

Kelley, William D. *Speeches, Addresses and Letters on Industrial and Financial Questions.* Philadelphia, 1872.

Memorial Addresses on the Life and Character of William D. Kelley, Delivered in the House of Representatives and the Senate, 51st Congress, 1st Session. Washington 1890.

Kenrick, Mrs. W. Byng (ed.). *Chronicles of a Nonconformist Family, the Kenricks of Wynne Hall, Exeter and Birmingham.* Birmingham, England, 1932.

Latrobe, Benjamin Henry. *The Journal of Latrobe.* New York, 1905.

Leland, Charles Godfrey. *Memoirs.* New York, 1893.

Pennell, Elizabeth Robins. *Charles Godfrey Leland, a Biography.* 2 vols. New York, 1906.

Ames, Mary Lesley (ed.). *Life and Letters of Peter and Susan Lesley.* 2 vols. New York, 1909.

Maclay, Edgar S. (ed.). *Journal of William Maclay.* New York, 1890.

Martineau, Harriet. *Retrospect of Western Travel.* 2 vols. New York, 1838.

———. *Autobiography.* 2 vols. Boston, 1877.

May, Samuel J. *Some Recollections of Our Antislavery Conflict.* Boston, 1869.

———. *Memoir.* Boston, 1873.

Melish, John, *Travels through the United States of America in the Years 1806 & 1807, and 1809, 1810 & 1811.* 2 vols. Philadelphia, 1815.

———. *A Geographical Description of the United States.* Philadelphia, 1816.

Hallowell, Anna Davis (ed.). *James and Lucretia Mott, Life and Letters.* Boston, 1884.

Cromwell, Otelia. *Lucretia Mott.* Cambridge, Mass., 1958.

Hare, Lloyd, C. M. *The Greatest American Woman, Lucretia Mott.* New York, 1937.

Tolles, Frederick B. *Slavery and "The Woman Question." Lucretia Mott's Diary of Her Visit to Great Britain to Attend the World's Anti-Slavery Convention of 1840.* Haverford, Penna., 1952.

Priestley, Joseph, *Works.* No definitive edition available. Sixty volumes, published in various places, 1769–1809, were examined. The following were used in the text:

From *Discourses on Various Subjects, Including Several on Particular Occasions.* Birmingham, England, 1787.

"A Prefatory Discourse Relating to the present State of those who are called Rational Dissenters." Prefaced to "A Sermon preached at the New Meeting, Birmingham, November 3, 1782."

"The Importance and Extent of Free Inquiry in Matters of Religion: A Sermon Preached Before the Congregations of the Old and New Meeting of Protestant Dissenters at Birmingham. November 5, 1785."

Letters to a Philosophical Unbeliever. Northumberland, Penna., 1794.

Unitarianism explained and defended, in a Discourse, delivered in the Church of the Universalists, at Philadelphia, 1796. Philadelphia, 1796.

Discourses on the Evidences of Revealed Religion. 2 vols. Philadelphia, 1796–1797.

Observations on the Increase of Infidelity. Philadelphia, 1797.

Volney's Answer to Dr. Priestley. Philadelphia, 1797.

Letters to Mr. Volney, occasioned by a work of his entitled Ruins and by his letter to the Author. Philadelphia, 1797.

An Address to the Unitarian Congregation at Philadelphia. Delivered Sunday, March 5, 1797. Philadelphia, 1797.

Letters to the Inhabitants of Northumberland. Northumberland, Penna., 1799.

Memoirs of Dr. Joseph Priestley, to the Year 1795, Written by Himself; With a Continuation, to the Time of his decease, by his son, Joseph Priestley: and observations on his writings, by Thomas Cooper, . . .: and the Rev. William Christie. 2 vols. Northumberland, Penna., 1806.

Rutt, John Towill. *Life and Correspondence of Joseph Priestley, L.L.D., F.R.S. &c.* 2 vols. London, 1831.

Park, Mary Cathryne. "Joseph Priestley and the Problem of Pantisocracy." Ph.D. dissertation, University of Pennsylvania, 1947. Published in *Proc. Del. Co. Instit. of Science,* XI (1947), 1–60.

Smith, Edgar F. *Priestley in America, 1794–1804.* Philadelphia, 1920.

Holt, Anne. *A Life of Joseph Priestley.* London, 1931.

F[urness], H[orace] H[oward]. *F[airman] R[ogers]: 1833–1900.* Philadelphia, 1903.

Corner, George W. (ed.). *The Autobiography of Benjamin Rush.* Princeton, 1948.

Jeyes, S. H. *The Russells of Birmingham.* London, 1911.

Sartain, John. *The Reminiscences of a Very Old Man, 1808–1897.* New York, 1899.

Adams, Herbert B. *The Life and Writings of Jared Sparks.* 2 vols. Boston, 1893.

Biddle, Edward and Fielding, Mantle. *The Life and Works of Thomas Sully (1783–1872).* Philadelphia, 1921.

Catalogue of the Memorial Exhibition of Portraits by Thomas Sully, Pennsylvania Academy of the Fine Arts. Philadelphia, 1922.

Sumner, Charles, *Works.* 15 vols. Boston, 1870–83.

Pierce, Edward L. (ed.). *Memoir and Letters of Charles Sumner.* 4 vols. 1877–93.

Memoir of Charles Toppan. Old Newbury, Mass., 1880.

Sheppard, John M. *Reminiscences of the Vaughan Family, and more particularly of Benjamin Vaughan, LL.D.* Boston, 1865.

Ford, Worthington Chauncey (ed.). *The Writings of George Washington.* 14 vols. New York, 1891.

Fitzpatrick, John C. (ed.). *The Writings of George Washington, 1745–1799.* 39 vols. Washington, 1931–44.

Barnes, Gilbert H. and Dumond, Dwight L. (eds.). *Letters of Theodore Dwight Weld, Angelina Grimké Weld and Sarah Grimké, 1822–1844.* 2 vols. New York, 1934.

Wilson, Bird. *Memoir of the Life of the Right Reverend William White, D.D.* . . . Philadelphia, 1839.

ORGANIZATIONS

Members and Correspondents of the Academy of Natural Sciences of Philadelphia, 1868. Philadelphia, 1868.

Members and Correspondents of the Academy of Natural Sciences of Philadelphia, November 1, 1893. Philadelphia, 1893.

American Philosophical Society. *Early Proceedings, Compiled by one of the Secretaries from the manuscript Minutes of its Meetings from 1744 to 1838.* Philadelphia, 1884.

———. *Year Book, 1956.* Philadelphia, 1957.

Du Ponceau, Peter Stephen. *An Historical Account of the Origin and Formation of the American Philosophical Society Held at Philadelphia for Promoting Useful Knowlege.* Philadelphia, 1914.

The Anti-Slavery History of the John-Brown Year; Being the Twenty-Seventh Annual Report of the American Anti-Slavery Society. New York, 1861.

The Charter, By-Laws, and 75th Annual Report of the Athenaeum of Philadelphia. Philadelphia, 1890.

A Century of the First Day or Sunday-School Society: A Sketch of the Beginning of Sunday Schools in Philadelphia. Philadelphia, 1891.

Semi-Centennial Celebration of the Franklin Fire Insurance Company of Philadelphia, June 25, 1879. Philadelphia, 1879.

First Annual Report of the Proceedings of the Franklin Institute . . . to which are prefixed the Charter, Constitution and By-Laws . . . with a list of the Members and Officers for 1824 and 1825. Philadelphia, 1825.

Centenary of the Franklin Institute of Pennsylvania, 1824–1924. Philadelphia, 1924.

Wright, Sydney L. *The Story of the Franklin Institute*. Philadelphia, 1938.

Historical Society of Pennsylvania. *Charter and By-Laws, with a List of the Officers, and of the Members of the Executive Council, Since the Organization of the Society*. Philadelphia, 1880.

Carson, Hampton L. *A History of the Historical Society of Pennsylvania*. 2 vols. Philadelphia, 1940.

A History of the Insurance Company of North America. Philadelphia, 1885.

Lea and Febiger. *One Hundred and Fifty Years of Publishing, 1785–1935*. Philadelphia, 1935.

Musical Fund Society of Philadelphia. *Act of Incorporation, approved February 22, 1823, Amendment Thereof, approved April 28, 1857, and By-Laws, . . . Together with a list of Officers and Members, Historical Data, and List of Portraits*. N.p., 1930.

Goepp, Philip H. (ed.). *Annals of Music in Philadelphia and History of the Musical Fund Society from its Organization in 1820 to the Year 1858*. Philadelphia, 1896.

Henderson, Helen W. *The Pennsylvania Academy of the Fine Arts and Other Collections of Philadelphia*. Boston, 1911.

Boyd, James, *A History of the Pennsylvania Horticultural Society, 1827–1927*. Philadelphia, 1929.

Morton, Thomas G. and Woodbury, Frank. *The History of the Pennsylvania Hospital, 1751–1895*. Philadelphia, 1895.

Pennsylvania Institution for the Instruction of the Blind, *Annual Reports of Managers, 1834–1860*. Philadelphia, 1834–60.

Bibliography

Burgess, George H. and Kennedy, Miles C. *Centennial History of the Pennsylvania Railroad Company, 1846–1946.* Philadelphia, 1949.

Wilson, William Bender. *History of the Pennsylvania Railroad Company with Plan of Organization, Portraits of Officials and Biographical Sketches.* 2 vols. Philadelphia, 1895.

The Philadelphia Club, 1834–1934, Being a Brief History of the Club for the First Hundred Years of Its Existence, Together with Its Roll of Officers and Members to 1934. N.p., 1934.

Memoirs of the Philadelphia Society for Promoting Agriculture. Vol. I. Philadelphia, 1808.

Memoirs of the Philadelphia Society for the Promotion of Agriculture. Vol. VI. Philadelphia, 1939.

A History of the Schuylkill Fishing Company of the State in Schuylkill, 1732–1888. Philadelphia, 1889.

An Historical Sketch of the Origin and Progress of the Society of the Sons of St. George, Charter, By-Laws and Permanent Resolutions, Together with an Alphabetical List of the Names of Members and Associates, Officers, etc., April 23, 1772—April 23, 1872. Philadelphia, 1872.

University of Pennsylvania. *Biographical Catalogue of the Matriculates of the College, . . . 1749–1893.* Philadelphia, 1894.

———. *Catalogues, 1855–1861.* Philadelphia, 1855–61.

Cheyney, Edward Potts. *History of the University of Pennsylvania, 1740–1940.* Philadelphia, 1940.

Carson, Hampton L. *The Centenary of the Wistar Party.* Philadelphia, 1918.

History of the Wistar Association. Philadelphia, 1945.

GENERAL

Adams, Henry. *History of the United States During the First Administration of Thomas Jefferson.* 2 vols. New York, 1921.

American Slavery. A Protest against American Slavery by 173 Unitarian Ministers. Boston, 1845.

Anon. *Wealth and Biography of the Wealthy Citizens of Philadelphia.* Philadelphia, 1845.

Appletons' Cyclopaedia of American Biography. Vol. II. New York, 1887.

Barnes, Gilbert Hobbs. *The Antislavery Impulse, 1830–1844.* New York, 1933.

Belcher, Joseph. *The Religious Denominations in the United States.* Philadelphia, 1864.

Binney, Horace. *Leaders of the Old Bar.* Philadelphia, 1859.

Bowers, Claude G. *Jefferson and Hamilton*. Boston, 1925.

Buckingham, J. S. *America, Historical, Statistic, and Descriptive*. 3 vols. London, n.d.

A Century of Population Growth from the First Census of the United States to the Twelfth, 1790–1900. Washington, 1909.

Clark, Edward W. *A Record of the Inscriptions on the Tablets and Grave-Stones in the Burial-Grounds of Christ Church, Philadelphia*. Philadelphia, 1864.

Cochran, Thomas C. and Miller, William. *The Age of Enterprise*. New York, 1949.

Cole, Arthur Charles. *The Irrepressible Conflict, 1850–1865*. New York, 1934.

Cuthbert, Norma B. (ed.). *Lincoln and the Baltimore Plot*. San Marino, Calif., 1949.

DeGarmo, James M. *The Hicksite Quakers and Their Doctrines*. New York, 1897.

Drake, Thomas E. *Quakers and Slavery in America*. New Haven, 1950.

Du Bois, William E. B. *The Philadelphia Negro*. Philadelphia, 1899.

Eliot, Samuel A. (ed.). *Heralds of a Liberal Faith*. Vol. III. Boston, 1910.

Fielding, Mantle. *Dictionary of American Painters, Sculptors, and Engravers*. Philadelphia, n.d.

Fish, Carl Russell. *The Rise of the Common Man, 1830–1850*. New York, 1927.

Franklin, John Hope. *From Slavery to Freedom*. New York, 1948.

A Full and Complete Account of the late Awful Riots in Philadelphia. Philadelphia, 1844.

Gabriel, Ralph H. *The Course of American Democratic Thought*. New York, 1940.

Great Union Meeting, Philadelphia, December 7, 1859. Philadelphia, n.d.

Griswold, Rufus Wilmot. *The Republican Court or American Society in the Days of Washington*. New York, 1885.

Groce, George C. and Wallace, David H. (eds.). *The New-York Historical Society's Dictionary of Artists in America (1564–1860)*. New Haven, 1957.

A Guide to Laurel Hill Cemetery Near Philadelphia. Philadelphia, 1851.

Hart, Alfred Bushnell. *Slavery and Abolition, 1831–1841*. New York, 1906.

Henry, Frederick P. (ed.). *Standard History of the Medical Profession of Philadelphia*. Chicago, 1897.

Hidy, Ralph W. *The House of Baring in American Trade and Finance*. Cambridge, Mass., 1949.

Bibliography

Jackson, Joseph. *Encyclopaedia of Philadelphia.* 4 vols. Harrisburg, 1933.

————. *Literary Landmarks of Philadelphia.* Philadelphia, 1939.

James, Reese D. *Old Drury of Philadelphia, A History of the Philadelphia Stage, 1800–1835.* Philadelphia, 1932

Johnson, Allen and Malone, Dumas (eds.). *Dictionary of American Biography.* 20 vols. New York, 1929–36.

Jones, Rufus M. *The Later Periods of Quakerism.* 2 vols. London, 1921.

Joyce, J. St. George. *Story of Philadelphia.* N.p., 1919.

Krout, John Allen and Fox, Dixon Ryan. *The Completion of Independence, 1790–1830.* New York, 1944.

Lippincott, Horace M. *Early Philadelphia, Its People, Life and Progress.* Philadelphia, 1917.

MacDonald, William. *Jacksonian Democracy, 1829–1837.* New York, 1906.

Macy, Jesse. *The Anti-Slavery Crusade.* New Haven, 1921.

Martin, John Hill. *Bench and Bar of Philadelphia.* Philadelphia, 1883.

McMaster, John Bach. *A History of the People of the United States.* Vols. II–VII. New York, 1885.

Mease, James. *The Picture of Philadelphia,* Philadelphia 1811.

Morgan, George. *The City of Firsts.* Philadelphia, 1926.

Munsell's (pub.). *American Ancestry.* Vol. IV. Albany, 1889.

Mueller, Henry R. *The Whig Party in Pennsylvania.* New York, 1922.

Nevins, Allen. *American Social History as Recorded by British Travellers.* New York, 1923.

————. *Ordeal of the Union.* 2 vols. New York, 1947.

Nichols, Roy F. *Advance Agents of American Destiny.* Philadelphia, 1956.

Oberholtzer, Ellis Paxson. *The Literary History of Philadelphia.* Philadelphia, 1906.

————. *Philadelphia, A History of the City and Its People.* 4 vols. Philadelphia, n.d.

One Hundred Years in Philadelphia, 1847–1947. Philadelphia *Evening Bulletin* Anniversary Book. N.p., n.d.

Philadelphia and Popular Philadelphians. Philadelphia, 1891.

Philadelphia *City Directories.* Philadelphia, 1785–1860.

Proceedings of the Great Union Meeting, held in the Large Salon of the Chinese Museum, Philadelphia, on 21st November, 1850. . . . Philadelphia, 1850.

Report of the Proceedings of the Town Meeting in the City of Philadelphia, July 7th, 1828. N.p., n.d.

305

Repplier, Agnes. *Philadelphia, The Place and the People.* New York, 1899.

Ritter, Abraham. *Philadelphia and Her Merchants.* Philadelphia, 1860.

Sachse, J. F. *The Religious and Social Conditions of Philadelphia during the first decade under the Federal Constitution, 1790–1800.* Philadelphia, 1900.

Scharf, J. Thomas and Westcott, Thompson. *History of Philadelphia, 1609–1884.* 3 vols. Philadelphia, 1884.

Schlesinger, Arthur M., Jr. *The Age of Jackson.* Boston, 1945.

Siebert, Wilbur H. *The Underground Railroad from Slavery to Freedom.* New York, 1898.

Simpson, Henry. *The Lives of Eminent Philadelphians Now Deceased.* Philadelphia, 1859.

Smith, Edgar Fahs. *Chemistry in America.* New York, 1914.

———. *Chemistry in old Philadelphia.* Philadelphia, 1919.

Sonne, Niels Henry. *Liberal Kentucky, 1780–1828.* New York, 1939.

Stauffer, David McNeeley. *American Engravers Upon Copper and Steel.* 2 vols. New York, 1907.

Still, William. *The Underground Rail Road.* Philadelphia, 1872.

Sweet, William Warren. *The Story of Religions in America.* New York, 1930.

Thomas, Abel C. *A Century of Universalism in Philadelphia and New-York, with Sketches of its History in Reading, Hightstown, Brooklyn, and Elsewhere.* Philadelphia, 1872.

Tocqueville, Alexis de. *Democracy in America.* 2 vols. New York, 1904.

Toppan, Robert Noxon. *A Hundred Years of Bank Note Engraving in the United States.* New York, 1896.

Turner, Edward Raymond. *The Negro in Pennsylvania.* Washington, 1911.

Tyler, Alice Felt. *Freedom's Ferment.* Minneapolis, 1944.

University of Pennsylvania. *Biographical Catalogue of the Matriculates of the College . . . 1749–1893.* Philadelphia, 1894.

Watson, John F. *Annals of Philadelphia and Pennsylvania . . .,* ed. Willis P. Hazard. 3 vols. Philadelphia, 1881.

Wilson, Arthur Herman. *A History of the Philadelphia Theatre, 1835 to 1855.* Philadelphia, 1935.

Articles and Periodicals

Ames, Charles Gordon. "William Henry Furness," *Harvard Graduates' Magazine,* June, 1896. Reprint.

American Philosophical Society. "Officers [1769–1934]," *Proc. Amer. Phil. Soc.,* LXXIII (1934), 371–97.

Bibliography

"Black Letters; or Uncle Tom-Foolery in Literature," *Graham's Magazine*, XLII (February 1853), 209–15.

Bronk, Detlev W. "Joseph Priestley and the Early History of the American Philosophical Society," *Proc. Amer. Phil. Soc.*, XIVC (September 1942). Reprint.

Budd, Henry. "Thomas Sully," *Pa. Mag. of Hist. & Biog.*, VIIIL (April 1918), 97–126.

Christian Examiner, 1824–61.

Clothier, Isaac H. "Philadelphia in Slavery Days," Philadelphia *Public Ledger*, December 14, 1902.

"Despatches from the United States Consulate in New Orleans, 1801–1803," *Amer. Hist. Review*, XXXII (July 1927), 801–24.

Dorfman, Joseph. "The Jackson Wage-Earner Thesis," *Amer. Hist. Review*, LIV (January 1949), 296–306.

Eaton, Clement. "Winifred and Joseph Gales, Liberals in the Old South," *Jour. of South Hist.*, X (November 1944), 461–74.

Frazer, Persifor. "The Franklin Institute; Its Services and Deserts," *Jour. Frank. Instit.*, CLXV (April 1908). Reprint.

Francis, Russell E. "The Religious Revival of 1858 in Philadelphia," *Pa. Mag. of Hist. & Biog.*, LXX (January 1946), 52–77.

Hale, Edward Everett. "Reminiscences of the Unitarian Pulpit, III, William Henry Furness," *Christian Register*, LXXVIII (March 2, 1899), 239–43.

Hamlin, Talbot. "Some Greek Revival Architects of Philadelphia," *Pa. Mag. Hist. of & Biog.*, LXV (April 1941), 121–44.

The Journal of the Franklin Institute, 1826–61.

Mackay, Winnifred K. "Philadelphia During the Civil War, 1861–1865," *Pa. Mag. of Hist. & Biog.*, LXX (January 1946), 3–51.

Obituary notice, William Henry Furness, *The Athenaeum*, No. 3563 (February 8, 1896), p. 183.

———. *The Critic*, XXVIII (February 8, 1896), 99.

———. *The Nation*, LXII (February 6, 1896), 114–15.

Pettingill, George E. "Franklin, Priestley, and the Samuel Vaughan, Jr. Manuscripts, 1775–1782," *Jour. Frank. Instit.*, CCIIIL (March 1949), 195–204.

———. "Walter Rogers Johnson," *Jour. Frank. Instit.*, CCL (August 1950), 93–113.

The Port Folio, 1801–27.

Rosengarten, Joseph G. "Obituary Notice of the Rev. Dr. William H. Furness," *Proc. Amer. Phil. Soc.*, *Memor. Vol. I* (1900), 9–17.

Shryock, Richard H. "Historical Traditions in Philadelphia," *Pa. Mag. Hist. & Biog.*, LXVII (April 1943), 115–41.

Stetson, Sarah P. "The Philadelphia Sojourn of Samuel Vaughan," *Pa. Mag. Hist. & Biog.*, LXXIII (October 1949), 459–74.

"Unitarianism in Philadelphia," *Christian Examiner*, March and April, 1828, p. 170.

"Washington's Household Account Book, 1793–1797," *Pa. Mag. Hist. & Biog.*, XXX (April 1906), 159–86.

Whitaker, Arthur P. "Reed and Forde: Merchant Adventurers of Philadelphia," *Pa. Mag. Hist. & Biog.*, LXI (July 1937), 237–62.

Wolfgang, Marvin E. "John Melish, An Early American Demographer," *Pa. Mag. Hist. & Biog.*, LXXXII (January 1958), 65–81.

Other Sources

Gales's Independent Gazeteer, 1796–1797. Historical Society of Pennsylvania.

Framed list of Officers and Directors. Pennsylvania Academy of the Fine Arts.

INDEX

Abbot, Leonard, 133

Abolitionism (*see* Antislavery cause)

Academy of Music, 134, 217

Academy of Natural Sciences, 105, 120, 123–124, 137, 167, 199, 216, 278

Accountants' Society of Pennsylvania, 137, 278

Adams, John, 17, 28, 31, 50, 51, 52–53, 174, 185

Adams, Mrs. John, 31

Adams, John Quincy, 175, 213–214

Agnew, John, 100

Agriculture, Society for the Promotion of, 77, 82, 278–279

Alcott, Amos Bronson, 159, 165–166

Alder, Caleb, 33, 44, 276

Aldrich, Lyman D., 263

Alien and Sedition Acts, 52–53, 67

Allen, James, 247, 274

Allen, S. and M., and Company, 197

Allport, William B., 34, 35, 45, 246

American (and Health) Insurance Company, 279

American Anti-Slavery Society, 187, 189, 214

American Art Union Association, 199

American Association for the Advancement of Science, 124

American Bank Note Company, 128

American Beneficial Society, 105, 279

American Colonization Society, 189

American Daily Advertiser, 43

American Fire Insurance Company, 67, 105, 279

American Gallery of Art, 155

American Lady's Pocket Book, 44

American Literary Fair, 66, 98

American Philosophical Society, 21, 24, 26, 75, 78, 81, 94, 102, 106–107, 119, 123, 167, 199, 216–217, 221–222, 223, 279

American Revolution, 18, 22, 27, 109, 185, 225

American Tract Society, 222

American Type Founders' Company, 125

American Unitarian Association, 137, 219, 220

Ames, Charles G., 115, 200, 220, 224

Amusements, 132–133, 173–174, 203

Anderson, William V., 202, 263, 280, 283, 287, 290

Andrews, John, 47, 102

Animal magnetism, 204

Anti-French attitudes, 19, 23–24, 51

Anti-Negro riots, 185–186, 192, 202–203

Antislavery cause, 40, 42, 143, 157, 166–167, 178, 184–197, 199, 205–208, 213, 214–216, 224, 228–233, 234

Anti-Unitarian attitudes (*see* Hostility toward Unitarianism)

Architecture (*see also* individual architects), 118, 252

Arianism, 121

Armitage, George, 275

Art Union, 199

Artists and Amateurs Association, 199, 279

Artists' Fund Society, 154, 167, 199, 280

Associated Teachers in the City of New York, 21

Association of American Geologists, 124

Astley, Thomas, 73, 81, 82, 104, 246, 247, 263, 286, 292

Atheism, 34, 49–51

Athenaeum, 94, 105, 120, 167, 199, 203, 216, 280–282

Athenian Institute, 282

Audubon, John James, 119

Aurora, 24, 52, 62, 63, 83

Bache, Benjamin Franklin, 24, 62

Bache, Richard, 80

Bailey, Lewis, 247, 262

Index

Index

Ellis, Rufus, 223
Embargo Act, 82, 83
Emerson, Ralph Waldo, 114, 134, 149, 152, 164, 166, 176
Emerson, William, 49, 152, 165
Emery, Samuel, 261
English, Hugh, 265
English, James, 253
English, Robert, 253
English origins, 17, 36, 46, 54–55, 83, 84–85, 90–91, 107, 131–132, 133, 143, 162, 169, 218, 239
English sympathizers, 19, 23–24, 83, 84–85, 90–91, 218, 292–293
Engraving (*see also* individual engravers), 126–127, 155, 259–260
Epiphany, Church of the, 229
Episcopal Church, 17, 47, 49, 153, 165, 229, 239, 241
Esherick, Frederick, 258
Espy, George, 258
Espy, James P., 122, 167, 276, 279, 282, 285
Espy, Mrs. James P., 170, 293
Eustice, Mr., 220
Evans, Josiah, 256, 274
Evans, Whitten, 265
Evans, William H., 265
Everett, Prof., 115
Ewing, John, 47, 48–49, 65
Exchange Coffee House, 98

Fagan, John, 275, 281
Fairman, Caroline, 128, 149
Fairman, David, 127
Fairman, Ellen Gardiner, 128
Fairman, George W., 128, 215, 257
Fairman, Gideon, 126–128, 146, 149, 221, 259, 279, 281, 283, 285
Fairman, Mrs. Gideon, 170, 293
Fales, George, 130, 134, 202, 215, 248, 266, 281, 283, 285
Falkner, Matthew, 46
Farmers' and Mechanics' Bank, 67, 284
Farnham, Benjamin A., 149, 248, 266, 284, 287
Farnsworth, Jacob, 151, 266
Fay, Charles, M., 266
Federalist party, 18–19, 31, 47, 52–54, 62–63, 76, 83–84, 90

Fellowes, Caleb, 261, 281
Felton, Samuel Morse, 227–228, 233, 274, 278
Female Medical College, 217, 284
Fenno, John, 24, 54, 62
Finch, Francis, 248
First City Troop, 222
Five Per Cent Saving Fund Deposit and Loan Company, 284
Fletcher, Charles, 97, 130, 248, 262, 287
Fletcher, George, 97, 130, 147, 161
Fletcher, Hannah, 97
Fletcher, Levi, 97
Fletcher, Louis Veron, 130, 135
Fletcher, Melina Veron, 130
Fletcher, Thomas (Chestnut Street), 96–97, 101, 107, 109, 120, 122, 147, 167, 248, 262, 266, 283, 284, 285, 287, 290
Fletcher, Thomas (Walnut Street), 97
Ford, Catharine Bryan, 96, 107, 172
Ford, John, 96, 104, 107, 109, 147, 248, 266
Ford, Samuel C., 266
Fort Sumter, 234
Foster, Augustus John, 83–84
Foulke, William, 251
Founding of Philadelphia Unitarian Society, 17, 23, 25, 28, 32–34, 45
Fox, Samuel, 255
Franklin, Benjamin, 22
Franklin Fire Insurance Company, 284–285
Franklin House, 200
Franklin Institute, 100–101, 103, 105, 107, 120, 122, 124, 137, 167, 199, 216, 222, 285–286
Free Friends' burial-ground, 93
Free Soil party, 214
Freeman, James, 108
French Revolution, 19, 20, 36, 40, 49
French sympathizers, 19, 20, 24, 36, 37, 85, 185
Friedlander, Julius R., 171
Frothingham, Frederick K., 220
Fryer, George, 258
Fugitive Slave Act, 215–216, 229–230
Furness, Ann M., 148
Furness, Annis Jenks, 120, 121–122, 133, 152, 162, 164, 170, 173, 193, 195, 219, 291, 293

313

Index

Index

315

Index

Index

Index

Index

Index

Randall, Matthew, 98

Readers, lay, of Philadelphia Unitarian Society, 33, 34–35, 43–44, 246

Reed, Charles, D., 270, 290

Reed, Joseph, 80

Reed, William B., 233

"Reform Convention," 188

Reform spirit, 37, 126, 144–146, 162, 178, 202, 216, 234

Register of Births, Baptisms, Marriages, and Burials, 74, 91, 92

Reilly, Jane Sill, 202

Reliance Mutual Insurance Company, 291

Renshaw, William, 81, 98–99, 107, 262, 292, 293

Republican Natives of Great Britain and Ireland, 21

Republican party, 218, 225

Revivalism, 207–208

Revolution, American, 18, 22, 185

Revolution, French, 19, 20, 36, 40, 49

Riding Club, 291

Rioting, 185–189, 192–193, 202–203

Rittenhouse, David, 21, 41

Roberts, Algernon S., 249, 259, 281, 285, 286

Robertson, William H., 270

Rochefoucault-Liancourt, Duke de la, 41–42

Rodgers, W. H., 204

Rogers, Caroline Fairman, 128, 149–150, 205, 221

Rogers, Evans, 128, 149–150, 167, 168 194, 208, 221, 249, 270, 279, 281, 282, 283, 285, 286, 291

Rogers, Fairman, 221–222, 276, 278 279, 281, 282, 283, 285, 286

Rogers, Henry D., 222

Rogers, William, 23, 48

Rogers, William E., 149, 270

Ronaldson, James, 101

Ronaldson, Richard, 124–125

Rosine Association, 216, 291

Rotch, Thomas, 134, 146, 169, 278, 281, 289, 290

Roy, John, 34, 45

Royston, George, 33, 44, 45, 46, 47, 276

Royston, John, 33, 44, 45, 46, 47

Rush, Benjamin, 21, 25, 41, 54, 62, 65, 102

Rush, James, 165

Rush, Richard, 80

Rush, William, 118, 119

Russell, William (Englishman), 33, 35, 39–42, 261

Russell, William (Scottish educator), 165

Sacraments, 45, 92–93, 104

St. Augustine's Church, 203

St. Mary's Episcopal Church (Burlington, N.J.), 153

Saltmarsh, Seth, 259

Sanderson, Joseph M., 146, 169, 262, 288

Sansom, William, 62

Sartain, Emily, 155

Sartain, John, 154–156, 167, 190, 217, 220, 260, 280, 282, 289, 292

Sartain, (Kenneth) Samuel, 155–156, 217, 220–221, 260

Sartain's Union Magazine of Literature and Art, 155

Saturday Club, 221

Saulnier, Henry E., 129, 260, 282

Saulnier, John Joseph Marie, 92, 107, 270

Say, Thomas, 119

Schiller's centennial, 217

Schlatter, William, 96

Scholefield, John, 193, 249, 257, 281, 292

Schott, James, Jr., 160

Schroeder, Mr., 198

Schuylkill Fishing Company of the State in Schuylkill, 291

Schuylkill Navigation Company, 105, 118

Science, 20–21, 25, 26, 65, 68, 105, 119, 124, 261, 278

Scott, Thomas, 252

Sculpture, 118

Seal of Philadelphia Unitarian Society, 91

Second Unitarian Church, 219–220, 238

Sedition Act, 52

Select Council of Philadelphia, 90, 137, 167, 168, 202, 218, 284

Sergeant, Mrs. Elizabeth, 41

Sergeant, John, 64, 102, 106, 215

Sewing Circle, Ladies', 201

Sheffield (England) Register, 42

Shipbuilding, 66

Shippen, Charles, 107, 109, 249, 251

320

Index

Tevis, Joshua, 150, 169, 191, 192, 194, 196, 206, 249, 271, 284
Thackara, Samuel, 258
Thayer, Ziptheon, 272
Theatre, 119, 173, 198, 251, 276, 293
Thomas, Charles J., 152, 272
Thomas, Eliza, 152
Thomas, Jacob, 151, 249, 284, 285
Thomas, Joseph M., 152, 249, 272, 284, 289, 291
Thomas, Mary, 39
Thomas, Moses, 272, 282, 288, 290
Thomas, Nathaniel, 33, 34-35, 39, 44, 47, 71, 100, 246, 275
Thomas, Richard, 273
Thomas, Samuel H., 174, 250, 272, 282, 288
Thomas, Sarah, 100, 107
Thompson, George, 189
Tilghman, William, 80
Toby, Samuel, 260
Todhunter, Jane, 131
Todhunter, John, 292
Todhunter, Joseph, 131, 137, 147, 148, 169, 185, 189, 250, 272, 285, 293
Todhunter, Joseph, Jr., 282
Todhunter, Rachel, 153
Todhunter, William, 169, 272, 293
Tompkins, Daniel D., 102
Toppan, Charles, 127-129, 167, 260, 280, 282, 286
Tories, 185
Toulmin, Henry, 32-33
Toulmin, Joshua, 32-33
Towne, John H., 224, 260, 280, 286, 288, 289
Towne Scientific School, 224
Townsend, Charles, Jr., 151, 277
Townsend, Elisha, 151, 259
Transcendentalists, 166
Transportation, 61, 67, 105, 118, 274
Transylvania University, 122
Tredrick, Thomas, 272
Trendel, Thomas, 70, 73, 246
Trott, George, Jr., 272, 282
Trustees of Philadelphia Unitatian Society, 104, 247-250
Tryon, George W., 278
Tucker, James, 33, 44, 272
Tucker, William E., 130, 260
Tuesday Club, 63

Turner, John, 34, 35, 45, 46, 47, 246
Turner, William, 34, 44, 46, 47, 73, 104, 109, 246, 247, 250
Tyng, Dudley Atkins, 229

Uncle Tom's Cabin, 215
Underground Railroad, 186, 215-216
Union Academy, 125
Union Benevolent Association, 293
Union Insurance Company, 67, 293
Union League, 221
Union Magazine, 155
Union Mutual Insurance Company, 293
Unitarian Controversy, Boston, 108, 114-115
Unitarian doctrines (*see* Doctrines, Unitarian)
United States Coast and Geodetic Survey, 222
United States Gazette, 24
United States Insurance, Annuity and Trust Company, 144
United States Insurance Company, 67, 71
Universalists, 24, 28, 48, 70
University of Pennsylvania, 21, 25, 26, 33, 47, 64-65, 81, 94, 119-120, 134 217, 221, 222, 223-224, 230

Vaccination, 77
Van Buren, Martin, 168
Vaughan, Benjamin, 22, 51, 52, 74, 99, 101
Vaughan, John, 20, 22-23, 27, 36, 45-46, 66, 70, 73-78, 79, 80, 81-82, 101, 102, 104, 105-107, 108, 109, 121, 146, 148, 149, 154, 156, 164, 165, 167, 170, 171, 190, 191, 195, 201, 217, 223, 246, 247, 250, 272, 278, 279, 280, 282, 283, 286, 288, 289, 290, 293
Vaughan, Petty, 101
Vaughan, Samuel, 22, 76, 82, 91
Vaughan, William, 20, 90, 101
Vaughan Charitable Association, 201
Vaughan Sewing Circle, 201
Vaux, Roberts, 165
Vauxhall Gardens, 185
Veron, Lewis, 130, 147, 272, 288,
Veron, Timothy, 272

Index

Volney (Constantin, Comte de Volney), 50

Wallach, James William, 119
Waln, Jacob S., 80
Walnut Street Theatre, 198, 293
Walsh, Robert, 102, 106, 165
Walstein, James W., 197–198, 276
Walter, Thomas U., 118
War of 1812, 82, 83–85, 90–91, 94, 117, 134, 225, 227
Ward, John, 275
Ware, Henry, Jr., 116, 117, 165, 198
Ware, William, 116
Warren, James Cogan, 258
Warren, William, 272
Warriner, H. Ryland, 253
Washington, George, 18, 31–32, 42, 74–75, 76, 109, 174, 185, 195
Washington Benevolent Society, 99
Washington Grays, 129
Washington Hall Hotel, 99
Washington Mining Company, 200
Waters, Mrs., 41
Wealth of members, 147, 150, 194, 200
Weaver, William, 272
Webster, James, 124, 255
Weld, Theodore, 207–208
West, Benjamin, 102
Western Bank, 293
Western Saving Fund Society, 293
Wetherill, Edward, 250
Wetherill family, 102
Wharton, Daniel C., 273
Wharton, Robert, 62, 80
Wheeler, Ellen Sully, 228

Wheeler, John, 34, 44, 273
Wheeler, John H., 228
Whig party, 167–168, 174–175, 201, 202
Whiskey Rebellion, 76
White, Bishop William, 47, 49, 102, 154, 164, 170
Whitney, Thomas, 46
Whittle, Robert, 273
Whitwell's School, Mrs., 114
Willard Sidney, 115
Williamson, Passmore, 228
Winchester, Elhanan, 48
Winsor, Henry, 226–227, 250, 273
Wistar, Caspar, 65, 106
Wistar Association, 106–107, 293
Wistar Parties, 106–107, 165, 173
Wister, Annis Furness, 133, 229
Wister, Caspar, 133, 202
Wood, Elizabeth Ann, 152
Wood, George A., 250, 273
Wood, James, 96, 107, 273, 293
Woodhouse, James, 21, 65
Woodman, William, 46, 246, 276
Worrall, John, 277
Wright, Fanny, 186
Wyeth, John, 147, 282

XYZ Treaty, 185

Yarrow, John, 273, 284, 286, 289, 290
Yellow fever, 21, 35, 44–45, 46, 54, 61, 62, 64, 67
Young, Alexander, 114
Young, William, 34, 44, 70, 276
Young Men's Christian Association, 207